Michael Balcon

Michael Balcon: The Pursuit of British Cinema

Essays by Geoff Brown and Laurence Kardish
With contributions by David Puttnam and Adrienne Mancia

The Museum of Modern Art, New York

This book has been published in conjunction with
British Film, a retrospective codirected by the
Department of Film of The Museum of Modern Art,
New York, and the National Film Archive, British Film
Institute, London, and made possible by Pearson,
Goldcrest Films and Television Limited, and Thorn EMI,
London. Additional support has been provided by the
National Endowment for the Arts, the New York State
Council on the Arts, the British Council, and The Roy
and Niuta Titus Fund

Edited by Jane Fluegel
Designed by Antony Drobinski
Production supervised by Susan Schoenfeld
Type set by Concept Typographic Services, Inc., New York
Printed by Baronet Litho, Johnstown, N.Y.
Bound by Sendor Bindery, New York

The Museum of Modern Art
11 West 53 Street
New York, N.Y. 10019

Printed in the United States of America

Frontispiece: *Pool of London,* 1951, Basil Dearden

Contents

Michael Balcon and Charles Crichton on location, *Painted Boats*, 1945

Preface

David Puttnam

SIR MICHAEL BALCON was the central and outstanding figure in the creation of what is commonly termed the "British Film Industry." He wasn't the most gifted; David Lean, Alexander Korda, Carol Reed, Michael Powell, and any number of others must scrap over that distinction. "Mick" Balcon was simply the most "British"; wherever he worked, there lay the *heart* of British films. He described a British film as one that "projected Britain and the British character." Years later, I've yet to hear a more succinct or apt description.

Michael Balcon's career could be said to fall into four distinct phases:

1. Early Years—running Gaumont-British and Gainsborough, struggling against the overwhelming influence of the then all-powerful American and German industries. It was during this period that he discovered and promoted the talents of a young art director named Alfred Hitchcock and produced the original version of *The Man Who Knew Too Much* (1934).

2. Mid-Atlantic Period—head of M-G-M in England, not a personally happy time, but a stretch that produced at least one wonderful movie, *A Yank at Oxford* (1938).

3. Golden Years of Ealing—in my view, the most cohesively creative and vigorous period in British movies. *Kind Hearts and Coronets* (1949) remains my favorite.

4. Post Ealing—the later years with Bryanston and the BFI Production Board, when he attained his position as the Elder Statesman of British Cinema.

Like his contemporaries Irving Thalberg and David Selznick, Michael Balcon helped define the role of the Producer and found the niche that suited him ("less than a 'Mogul,' but more than a Production Executive"). He molded Ealing, his triumphant creation, after his own personality. It would appear to have been a truly democratic creative environment, without any hint of anarchy—that they saved for the plots! Balcon accepted majority votes, frequently against his own inclination, with a standing joke: "Well, if you fellows feel so strongly in favor, on my head be it." There may have been a slight sense of "officers and other ranks," the films may at times have seemed a bit puritanical, but those were just social facets of the postwar years. Balcon and his Ealing colleagues addressed themselves to an exhausted country wishing to be healed, amused, and reassured.

At the very start of his period at Ealing, Mick realized that he would never be able to compete on a financial level with the American majors or even with the dominant Rank Organisation at home. "In the absence of money," he decided, "we'll have to make do with talent"; thereafter, the secret of Ealing's success lay in Balcon's ability to spot creative potential and invest in it.

It was this, the quintessential quality of any producer worth the title, combined with his earnestness and loyalty to genuinely creative people, that enabled Mick to overshadow the lesser, if more powerful, figures surrounding him in the industry. He had no illusions about who actually made the films that "Tibby" Clarke, among others, wrote. Equally, no one else had any illusions about who ran Ealing, or whose dreams and attitudes were being projected.

Mick Balcon was fortunate that Ealing in its most significant creative period did not come into conflict with the principal elements that were to bring the British and American film industries to their knees in the sixties. Television, then in its infancy, was not yet a dominant competitor; cinema attendance was for most of the Ealing years on the increase. The period of lunatic "mega salaries" for stars, directors, and even executives had not yet dawned, and most significantly, the business was not yet dominated by lawyers nor in the hands of multinational conglomerates.

In fact, it was the filmmaking-comes-first exclusiveness characteristic of Ealing that created enmity and finally made it impossible to raise the £300,000 required to stave off collapse and subsequent sale in 1955. The distributors and bankers got their revenge for what they saw as a decade of Mick's high-handedness in the cause of creative integrity.

Given Britain's monopolistic distribution set-up and the envious hostility Mick had to deal with, it was no small miracle that under Balcon's aegis the great Ealing directors Alexander Mackendrick, Robert Hamer, Basil Dearden, and Charles Crichton, and later at Bryanston, Tony Richardson and Karel Reisz, all got their start. No less significant

Kind Hearts and Coronets, 1949, Robert Hamer (Dennis Price, Valerie Hobson)

were his postretirement years as chairman of the BFI Production Board, where in partnership with Bruce Beresford and Mamoun Hassan, now the head of the National Film Finance Corporation, he did much of the spadework for programs of which I, among others, am the grateful beneficiary. No more decent or kindly man ever lived, as the innate qualities of his over three hundred films attest. During his final years Mick became a beacon to those of us who dreamed of a regeneration of the British film. One of the great moments of my life was receiving the memorial Michael Balcon Award for services to the British film industry; and one of the saddest, opening *Chariots of Fire* and not having him there to share in the excitement of its success. I like to think *Chariots* was a film of which Mick would thoroughly have approved.

One evening in the middle of October 1977, I received a telephone call from one of the industry papers telling me that my friend had died and asking me to write an appreciation. With more than the odd tear I sat down and wrote it in the form of a letter to Lady Balcon. I don't think I can do better than end with an extract from what I wrote that night.

It was only in conversation with Sir Michael that I finally came to terms with the reasons I work in the film industry; he convinced me by example that there was a way of salvaging pride out of what can be a rather tawdry business: that it could be carried out successfully, with taste and a sense of one's own dignity. How do you thank the man who gives you a sense of purpose and pride in what you do?

Speaking selfishly, I wasn't ready to lose him, nor am I quite sure how I will manage without him being around to talk to.... If in my own lifetime I can create the same amount of happiness, and in my departure as great a sense of loss, then I must surely have done something right. *(Screen International)*

Having said all that, I can only add that it's the quality and integrity of Mick Balcon's films that are his very best epitaph.

Acknowledgments

Michael Balcon: The Pursuit of British Cinema is published on the occasion of British Film, a comprehensive two-part exhibition of which the films produced by Sir Michael Balcon comprise the first part. The second part, an extensive and critical ninety-year history, will be presented chronologically, tracing the specific traditions and illuminating the various aspects that collectively distinguish British film, whose rich and consistent history we hope will now become known in America.

This project would not have been possible without decades of work in acquiring and preserving British films by the staff of the National Film Archive, a division of the British Film Institute, London. In 1985 the National Film Archive will celebrate its 50th year, as will The Museum of Modern Art's Department of Film. Our close collaboration during our joint anniversaries is both fitting and appropriate. The shape and content of the exhibition were determined by the curatorial staff of both institutions, and the majority of prints screened during British Film have been borrowed from the National Film Archive. We would like to give special thanks to Sir Richard Attenborough, Chairman, and Anthony Smith, Director, the British Film Institute, for their energetic determination to bring this project to the United States, and to David Francis, Curator of the National Film Archive, for so generously making available to us many archival prints, some of which have been newly struck for this retrospective.

We are deeply grateful to Goldcrest Films and Television Limited for its enthusiastic sponsorship of British Film, and to its Chairman and Chief Executive, James G. Lee, for his generous and unfailing support. Goldcrest Films and Television Limited is the leading British company financing, producing, and distributing feature films and television programs in that country. Since its founding in 1976, Goldcrest has been associated with such important British films as Chariots of Fire, Gandhi, Local Hero, Moonlighting, and the television series First Love and The Far Pavilions.

We also thank David Puttnam, producer of Chariots of Fire and The Killing Fields, among numerous other films, who was the recipient of the first Michael Balcon Award for services to the British film industry and who kindly authored the preface to this book.

Additional assistance, for which we are most grateful, has been provided by the National Endowment for the Arts, Washington, D.C., the New York State Council on the Arts, the British Council, London, and The Roy and Niuta Titus Fund.

Our closest collaborators—in fact co-directors—on British Film are our colleagues at the BFI National Film Archive: Clyde Jeavons, Deputy Curator; Scott Meek, former Feature Films Officer; Elaine Burrows, Viewings Supervisor; David Meeker, Print and Copyright Research. We are indebted to them for their perseverance, patience, wit, and love of meeting over a good lunch. It has been a joy working with them, as it has been also with Michelle Snapes, Head of the BFI Stills, Posters, and Designs Collection, whom we gratefully thank for the photographs she gathered together for this publication, and for the loan of Ealing posters. We also thank Gillian Hartnoll, Head of the BFI's Library Services, who had the exhausting task of providing documentation for program notes and for preparing the thorough bibliography, with assistance from Joan Ingram and Virginia Hennessy, which concludes this book. The help of Patricia Perilli, Markku Salmi, Peter Tasker, and Linda Wood in gathering information for program notes is also gratefully acknowledged.

We are delighted that Geoff Brown, who has already written so comprehensively on Balcon, agreed to author an original essay for Michael Balcon: The Pursuit of British Cinema. He gave freely of his counsel and advice throughout the preparation of this book. We thank him as well for providing the subtitle of the Balcon series.

We thank Geoffrey Nowell-Smith, Head of Publishing at the BFI, for his support of this book and for undertaking to publish a new book, edited by Charles Barr, on the broad aspects of British film history to be examined in Part II of the series. We also extend our appreciation to Charles Barr and the contributors to the book under his direction. Other BFI staff members we would like to thank for their advice and support are John Gillett, Penelope Houston, Carole Myer, and John Pym. For their help we also thank Rachel Daley and Jane Hockings. For their patience while we spent many hours viewing we thank Clive Truman and Tim Cotter, who made certain all the prints were on schedule.

We very much appreciate the cooperation of Thorn EMI and the Rank Organisation, London, for giving us permission to screen British films not otherwise available in the United States; we would like to thank for their involvement Gary Dartnall, Michael Bromhead, and R. J. Payton, Thorn EMI Film Distributors

Cheer Boys Cheer, 1939, Walter Forde (Edmund Gwenn, Peter Coke)

Ltd.; and F. P. Turner and K. C. Robertson, Rank Film Distributors Ltd.

In the United States we are grateful to a number of organizations and individuals who have loaned us films for this exhibition; A. William J. Becker III, Saul J. Turell, and Ian Birnie of Janus Films; Charles Benton, Allen J. Green, Douglas Lemza, and George Feltenstein of Films Incorporated; Don Krim of Kino International; and John Poole and Peter Meyer of Corinth Films.

Our particular and very special thanks go to William K. Everson, whose knowledge of and enthusiasm for British filmmaking and British film history informed and guided us. Stewart Grainger and other staff of the British Information Services were of great assistance. Also advising and encouraging us were colleagues and friends Lindsay Anderson, John Croydon, Joel Doerfler, Jake Eberts, John Ellis, Alex Gordon, Sheldon Gunsberg, Stephen Harvey, Howard Mandelbaum, Daniel Pearl, Tony Rayns, Richard Roud, Jillian Slonim, Colin Sorensen, Elliott Stein, T. B. Urs, and Ken Wlaschin.

In preparing *Michael Balcon: The Pursuit of British Cinema,* we found certain texts particularly helpful, and these are listed in the bibliography. Three of the most useful books we wish to cite here: Charles Barr's *Ealing Studios,* George Perry's *Forever Ealing,* and *Der Produzent: Michael Balcon und der englische Film,* edited by Geoff Brown and published by the Stiftung Deutsche Kinemathek, West Berlin. We are thankful to Helga Belach and Eva Orbanz for permitting us to print material originally compiled for that publication. Rachael Low's comprehensive research on the history of the British film industry has proved an invaluable resource in planning both book and series. We wish to acknowledge our debt to her scholarship.

At The Museum of Modern Art, Richard E. Oldenburg has been an enthusiastic supporter of this exhibition and publication, and we appreciate his willingness to assist wherever possible. We are indebted to Mary Lea Bandy, Director of the Department of Film, who initiated and orchestrated this publication and whose quick intelligence, organizational skill, and good cheer made *British Film* happen. To Catherine A. Surowiec go our most grateful thanks for the painstaking research she did for this book and for the comprehensive and illuminating chronology that appears herein. For the co-direction of the poster and stills exhibition accompanying *Michael Balcon,* we warmly thank Michelle Snapes of the BFI and Mary Corliss, head of the Museum's Film Stills Archive. For his cooperation and assistance in installing the exhibition we thank Jerome Neuner, Production Manager in the Department of Exhibitions.

We also wish to thank our other colleagues in the Department of Film for their unstinting cooperation, particularly Eileen Bowser, Curator, and Jon Gartenberg, Assistant Curator of the Archives, who have provided a number of prints for the series. We thank Robert Beers for his meticulous job in compiling the index, and Howard Feinstein for researching, compiling, and editing the program notes that attend each screening. We are grateful to Charles Silver, Supervisor of the Film Study Center, and his Assistants Ron Magliozzi and Ed Carter, for making documentation available throughout the difficult period of Museum construction. We are also grateful to Jytte Jensen, who with a smile holds our office together, and to Rachel Gallagher and Laura Winston.

To Jane Fluegel who edited *Michael Balcon* our most profound thanks are given. Her perspicacity, discernment, and humor were of fundamental assistance in preparing this book. We also owe a special thanks to Tony Drobinski who designed the book, and to Nancy Kranz and Susan Schoenfeld of the Publications Department for their support throughout.

The work of promoting and publicizing a retrospective of this complexity is enormous, and we are grateful for the calm but effective way Stuart Klawans drew attention to this exhibition. Thanks also go to John H. Limpert, Jr., and Darryl Brown of the Development Office for their continued support of our programs and to Virginia Coleman and Cathy Lehman of Special Events for their assistance.

For their concern in giving audiences the sharpest image, and for their dedication, we thank our incomparable projectionists, Jeffrey Schulman, Janet Seth, and Gregory Singer. We are also grateful to James Loonam who keenly supervises all print traffic.

We would like to mention dear friends whose warm support and kind interest helped us enormously, Lillian Gish and James Frasher.

To Michael Balcon, a gentleman who devoted his life to films, and especially to forging a British cinema, and to his "team," we are forever grateful. And finally, to Iris Barry, our own British-American connection, we wish to dedicate *British Film.* Like Michael Balcon, Iris Barry was born in Birmingham and made her way to London, where she was one of the founders of The Film Society. She came to The Museum of Modern Art in 1932 and in 1935 became the first curator of film. She was a pioneer and we salute her memory.

Adrienne Mancia and Laurence Kardish

Introduction

Adrienne Mancia

You see, if you think about Ealing at those times—I've often examined it myself—what were we? We were middle-class people brought up with middle-class backgrounds, with rather conventional educations. And although many people thought we were radical in our point of view, we were not tearing down all the institutions in our films. We didn't think in terms of Marxism or Maoism, or Lévi-Strauss or Marcuse, or anything like that. We were people of the immediate post-war generation, we voted Labour for the first time after the war; that was our mild revolution. We had great affection for British institutions and the comedies were done with affection. And I don't think we would have thought of tearing down institutions unless we had a blueprint for what we wanted to put in their place. Of course we wanted to improve them, or to use the cliché of today, to look for a more just society in the terms that we knew. And the comedies were, if you like, a mild protest—but a protest about nothing more sinister than the regimentation of the times, after a period of war. I think we were going through a mildly euphoric period then—believing in ourselves and having some sense of, yes it sounds awful, national pride. And if I were to think and think I couldn't give you a deeper analysis. . . .

Michael Balcon in an interview with John Ellis

THE EXHIBITION IS *British Film*. The first part of the series focuses on Michael Balcon, producer. Balcon (1896–1977) would probably assent to this modest, workmanlike appellation. His style, after all, was understatement. His career, accomplishments, and dedication nonetheless indicate a much more significant and influential role in the British film industry, and it will be made clearer in the program at The Museum of Modern Art and in the essays of this catalog.

It is a quarter of a century since Michael Balcon's last production for Ealing, the studio synonymous in the mind of the public with Balcon, comedy, and Alec Guinness. It is true: Balcon's character and purpose were more or less imprinted in every frame of Ealing films, which, beginning in 1938, he supervised when he took over as production chief from Basil Dean. That Ealing was synonymous with comedy is the illusion many of us grew up with. Although comedies—many lovable and some not so lovable—were a staple at Ealing, the range of films was extensive and varied; less than a third were comedies. As for Guinness, his international reputation

did originate in the memorable portraits he created for Balcon—culminating in his tour-de-force in the 1949 *Kind Hearts and Coronets* (eight roles, one as a woman). It was, perhaps, the only instance at Ealing where the star not the company was of primary importance.

When Balcon took over Ealing, he had already had considerable experience in the film industry. He grew up in Birmingham, where he caught the "film bug" from his friend and fellow Birminghamian Victor Saville, and the two young enthusiasts jumped into film distribution. Before long, they were in London and ready for the adventure of film production. Saville went on to become an elegant director, and Balcon, together with another hopeful from his hometown, Graham Cutts, launched into production of their first feature: the silent *Woman to Woman* (1923). In 1924, Balcon and Cutts founded Gainsborough at Islington Studios. From Gainsborough came the early films of Alfred Hitchcock and Ivor Novello, among others, all signalled by the logo of the Gainsborough lady in the big hat.

By 1931, Balcon was dividing his responsibilities between Gainsborough and Gaumont-British, which produced at the Lime Grove Studios, Shepherd's Bush. It was during this period, from 1931 to 1936, that Balcon nurtured his association with filmmakers and technicians—many of whom followed him to Ealing. Productions during this period ranged from thrillers such as *Rome Express* (1932) with Conrad Veidt, to musicals with Jessie Matthews, to Robert Flaherty's documentary, *Man of Aran* (1934). In brief, Balcon was already working in diverse genres and sharpening his production and administrative talents.

Balcon's reputation was such that by 1936, Metro-Goldwyn-Mayer asked him to head their British unit. The relationship was an uneasy one, and Balcon produced a single picture for M-G-M, *A Yank at Oxford* (1938), before he ended his contract and accepted the challenge at Ealing.

Ealing was the studio that gave us the comedy/singing stars Gracie Fields and George Formby. They were popular with working-class audiences and were nourished by the production talents of Basil Dean, who had worked out of Ealing since 1931, on land originally owned by the film pioneer

It Always Rains on Sunday,
1947, Robert Hamer
(Googie Withers)

Will Barker. Dean made entertainments designed to appeal to a wide audience. He also instituted the cozy atmosphere that Ealing was later known for. At Ealing Balcon was not so much an innovator as one who continued the tradition established by Dean and his colleagues (one notable exception being Balcon's preference for original screenplays, as opposed to Dean's tendency, out of keen interest and involvement in the theater, toward literary adaptations). Balcon's job was to bring financial stability to a troubled studio. It was at Ealing that Balcon, then in his forties, would consolidate his position, become conscious of his calling, and create a legend. Balcon and company were Ealing, and Ealing films at their best earned laurels for a none-too-healthy British film industry.

Balcon has been singled out for this exhibition for several reasons. His career spanned over forty years of British film history; he was associated with and encouraged some of the finest artists and craftsmen in the industry; and, if one had to point to one film professional who is quintessentially English, Balcon would win hands down. Communicating Britishness was a moral responsibility he shouldered, and he was the committed spokesman for an independent national cinema. Once his course was set, he never wavered.

There is a catch, however. Balcon's celluloid England was as he believed it to be, or wanted it to be, and how he wanted the audience to believe it. It was working/middle class, liberal, traditional, comfy, and parochial, with a strong sense of community where—when everybody pulled together—things usually worked out for the best. In other words, England was very much like his domain at Ealing. That is how Balcon saw it and that is how he managed his studio: as a democratic team with "Mick" Balcon as head coach.

G. Campbell Dixon, the film critic, put it this way:

If I must generalise, I should say the secret is this—that of all our film producers Mickey Balcon is the most English, judged by the spirit and style and content of his pictures.... Sometimes the openers have plodded, the cutting has been slow, point a trifle dull and backward, the slips too conspicuous. But aren't these in the English character?... In Ealing films you will find the whole face of England, from Welsh mines and leafy lanes to suburban gardens and the bar you instantly recognise as your own local.

It is not difficult to understand why the radical young men of the sixties reacted against the snugness and smugness of Balcon's vision. Times had changed; the sense of national purpose that held the country together during the war and postwar years, and that Balcon struggled to identify, had blurred (a situation not dissimilar to the New Wave revolt by the *Cahiers du Cinéma* critics in France in the same years). Viewed in retrospect, however, the cinema of protest had precedents and roots in Balcon's films.

It Always Rains on Sunday (1947), directed at Ealing by Robert Hamer, is surprisingly bleak on the surface—and in substance—and on close analysis, one sees that the theme of discontent is a subtext of many Ealing films. *Sunday* communicates not only the drabness of a working-class environment but also an atmosphere of claustrophobia, frustration, pettiness, irritability, and—what was a bête noire at Ealing—sexual repression. The ending is a pathetic accommodation, however, achieved only by resignation. If the family structure is to remain intact, true feelings have to be suppressed. By the midsixties, these feelings were ripe for explosion.

One of Balcon's striking contributions was the convincing look of a film. The story could be fanciful, but the setting and atmosphere had to be real enough. It usually was, because Balcon believed in shooting on location with attention to believable detail. He was aided in this by Alberto Cavalcanti, whom Balcon was perceptive enough to bring to Ealing. Cavalcanti was a pioneer of documentary film as well as an accomplished narrative filmmaker. The ebullient "Cav" stimulated Balcon's team and, by his presence, helped mark Ealing productions with the stamp of authenticity.

It was Balcon's conviction that he had a mandate to create an indigenous cinema. He "stubbornly chose to be stubbornly English" in the face of competitive Hollywood entertainment. Even after he sold Ealing to the British Broadcasting Corporation in 1955, he struggled to continue production and to find solutions for the British film industry. He was for a brief period chairman of Bryanston, which gathered together some angry young Turks who had little in common with Balcon's insular world. Balcon also welcomed television, and in the sixties saw Pay TV as a means of survival for an ailing film industry (Balcon even served as a director of Border Television until 1970). He also appreciated the task of the British Film Institute, donating his papers to it and serving as Chairman of the BFI Production Board.

Finally, this tribute to Michael Balcon is a tribute as well to his associates and collaborators, the "team" as he would have put it. No producer was ever more conscious of the collaborative nature of filmmaking. His achievements were also theirs, as he noted: "A film producer is only as good as the sum total of the quality of the colleagues with whom he works, and in this respect I have been uniquely fortunate."

The Lavender Hill Mob, 1951, Charles Crichton (Stanley
Holloway, Alec Guinness)

A Knight and His Castle

Geoff Brown

ONCE UPON A TIME there was a true doughty knight of the British cinema, Sir Michael Balcon by name. Everything he did and touched was quaint, modest, and quintessentially English. No squat factory home for him: Sir Balcon lived in a funny little studio with rose gardens and beehives, picturesquely perched on Ealing's village green on the western edge of the London sprawl. He hatched his films at a splendid Round Table, in fatherly discussion with loyal, loving henchmen: droll comedies like *Whisky Galore!* (1949), *Passport to Pimlico* (1949), *The Lavender Hill Mob* (1951), celebrating the quirks and mild anarchy of ordinary British folk—films loved by all, including discerning foreigners. Periodically, Sir Balcon went off on crusades—against overweening American interests, Government bureaucracy, film-industry monopolies—and his bulldog tenacity brought him back victorious. Sir Balcon only fell down, perhaps, in rescuing damsels in distress: few ladies resided at Ealing Castle, with the principal exception of Princess Googie Withers. It was a happy life until the dastardly Baron Television robbed Sir Balcon of his castle in 1955, forcing him to decamp to Boreham Wood, which sounds romantic but wasn't. Sir Balcon, however, was too British to die of a broken heart; though his films and his henchmen were never quite the same again, he battled on cheerfully, rattling his British saber to the end (1977).

Critical evaluation of Balcon may well be subtler than this fairy-tale version suggests, yet the reality of his important career as a British film producer remains clouded by cozy nostalgia and easy assumptions. Comedies form only a fraction of Ealing's total output, and among the comedies there is wide variety in style and achievement. There is little coziness about Robert Hamer's *Kind Hearts and Coronets* (1949) or Alexander Mackendrick's *The Man in the White Suit* (1951); there are few good jokes in the limp show-business satire *The Love Lottery* (1954) or the tepid farce *Who Done It?* (1956).

Balcon himself has his own image, first affixed during the Second World War, when he became the unofficial spokesman for a film industry fighting to continue production and entertain the British public with relevant, patriotic entertainment. The image needs no dismantling, but modifications would be helpful; at various times in his career from 1922, the knight of the British cinema found himself working for transatlantic interests. Balcon reached Ealing and his distinctive kind of modest, indigenous filmmaking through a long process of trial and error. The process is worth examining carefully, for it reveals valuable information about Balcon's habits and capabilities, and the fluctuating health of that perennially ailing (and perennially surviving) patient, the British film industry.

Balcon's first filmmaking home was in Islington, London, where Famous Players-Lasky Productions had established a tentative British outpost in a converted Metropolitan Railway powerhouse, next to a canal. Like many London studios, the Islington building had no surrounding ground for outside locations; the two studio floors were also positioned on top of each other. For the tiny company of Balcon, Victor Saville, and Jack Freedman—already experienced in exhibition and advertising—it nonetheless was a good place to begin.

Their chosen subject was *Woman to Woman* (1923), based on a sentimental play concerning an amnesiac British army officer who discovers his sordid past during a soirée with his aristocratic wife. Needing a carrot to dangle before American audiences, they secured Betty Compson from Hollywood at an inflated salary of £1,000 per week. The carrot worked on both sides of the Atlantic, though no one seemed inclined to bite a second time when Compson appeared in the hastily conceived *The White Shadow* (1924), advertised as featuring "the same Star, Producer, Author, Hero, Cameraman, Scenic Artist, Staff, Studio, Renting Company as *Woman to Woman*." The same cast and crew, perhaps; the effect, though, was far different.

The advertisement points to one Balcon characteristic that runs right through to his chairmanship of Bryanston in the early sixties: his belief in nurturing a family of colleagues, transported from film to film, studio to studio. As in all the best families, there would be grumbles, rows, broken crockery, haughty departures, humble returns, and the occasional irredeemable rift. By the end of the thirties, for instance, relationships with Saville—who shared Balcon's Birmingham upbringing and early struggles—were seriously soured by the tribulations of working for M-G-M British. Other family members—acquired from Islington's resident staff—included studio manager Harold Boxall, art director C. W. Arnold, and electrician George Gunn. All these paled before the talent of Alfred Hitchcock, first employed at Islington as a title-card designer and odd job man, and accorded director status with *The Pleasure Garden* (1926), filmed in Munich.

By this time, Balcon had consolidated his position. Having formed his own company, Gainsborough Pictures, in 1924, he was also now the sole owner of the Islington studios. Various talents with intellectual credentials clustered round: Adrian Brunel and Ivor Montagu, brimming with knowledge of cinema's international trends through their connections with the Film Society in London and their own work editing foreign films for British consumption; writer Angus MacPhail and editor Ian Dalrymple, from Cambridge University. Among performers, Balcon's chief British glory was Ivor Novello, the young actor-dramatist-composer who looked beautiful enough to delight both sexes, and appeared in nine Gainsborough films between 1925 and 1930.

Personal frictions added to the adventures of production. Director Graham Cutts bitterly resented the meteoric rise of Hitchcock, his former assistant. Balcon found himself caught between the rival tastes of Gainsborough's distributor C. M. Woolf and his own young cinema enthusiasts. Woolf believed in British films, but not in highbrow British films; Brunel was even asked to resign from the Film Society's council, lest Gainsborough's product became tainted through association. Films that Woolf thought not merely tainted but actually diseased received the cold shoulder. Hitchcock in particular suffered: *The Pleasure Garden* and *The Mountain Eagle* (1926) spent long months on the shelf, and *The Lodger* (1926) was reedited. For *The Lodger* the delay proved beneficial. "It is possible that this film is the finest British production ever made," *The Bioscope* ventured at the time.[1] Even now, it stands preeminent among British silents for the sophisticated use of poetic atmosphere, symbols, and camera tricks to convey the melodrama of Jack the Ripper.

The general output of Balcon's bright young men rarely matched their capabilities or hopes. The quirky fun Brunel displayed in his burlesque shorts could find little outlet in the wartime sentimentalities of *Blighty* (1927, p. 45) or the lush romance of *The Constant Nymph* (1928). As Film Society members, Brunel, Montagu, MacPhail, and company absorbed the experimental practices of Eisenstein, Pudovkin, and the stylistic triumphs of Germany; as Gainsborough employees they knew the techniques of Russian montage would be wasted on the small emotions of middle-brow fiction and popular West End plays. Balcon, trapped in the middle, seemed to have fitful powers

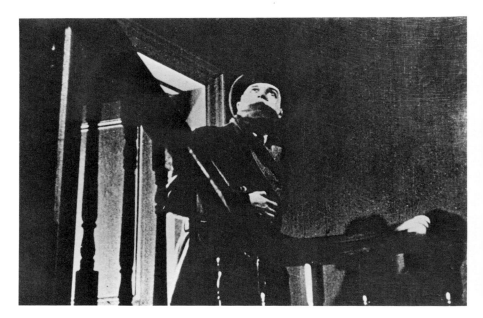

The Lodger, 1926, Alfred Hitchcock (Ivor Novello)

over the selection of material. He picked *The Lodger* as a property for Hitchcock, but it was Woolf who instigated *The Vortex* (1928, from Noël Coward's sensational play); it was Woolf, too, who insisted Brunel's *A Light Woman* (1928) be transferred, unhelpfully, to a Spanish setting. Woolf's words in all things could not be ignored; his distribution company W and F was vital to the company's financial well-being.

Balcon's position became further complicated by changes in Gainsborough's structure. In 1927, W and F was absorbed by the new Gaumont-British Picture Corporation, which combined facilities for production, distribution, and exhibition. Gainsborough sheltered under the same umbrella; some independence was lost as a result, but financing was found to place the company on a firmer footing as Gainsborough Pictures (1928) Ltd.

Life as an associate of Gaumont-British brought its own problems. The 1927 Cinematograph Films Act intensified the struggle between British and American concerns for exhibition in Britain. Financial warfare erupted above Balcon's head, involving Gaumont board members Maurice and Isidore Ostrer, Hollywood's William Fox, and a holding company called the Metropolis and Bradford Trust. Whoever held controlling interest in Metropolis and Bradford also held controlling interest in 65 percent of Gaumont's ordinary share capital. Fox's threatened takeover was neatly obstructed by a change in Metropolis's constitution, effected during July 1929, restricting the buying powers of any foreign national.

Balcon had his own practical headaches in the summer of 1929. Films now talked, creating havoc on production schedules and the studio site. Films not overly promising even as silent movies were further

Sunshine Susie, 1931, Victor Saville (Owen Nares, Renate Müller)

imperiled by the insertion of sound effects, portions of synchronized dialogue, and the odd song. Steam trains could be heard puffing, whistling, and crashing in *The Wrecker* (1929). In *Taxi for Two* (1929), twenties matinee idol John Stuart mouthed occasional sweet nothings to Mabel Poulton, a silent heroine revealed by the microphone as an undisguisable Cockney. At first Balcon commanded none of the proper equipment. Some films had their sound clothes fitted by RCA in New York; a sound remake of *Woman to Woman* (1929) and a version of R. C. Sherriff's hit play *Journey's End* (1930) were both produced in Hollywood in collaboration with the Tiffany-Stahl company. Gradually the Islington studio was equipped for sound. To insulate sets, studio walls were wrapped round with wood, but on January 18, 1930, the wood—and the studio—caught fire, fatally trapping one studio employee and further disrupting production.

It took some time for Gainsborough films to find their feet in the thirties. Talented directors such as Saville and Walter Forde began to get results in 1931. Forde scored particularly with a remake of the thriller *The Ghost Train,* featuring Jack Hulbert and Cicely Courtneidge, eccentric stars of stage revues. Saville capped two careful theatrical adaptations, *Hindle Wakes* (p. 46) and *Michael and Mary,* with a popular version of the German hit musical *Die Privatsekretärin,* retitled *Sunshine Susie.*

The year of decisive change was 1932. Share manipulations brought Gainsborough closer into the Gaumont-British organization. Balcon had been given increased responsibilities, supervising all Gaumont-British production. Gaumont's studio at Lime Grove, Shepherd's Bush, was especially expanded to prepare for the future, at a reputed cost of £250,000. The building eventually housed five stages—placed, in true British fashion, one on top of the other. The thriller *Rome Express* took up residence first, and the press was invited for a jamboree. The set of a Paris railway station (with a meticulously detailed wooden steam engine) was much admired; no one had kind words when the freight elevator used to transport Lady Margot Asquith and various guests became stuck between floors for some twenty minutes. The elevator apart, Balcon had a spanking new studio under his thumb and a corporation with its own cinema chain to display the product. The problem now was to keep both studio and cinemas stocked with films.

What kind of films, though? To judge by an article published in *The Era* shortly after Balcon was appointed Gaumont's production chief, they were going to be British to the core. "Sincerity Will Make the Film English," the headline screamed. Balcon—pictured with the usual smile, moustache, and pocket handkerchief of the period—declared that the time had now come to "concentrate on the fashioning of the essential 'English Picture'" and to purge films of "foreign poison." He further observed: "The conditions of our industry are such that we are compelled by its exigencies to be true to ourselves.... We have to make films which express England."[2] Balcon's personal inclinations differed sharply from company policy, however: the actual Gaumont-British product bent over backward to accommodate American (and European) talents and sensibilities.

No doubt encouraged by the world success of Alexander Korda's *Private Life of Henry VIII* (1933), Gaumont-British began aiming their films at the lucrative American market. There was also a kind of royal assent in the Prince of Wales' edict: "Trade follows the film"; British films shown abroad, the argument went, would stimulate interest in other national products. Balcon was dispatched on regular talent hunts for

directors and performers who might give his product
some Hollywood sheen and a head start at the American box office. Scripts, too, came under review; Gaumont appointed an adviser, one Charles de Grandcourt, solely to weed out expressions he thought
Americans would not understand, such as "fortnight,"
or "pavement," or "braces." At first de Grandcourt sat
in New York, sending memos of doubtful worth. He
then crossed the Atlantic and bothered everyone at
close quarters.

Gaumont's first big American push came in 1934
with a distribution deal arranged through Fox. Individual films gathered respectable notices and business in
New York—Jessie Matthews's musicals were particularly popular—but distribution outlets in the rest of the
country were less eager to promote British fare. Balcon
himself admitted difficulties over American acceptance
of homegrown comedies, Jack Hulbert's in particular.
"So we are making slight alterations in the type of
character he portrays in his films this year,"[3] Balcon
wrote in *Film Weekly*—though it would take more than
slight alterations to change the effect of Hulbert's over-
whelmingly jaunty demeanor, his jutting chin and
gangling limbs.

Gaumont's American policy ensured work in Britain
for a number of talented performers and technicians.
Cameramen Phil Tannura and Charles Van Enger displayed their expertise in *I Was a Spy* (1933), *Friday the
Thirteenth* (1933, p. 47), and Tom Walls and Will Hay
comedies. Sylvia Sidney appeared in Hitchcock's *Sabotage* (1936); upcoming Robert Young partnered Jessie
Matthews in *It's Love Again* (1936) and Madeleine Carroll in *Secret Agent* (1936). Walter Huston's customary
vigor enhanced the ambitious biography of Cecil Rhodes, *Rhodes of Africa* (1936). Talent on the way down, ill
at ease in the Hollywood of the thirties, also found a
temporary British home: old-fashioned actors, way-
ward writers, and directors such as Charles Reisner.

Balcon's connections with Germany date from the
twenties. There were distribution and co-production
deals: Woolf acquired UFA product for British release;
Hitchcock and Graham Cutts directed films in Munich
and the UFA studios at Neubabelsberg. German technicians also began working for Gainsborough and
Gaumont-British in England, and the numbers
increased once Europe's political horizons darkened.
Cameramen Mutz Greenbaum, Otto Kanturek, and
Günther Krampf and art directors Alfred Junge, Oscar
Werndorff, and Ernö Metzner all gave their productions a lustrous and imaginative visual surface. Metzner
in particular turned the elaborate musical *Chu-Chin-
Chow* (1934) into a cornucopia of mock-Arabic design;
his sets for *The Tunnel* (1935) surpassed those in the
German original for sleekness and fantasy. Balcon presented these illustrious talents to his homegrown work

Top: *Rome Express*, 1932,
Walter Forde (Esther
Ralston, Finlay Currie)

Left: *The Tunnel*, 1935,
Maurice Elvey (Madge
Evans, Richard Dix)

force as teachers as well as studio colleagues, partly, perhaps, to justify the superior income his émigrés enjoyed; their lessons, at any rate, were readily absorbed. The co-productions themselves, generally filmed in Berlin alongside German and French versions, seem less notable now than their personnel. The films were never particularly successful with the public, and they were also denied British registration by the Board of Trade. Artistically speaking, this seems justified; for all the British antics of Sonnie Hale, Ernest Thesiger, Jack Hulbert, and Cicely Courtneidge, films such as *Happy Ever After* (1932) and *Early to Bed* (1933) remained locked in their world of German musical whimsy.

Balcon's difficulties at Gaumont-British extended beyond the implementation of dubious policies. His superiors also gave him star contracts he little relished. There was Tom Walls, the stage actor-producer long associated with the Ben Travers Aldwych Theatre farces, employed by Gaumont-British at Woolf's specific request. Walls's contract stipulated choice and approval of both story and cast, as well as the right to direct. The result was *A Cuckoo in the Nest* (1933), *Turkey Time* (1933), and eight other cinematically

impoverished comedies, kept alive now by their wholesale reliance on vanished styles of humor and theatrical performance.

Walls's shooting schedules were periodically interrupted for visits to race meetings; those of George Arliss regularly stopped at 3:45 P.M. for a nice cup of tea. Mr. Arliss, as he was cautiously called, proved another difficult acquisition. His American fame and impressive bearing were sufficient to secure an absurdly favorable contract and colossal salary. Balcon resisted, but awkward vehicles for his old-world acting were dutifully trundled out. For his opening venture, *The Iron Duke* (1934), Arliss reputedly received £40,000 (plus a banquet at the Savoy hotel, where the menu proudly offered "Le haddock George Arliss").

There was also Jack Hulbert, a man, Balcon recalled in 1947, with "the persistence of a road drill and the staying power of the Pyramids."[4] Yet it was a road drill worth the battle. Americans might have scratched their heads at his comedy style, but British audiences loved his eccentric nonchalance and the zany twitterings of his customary partner, Cicely Courtneidge. Several vehicles were directed by Forde; *Bulldog Jack* (1935) in particular benefits from a breezy pace and the clever

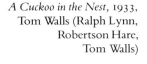

A Cuckoo in the Nest, 1933, Tom Walls (Ralph Lynn, Robertson Hare, Tom Walls)

manipulation of lighting and décor for comic effect. Balcon's biggest and best British star, however, was undoubtedly Jessie Matthews, whose idiosyncratic looks and charming way with a song and dance were showcased in *Evergreen* (1934), *First a Girl* (1935), and *It's Love Again* (1936), all persuasively directed by Saville. Here was a talent that Hollywood had eyes for; even before her film career began, she made a test for Paramount in 1929. After the American success of *Evergreen,* the offers mounted. There was talk of an M-G-M film, an RKO musical with Fred Astaire.

Directors, too, sometimes descended on Balcon from above. Woolf requested the employment of Albert de Courville, a stage producer of lavish spectacles; he made six films for Gaumont-British between 1932 and 1936. Other directors, such as Sinclair Hill and Maurice Elvey, proved longer on experience than flair. To counterbalance the veterans, Balcon promoted choice new talent acquired through the corporation's scheme for hiring university graduates. Robert Stevenson, from Cambridge, wrote Gainsborough scripts from 1931; by 1932 he was co-directing and supervising UFA collaborations and a Jack Hulbert musical. Pen Tennyson, great-grandson of the poet, climbed the ladder to direct two travel shorts and serve as assistant director on major features such as *The Good Companions* (1933) and *The Man Who Knew Too Much* (1934, p. 48). Tennyson and Stevenson continued their association with Balcon at Ealing; Tennyson, in particular, was regarded by Balcon with warm affection—"second only to that for my own son," he wrote in his autobiography.[5]

Balcon's brightest directing talents were Saville and Hitchcock. Saville occasionally had to apply his professional skills to unmanageable material such as *The Iron Duke* (1934) and *Me and Marlborough* (1935), but his Jessie Matthews musicals remain indestructible examples of craftsmanship. Hitchcock's achievement was more remarkable, for the thrillers he made at Gaumont-British both salvaged his uncertain reputation and swiftly established their own genre within British cinema. Since the triumph of *The Lodger* (1926), Hitchcock had worked for John Maxwell's British International Pictures on a mixed bag of thrillers and literary adaptations; he returned to Balcon's orbit as a fretful freelance, directing a musical, *Waltzes from Vienna* (1934), with dwindling interest. Balcon encouraged his return to the urban crime milieu of *The Lodger,* and a contract for five films was duly prepared. Michael Powell, still in his twenties, also found employment, directing between 1933 and 1935 four short features that give little hint of the flamboyant films to come.

Hitchcock soon resumed his battles with Woolf. While Balcon was off on an American spending spree, Woolf viewed *The Man Who Knew Too Much* (1934) and

Top: *Bulldog Jack,* 1935, Walter Forde (Jack Hulbert, Claude Hulbert)

Left: *First a Girl,* Ogden's cigarette card, ca. 1935

First a Girl, 1935, Victor
Saville (Jessie Matthews,
Sonnie Hale)

The Good Companions,
1933, Victor Saville (John
Gielgud, Jessie Matthews)

The Phantom Light, 1935,
Michael Powell (Gordon
Harker, Herbert Lomas)

Sabotage, 1936, Alfred
Hitchcock (set)

deemed it unfit for exhibition; luckily Balcon returned from abroad and intervened himself. Woolf's opposition to sophisticated cinema may also have affected the career of Anthony Asquith. Certainly, after directing the whimsical, René Clairlike comedy *The Lucky Number* (1933), Asquith only found minor work—staging the second-unit naval flurries in Forde's *Forever England* (1935) and supervising the English edition of Willi Forst's film on Franz Schubert, *The Unfinished Symphony* (1934).

Surveying the Gaumont-British output of Balcon's tenure, one is impressed by the sheer bulk of celluloid created both at home and abroad. Fourteen feature films were released during 1932. Production increased apace, and 1933 saw twenty-five films, including three UFA co-productions in Berlin. The year 1934 brought twenty-two more, with ventures into Vienna, France, and the Aran Islands off Ireland. The same number emerged during 1935; the total for 1936 was nineteen, including one co-production in Australia. Various production units were also busy in Canada, Africa, and India; Balcon himself was often on business in America.

With such hectic schedules and itineraries, Balcon had little opportunity to ensure strict quality control, let alone operate a coherent program policy. The *Era* article's fighting words about sincerity, naturalness, and "the perfect English film" crumbled before practicalities. Yet the idealistic impulse survived, and flowered again in print in a 1936 article called "Putting the *Real* Britain on the Screen."[6] After five years of headaches, Balcon acknowledged his practical difficulties: "We haven't felt much like experimenting with subjects which might not have suited the tastes of people overseas." But now, Balcon argues, the industry is primed for truly patriotic endeavors, wooing the world with films about Britain and the Empire. Among Gaumont-British product, he singles out *Forever England* (1935, Forde); an army adventure, *O.H.M.S.* (1936, released 1937, Raoul Walsh); an historical drama, *Tudor Rose* (1936, Stevenson; p. 52); and Hitchcock's forthcoming *Sabotage* (1936, due to feature "more of the real London than any other film yet made"). Balcon then moves on to a lyrical affirmation of patriotic possibilities:

We see the dramatic entertainment in the life of the farmer on the fells of the North, of the industrial worker in the Midlands, of the factory girls of London's new industrial areas, of the quiet shepherds of Sussex. I believe that the sweep of the Sussex Downs against the sky makes as fine a background to a film as the hills of California; that Kentish and Worcestershire orchards and farms are as picturesque as the farmlands of Virginia; that the slow talk of labourers round an English village pub fire makes as good dialogue as the wise-cracks of "City Slickers" in New York.

Practicalities, suddenly, are forgotten. The Balcon who urged British films to move and talk faster to ease their acceptance in America is now proposing the slow talk of laborers round an English village pub fire. One fears, too, for the dramatic viability of quiet Sussex shepherds.

The article, interestingly, makes no mention of Robert Flaherty's *Man of Aran* (1934; p. 51), one of the few instances of experimentation at Gaumont-British, known to intimates as "Balcon's Folly" during production. By finding employment for the romantic documentary maker of *Nanook of the North* (1922) and *Moana* (1926), Gaumont-British hoped to win cultural prestige unlikely to be achieved by the rest of their program. Balcon fretted over the mounting expense, but cheered himself up by regularly screening the spectacular storm scenes to studio doubters. Once completed, Flaherty's fond treatment of the Aran Islanders' battles with raw nature became subjected to the blare of commercial marketing. Irish Guards played folk music at the London premiere; the company's Wardour Street windows proudly displayed a stuffed basking shark, especially shortened in the middle to fit the available space. Despite mixed reviews, prestige did follow; yet this meeting of documentary and commercial cinema had no immediate successors. It took the special circumstances of the Second World War for the merger to become firmly established.

Ironically, while Balcon looked forward to the great British—and Gaumont-British—films of the future, his own organization experienced a financial and man-agerial earthquake. For 1935, profits had been £12,000; 1936 saw a loss of £97,000. The production schedule, hastily expanded, had resulted in too many films that too few wanted to exhibit or watch. For Balcon, matters were complicated by the increasing prominence of Maurice Ostrer in production decisions; rumors of share transactions also hung in the air, involving, first, Twentieth Century–Fox and, second, John Maxwell of British International Pictures. Although neither deal came to fruition, it seemed prudent for Balcon to move elsewhere.

So in 1936 Balcon left Gaumont-British, and the Shepherd's Bush studio began to wind down production, leaving only the company's instructional unit in residence. With mingled timidity and hope, Balcon signed on with M-G-M British—a new venture designed by M-G-M to produce quality films in England with British subject matter. Only one Balcon film resulted: *A Yank at Oxford* (1938), directed by Jack Conway, a popular success, polished and entertaining, made at Denham studios in a style far more Yank than Oxford.

For Balcon, the venture represented one more attempt to make British films commercially attractive to the American market. The transatlantic venture of Gaumont-British may have failed through inadequate talent and half-hearted promotion, but with the full force of M-G-M behind him, better things might be expected—or so Balcon reasoned. M-G-M's expectations were more equivocal. During his six-month session in Hollywood to observe production techniques,

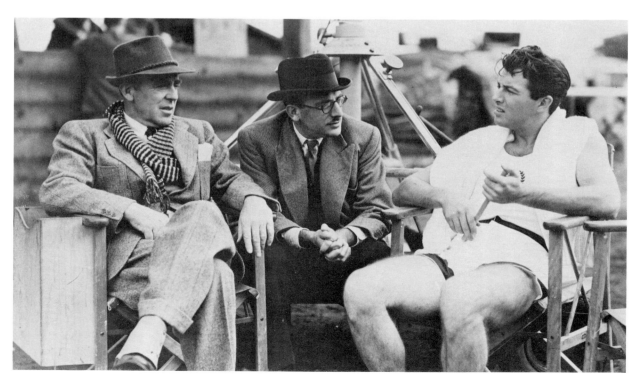

Jack Conway, Michael Balcon, and Robert Taylor on location, *A Yank at Oxford*, 1938

Cheer Boys Cheer, 1939,
Walter Forde (Graham
Moffatt, Jimmy O'Dea,
Moore Marriott)

Balcon was continuously forced to click his heels; when Louis B. Mayer descended on London in the summer of 1937, he took pains to harangue Balcon near an open window, within earshot of studio employees. Following completion of *Yank,* Balcon saw his own former colleague, Saville, receive the plum assignments. The expected announcement finally came in June 1938: Balcon's contract was terminated, and Saville produced the remaining M-G-M British films, *The Citadel* (1938) and *Goodbye, Mr. Chips* (1939).

Balcon may have been hired simply as a figurehead, a respected British producer with respectable credentials useful for demonstrating M-G-M's good faith (the entire venture had been mounted when American interests were wooing the British film trade before the renewal of the Cinematograph Films Act). At all events, the war curtailed further production. Saville remained as an M-G-M producer in Hollywood; Balcon retreated to Ealing, the picturesque studio on the village green, where life was a lot simpler and a lot more British.

Ealing Studios had been built in 1931, and for seven years it was the home of Associated Talking Pictures (ATP). During those years ATP experienced the typical vicissitudes of a British production base. Distribution in the American market (through RKO) failed to meet expectations; the need to supply regular product strained available talent and facilities. The production policy of Basil Dean, an experienced theater producer, was erratic. There were well-groomed versions of British plays and novels, and such cultural novelties as *Whom the Gods Love* (1936), a life of Mozart. The films that made money, however, were the boisterous comedies of Gracie Fields and George Formby—two talents from the industrial north of England who faced adversity with a song, a grin, and a pratfall.

Yet if ATP's product was uncoordinated, Dean sowed the seeds of a fruitful studio philosophy. Employees were encouraged to regard the studio as a family home. A sign on the walls declared: "The Studio with the Team Spirit"; the canteen, dubbed "The Inn," had its own walls painted a boisterous red. Outside the studio gates, the Red Lion pub stood with open arms. Balcon in time intensified the family atmosphere and added extra quaintness to the studio setting, placing beehives in the flower garden.

Balcon arrived at Ealing in 1938 as an independent producer with modest plans for a remake of Edgar Wallace's thriller *The Ringer,* financed as a cooperative venture. A summer of organizational changes at ATP left him in full charge of studio production; thereafter, the ATP name was gradually phased out in favor of Ealing Studios, previously used for the company owning the studio space. Grand thoughts of conquering world markets with transatlantic concoctions were now swept aside. Balcon adjusted his perspective to the small, the cheap, and the indigenous: "I have no intention of talking about spending millions of pounds on pictures; . . . that sort of talk is bad for films and bad for the industry."[7] He might have added that he hadn't millions of pounds to spend, anyway. He also confronted once more the problem of America. "I am sure we can get into the American market, but it will be with films of genuine British character. We shall become international by being national."[8] There could be no doubting the national identity of Balcon's early Ealing films: "A British Picture," the final frames declared in lettering superimposed over a Union Jack, "Made and Recorded at Ealing Studios, London."

The early films declared their national identity simply through their genres. *The Ware Case* (1938, Stevenson) revised a courtroom melodrama first staged in 1915. The *Ringer* remake, *The Gaunt Stranger* (1938, Forde), returned to the bottomless barrel of Wallace crime thrillers, which had provided Balcon with harmless material during the difficult months of the early thirties. Sidney Gilliat wrote a lively script that would have appalled Charles de Grandcourt with its topical British references to the popular organist Reginald Foort and the fey columnist Godfrey Winn. There was little chance of becoming international with such cheerfully parochial product. Balcon continued production of ATP's George Formby farces, beginning with *Trouble Brewing* (1939, Anthony Kimmins); four more followed. Irish comedian Jimmy O'Dea provided a further regional accent in *Let's Be Famous* (1939, Forde) and the fascinating *Cheer Boys Cheer* (1939, Forde).

Cheer Boys Cheer is a comedy about beer and breweries. It brings the first flickerings of the comic national consciousness that would flourish in the classic Ealing comedies, some ten years in the future. The old-fashioned Greenleaf brewery, its product advertised as "the beer of Old England," faces ruthless competition from the Ironside company, whose dictator boss is briefly glimpsed reading *Mein Kampf.* By some clumsy plot stratagems, Greenleaf's small community enterprise wins, and the beer of Old England maintains its peerless quality. Yet if the underlying themes suggest future Ealing celebrations of quaint individuality, the style and performers remain tied to prewar traditions. Where Ealing's later comedies offer a blended ensemble of actors, here the cast pursues wildly different paths. C. V. France, as the benign Greenleaf boss, offers sweet character acting; Peter Coke, from the stage, leaps about in the bullying theatrical manner of the time; Nova Pilbeam, young heroine of *Tudor Rose,* spreads upper-class haughtiness and vowels. Jimmy O'Dea oozes music-hall blarney, while Moore Marriott and Graham Moffatt (previously stooges to Will Hay) provide their customary brand of ragamuffin slapstick. There is abundant energy and attack, but no united front.

In a sense, this was true of all Balcon's early output at Ealing. Familiar and trusted colleagues gathered round him—MacPhail as script editor; Werndorff as art director; Forde, Stevenson, and Tennyson as directors—but the product had little group identity. Balcon, operating as an executive producer, left his directors to paddle their own canoes in the company of associate producers. Forde, paired with Balcon's brother Chandos, concentrated on good-humored farces; Stevenson, also linked with Chandos, directed the period romp *Young Man's Fancy* (1939) and a mordant romantic comedy, *Return to Yesterday* (1940). Formby's vehicles were provided by director Anthony Kimmins and producer Jack Kitchin, a team unchanged since ATP days.

Balcon's protégé Pen Tennyson made the pivotal contribution to the Ealing of the future. His first feature, *There Ain't No Justice* (1939), was advertised with the legend "Real people—real problems—a human document—supercharged with action." The people in this drama of boxing racketeering were not always real in the documentary sense; some of the cauliflower ears were only imitations, affixed with cellophane tape. Yet Tennyson consciously tried to lead his audiences into the seedier, more deprived corners of British life; and the leading performers (Jimmy Hanley and Phyllis Stanley) had the virtues of youth and freshness. In a lecture entitled "Realism or Tinsel?" delivered in 1943 to the Film Workers Association at Brighton,[9] Balcon duly mentioned *There Ain't No Justice* as the film that provided "food for thought" in its avoidance of commercial trumpery.

Tennyson's second film, *The Proud Valley* (1939), pursued the same approach with more confidence,

Let George Do It!, 1940, Marcel Varnel (Coral Browne, George Formby)

though Paul Robeson's outsize personality proved difficult to integrate into the portrait of a struggling Welsh mining village. The outbreak of war on the third day of production brought important changes to the film's conclusion: instead of establishing a cooperative, the unemployed miners work in consort with their bosses, putting shoulders to the national wheel to help the war effort. "Listen, Sir John," their spokesman argues at the London head office, "we heard you say that tomorrow we may be at war. In that case you know the risks that will have to be faced in the trenches, in the sky, on the sea; aye, and by our women and children in their homes. Coal in wartime is as much a part of our national defense as guns or anything else, so why not let us take our chance down the pit?"

Substitute cinema in those lines for coal, and one might have a speech by Michael Balcon. In the uneasy months before September 1939, he gave much thought to the British film industry's possible role in wartime, but a memorandum sent to the Government received cursory acknowledgment. When war became a reality, a series of bureaucratic battles had to be fought simply to keep the industry's production line rolling. Public cinemas were temporarily closed because of their vulnerability to aerial attack. Studio space was requisitioned for the storage of ammunition, overcoats, and other paraphernalia of armed combat. Studio personnel joined, or returned to, the fighting forces. Balcon's staff losses included his own brother Chandos, Formby's mentors Kimmins and Kitchin, managerial assistant Reginald Baker, and Tennyson—who died in 1941, serving with the Fleet Air Arm.

Ealing itself faced requisition, though Balcon managed to make the Board of Trade change its mind. He also helped win another victory over quota regulations. Discovering the Board's plans for repealing the 1938 Cinematograph Films Act, which would effectively leave the native industry stunted, Balcon made the issue public. In the London *Evening News* on September 8, 1939, Balcon implored audiences and Government to support "films of a character which will be of national use at this time," noting that "the collapse of British film production in Britain during the last war, and the consequent foreign domination of this market, should surely have taught us a lesson." The Board of Trade ultimately agreed, and kept the annual quota of British productions at their prewar level of 15 percent.[10]

Balcon's patriotic fervor even led him into harsh attacks in the press on the British talents and former colleagues now working in America. Hitchcock was working with David O. Selznick on *Rebecca;* Stevenson, a declared pacifist, was also with Selznick discussing projects; Saville was producing at Culver City. Hitchcock particularly came under fire: "I had a plump young technician in my studio, whom I promoted from department to department. Today he is in Hollywood, while we who are left behind short-handed are trying to harness the films to our great national effort."[11] Hitchcock's reply mentioned the producer's own Hollywood adventures, "which have invariably wound up unfortunately for Balcon. He's a permanent Donald Duck."[12] Balcon always clung to his employees and looked upon departing backs with the affronted pride of a possessive headmaster faced with the misdemeanor of a star pupil.

Along with the practical problems of maintaining

Ealing production, Balcon in 1939 also faced major decisions on aesthetic wartime tactics. What exactly were these "films of a character which will be of national use at this time"? He began tentatively, devising comedies with a war background. A film about evacuated children, *When the Children Came,* was planned in late September and abandoned; George Formby launched Ealing's war program in October with *Let George Do It!* (released in 1940).

"*It!*" in this context meant many things, from the singing of daft ditties like "Grandad's Flannelette Nightshirt" to the unmasking of Nazi spies in Norway. For wartime audiences, Formby's greatest action was probably his dream flight over Germany in a balloon. "Eh, windbag, Adolf," he yells, spotting Hitler addressing a rally, "put a sock in it.... Look out, Adolf, I'm coming to get you!" The balloon then descends, and the Führer is thumped. Such patriotic comic-strip farce continued throughout the war. When Formby left for the British studios of Columbia in 1941, Will Hay carried on the tradition in such rough-hewn, endearing films as *The Ghost of St. Michael's* (1941, Marcel Varnel) and *The Goose Steps Out* (1942, Dearden and Hay).

Serious drama with a war background proved more difficult to conceive. Government cooperation was essential to secure film stock and equipment, and to facilitate location shooting with the forces. But in the early months Government policy on film production and propaganda was difficult to decipher; only with the arrival in 1940 of Sir John Reith as Minister of Information and Jack Beddington as head of the Ministry of Information (MOI) Films Division did a coherent system emerge. One result was Ealing's string of short instructional films distributed by the MOI to all the nation's cinemas. *Salvage with a Smile* (1940, John Croydon) taught the virtues of saving scrap materials; *Dangerous Comment* (1940, John Paddy Carstairs) contributed to the campaign waged against "careless talk." Longer films surveyed the activities of the army, navy and the Fleet Air Arm.

Balcon's first dramatic war feature, *Convoy,* emerged in summer 1940, directed by Tennyson. Some 20,000 feet of film had been shot during convoy operations in the North Sea—vital raw material not just for Tennyson but for future Ealing directors working on maritime subjects. The results drew kind words from the House of Commons for its propaganda value, though seen from today's perspective the war against the Germans seems mild compared to the stylistic war waged between tinsel and reality.

The script's main characters are trapped in a melodramatic romantic triangle worthy of a stage drawing room; the German U-boat crew speak bad Cinema Esperanto ("Torpedo number *Zwei*"); binoculars and machine guns are regularly aimed at back-projection

Convoy, 1940,
Pen Tennyson

San Demetrio London, 1943, Charles Frend (Gordon Jackson, Michael Allen, Duncan McIntyre, John Coyle [?], Charles Victor, Frederick Piper, Robert Beatty)

The Next of Kin, 1942, Thorold Dickinson (Nova Pilbeam, Geoffrey Hibbert)

screens. Yet beneath this tinsel, a rough, ordinary surface can be observed. "It may give us a chance of action against enemy surface craft," Captain Clive Brook tells the crew in his customary ramrod style; but they know the reality this could mean: "Swimming in the North Sea with a leg off," someone mutters. For all the abundant class differences in the characters, the film acknowledges the communal endeavors of Britain at war. "We're patrolling the North Sea, not shooting for coconuts on Hampstead Heath," one officer proclaims.

Ealing's journey from tinsel to reality advanced considerably with the arrival of talent from the documentary movement. Alberto Cavalcanti was hired as a producer in 1940, after his status as a foreign alien made his position at the Government's Crown Film Unit vulnerable. Harry Watt, director of Crown's taut simulation of an RAF bombing raid, *Target for To-night* (1941), joined Ealing in 1942. Balcon must have sensed that such films reduced to smithereens the well-intentioned *Convoy,* or the subsequent, absurdly artificial *Ships with Wings* (1941), in which war seems a game played with toys and puppets. He was eager to use his documentary recruits as teachers, much as he had used the European émigrés at Gaumont-British.

Cavalcanti was the crucial figure in Ealing's stylistic

Went the Day Well?, 1942,
Alberto Cavalcanti (Frank
Lawton, Johnny Schofield,
Norman Pierce, C. V.
France, Basil Sydney [sec-
ond soldier])

development. New recruits such as Charles Crichton, Charles Frend, and Robert Hamer—all trained as editors—worked under him with great benefit. Balcon's own perception of cinema's possibilities deepened under Cavalcanti's influence; details in his 1943 "Realism or Tinsel" lecture were drawn, with due acknowledgment, from Cavalcanti's commentary for the National Film Library's compilation *Film and Reality* (1942).

If *Ships with Wings* presents Ealing's war output at its silliest, Watt's *Nine Men,* released early in 1943, reflects the sharp, lean, documentary prototype. For obvious reasons the drama of nine soldiers fighting for survival in a Libyan desert shelter was staged far from Libya, in a sandy corner of South Wales. But Watt and his producer, Charles Crichton, did everything else to keep tinsel at bay. The narrative was cut to the bare bones, with no extraneous twists (or female interest); most performers had regional accents unscathed by London drama schools or West End plays. One was Bill Blewitt, the Cornish postmaster discovered by Watt for a GPO film (*The Saving of Bill Blewitt*).

By the end of 1943, another key film was ready, *San Demetrio London,* based on the true story of a tanker crew crawling home across the Atlantic after a battering

from German guns. Here there is a further shift in the Ealing style. Studio artifice has crept back in—the Atlantic is clearly the Ealing special-effects tank—yet there is now sufficient emotional depth to situations and characters to render the fakery harmless.

Such films present one aspect of Balcon's notion of national character in wartime: groups of mixed backgrounds, yoked together in adversity, surviving—if not actually winning—with humor, and without rhetoric. Ealing's films centering on the Home Front shone a similar spotlight on group endeavor, though the light tended to be harsher, less flattering to the national ego. *The Next of Kin* (1942, Thorold Dickinson) and *Went the Day Well?* (1942, Cavalcanti) portrayed a Britain so cozy and slapdash that German spies and invading soldiers could operate with ease. *The Next of Kin,* originally planned as an army instruction film on security, describes how a trail of leaked information leads to a disastrous raid on a Nazi submarine base in France; cumulative shots of the dead and dying made Prime Minister Winston Churchill order cosmetic cuts (though the director claimed only 20 seconds were removed). Cavalcanti's *Went the Day Well?* produced a similarly lethal impact, with its picture of a rural English paradise slowly turning into a battleground.

The last Ealing film released in wartime, *They Came to a City* (1944), presents another aspect: the thoughtful drama of social regeneration and postwar hope. In terms of cinematic technique, few Ealing films could be more tedious; J. B. Priestley's play was transported from the West End with no alteration of cast and only modest changes in dialogue, leaving director Basil Dearden little to do but square up to actors spilling out words. The film's interest lies in the words themselves and the thoughts behind them. The city is a socialist Utopia, of which we see only the outside walls; a motley band of people is magically drawn to them, and debates the city's attractions and horrors. Balcon himself voted Labour for the first time in the 1945 General Election ("That was our mild revolution," he said in an interview with John Ellis in 1974).[13] The production of a film like *They Came to a City* was a step toward this revolution, encouraging audiences to consider the kind of peacetime Britain they wanted.

Indeed, one could interpret the whole of Balcon's Ealing career to date as the gradual formation of an ideal city equipped to survive the rigors of the British film industry and the demands of war. Just as individual Ealing films showed how Welsh, Scot, Cockney, English, and American could pull together to win the war, so Balcon showed by his creative management how documentary could combine with the commercial, how the slim traditions of British film could be rejuvenated and made to reflect its audience, building a fighting, nationalistic cinema.

British film production had not collapsed in the war, as Balcon and other industry leaders had first feared. Gainsborough flourished, as did Two Cities; Michael Powell and Emeric Pressburger let their imaginations rip; new directing careers were launched—David Lean, Launder and Gilliat, Laurence Olivier. For the first time British audiences seemed happy to see British rather than Hollywood films, and they saw them in increased numbers: cinema admission figures rose from 990 million in 1939 to 1.585 billion in 1945. The challenge now, for Balcon perhaps more than anybody, was to carry the victorious British film into the postwar world.

In the last months of the war, Balcon described his own vision of peacetime cinema in an article published in *Kinematograph Weekly,* "Let British Films Be Ambassadors to the World."[14] Balcon wanted to see on screen:

... Britain as a leader in Social Reform in the defeat of social injustices and a champion of civil liberties; Britain as a patron and parent of great writing, painting and music; Britain as a questing explorer, adventurer and trader; ... Britain as a mighty military power standing alone and undaunted against terrifying aggression.

In calmer prose he analyzed the part films could play in the projection of British achievement and values:

Fiction films which portray contemporary life in Britain in different sections of our society, films with an outdoor background of the British scene, screen adaptations of our literary classics, films reflecting the post-war aspirations not of governments or parties, but of individuals—these are the films that America, Russia and the Continent of Europe should be seeing now and at the first opportunity.

Balcon was far from alone in waving the Union Jack: intelligent observers of the film world in Britain and elsewhere looked to the medium as a universal language that could knit together the fractured world. But in Balcon's case the aggressive stance partly stemmed from his new position as the film industry's quasi-official spokesman. From his days in the twenties as the excited, eager independent producer—constantly referred to by his colleagues as "young Mickey Balcon"—Balcon had grown to assume the confident manner of the pugnacious, experienced statesman.

As with political statesmen, Balcon found that the hard facts of postwar life necessitated compromise. He had often fulminated against the crushing power of large film corporations; as a leading member of the Board of Trade's Cinematograph Films Council, he helped instigate its 1944 report, "Tendencies to Monopoly in the Cinematograph Film Industry." Ealing's own postwar survival, however, required association with the biggest British film monopolist of them all, J. Arthur Rank. Having begun as a propagandist for religious films in the thirties, Rank soon expanded his horizons and powers. By 1941, Gaumont-British Film Corporation, Balcon's old employer, was under his

Frieda, 1947, Basil Dearden (Flora Robson, David Farrar, Mai Zetterling)

Dead of Night, 1945, "The Haunted Mirror" episode, Robert Hamer (Ralph Michael, Googie Withers)

Dead of Night, 1945, "The Haunted Mirror" episode, Robert Hamer (Ralph Michael, Googie Withers)

thumb; at the time of the 1944 report he owned 56 percent of all studio space in Britain. Rank also controlled General Film Distributors (the major British distributor), two newsreels, and the Odeon cinema chain, and held the purse strings for the enterprising filmmakers grouped together as "Independent Producers" (among them David Lean and the Powell and Pressburger team).

By the terms of their agreement, the Rank Organisation guaranteed Ealing film distribution throughout Britain, provided half the budget (later increased to three-quarters), and offered the services of its contract artists. While Balcon may have been relieved to have Rank's financial cushion, the association brought other problems. Relations between Balcon and Rank's new troubleshooter, managing director John Davis, were cordial only on the surface. Monja Danischewsky's Ealing publicity department, responsible for innovative poster campaigns featuring the work of major British artists, was forced back to the conventional. As in the thirties, distribution arrangements sometimes favored American films rather than the homegrown product: returns for *The Overlanders* (1946; p. 70), for instance, were a fraction of those earned by its Hollywood companion on circuit double bills.

Moreover, Rank's cinema tactics in the forties did not fit in with the modest, indigenous product Balcon had

successfully cultivated in the past. Rank was once more aiming at the "impossible dream," loading British films with sufficient stars and spectacle to dazzle the American market. Some of its ambitions—and large budgets—duly crept into the Ealing program. *Scott of the Antarctic* (1948, Charles Frend; p. 68), Balcon's first color production, was festooned with the trappings of patriotic prestige; the historical romance *Saraband for Dead Lovers* (1948, Dearden; p. 67), similarly offered color and a solemn sense of occasion.

Ealing's postwar course inevitably took Balcon some distance from the triumphant prospectus of his 1945 *Kinematograph Weekly* article. Glimmerings of the vision can be seen here and there in Ealing's films of the late forties. Frend's *Scott of the Antarctic* dwelt on "Britain as a questing explorer." Classic British literature received attention with Cavalcanti's *Nicholas Nickleby* (1947), a Dickens adaptation crammed with incident but insufficient atmosphere. Frend's period drama *The Loves of Joanna Godden* (1947), set in Romney Marsh, Kent, was specifically mounted to satisfy Balcon and Frend's interest in "films with an outdoor background of the British scene." Balcon also renewed contact with the British Empire, last visited in Gaumont-British days. Harry Watt's *The Overlanders* inaugurated a series of Australian and African productions stretching through to 1959. The second, *Eureka Stockade* (1949), was conceived as the first of a Commonwealth series about the birth of democracy, though in Ealing's later foreign ventures exotic entertainment superseded education.

But it is hard to fit the celebrated Ealing comedies into the prospectus; when Balcon wrote about "films reflecting the post-war aspirations...of individuals," he assuredly didn't mean mild bank clerks robbing the Bank of England and smuggling out gold in Eiffel Tower souvenirs. Balcon reached these classic comedies through a roundabout route, as various genres and styles were attempted to replace the inspirational subjects of wartime. The war itself exerted dwindling appeal for both Ealing and British audiences. Dearden's *The Captive Heart* (1946; p. 65) extracted considerable emotion from the plight of prisoners of war; another Dearden film, *Frieda* (1947), agonized over a young German girl (Swedish import Mai Zetterling) who marries into a well-heeled English family. But after the unsuccessful release of Crichton's resistance drama *Against the Wind* (1948), Balcon put the war behind him; despite the craftsmanship of the film's direction, audiences shrank from the spectacle of drabness, treachery, and pain.

The supernatural omnibus film *Dead of Night* (1945) proved another dead end for Ealing, for all its popular and critical success. The film was mounted to celebrate studio expertise and resources. Cavalcanti (soon to leave Ealing) contributed two bravura displays of film-making technique, the episodes of the children's Christmas party and the ventriloquist obsessed with his dummy. Hamer's sequence, "The Haunted Mirror" provided a mordant analysis of the passions seething under the bland exterior of a man on the verge of marriage. Ealing used elements of the omnibus format again (*Train of Events*, 1949; *Dance Hall*, 1950; *Pool of London*, 1951, frontispiece), but the world of the irrational was henceforth avoided in favor of surface reality.

Ealing edged toward its peculiar brand of comedy by returning in part to the documentary spirit. Crichton's *Hue and Cry* (1947; p. 60) took cameras out into the devastated landscapes of East London and filled the screen with scampering boys foiling a criminal plot. Alexander Mackendrick's *Whisky Galore!* (1949) was filmed in the Scottish Hebrides ("To the west there is nothing—except America," the narrator declares in the opening seconds). Yet the kind of Britain Ealing comedy captured on film had little to do with precisely observed reality; the character types and environments, while always recognizable, were consciously given a rosy glow that made them appear fond projections of the popular imagination. There were elements of this in the prewar Ealing films such as the Greenleaf idyll of community enterprise in *Cheer Boys Cheer*. One thinks,

Whisky Galore!, 1949, Alexander Mackendrick (Wylie Watson, Gordon Jackson, Joan Greenwood, Bruce Seton, Gabrielle Blunt)

Passport to Pimlico, 1949, Henry Cornelius (Barbara Murray, Betty Warren, Raymond Huntley, Stanley Holloway, Basil Radford, Naunton Wayne)

too, of a prophetic sliver of dialogue in Forde's spy thriller *The Four Just Men* (1939), in which a character declares himself in love "with all the roads and rivers, the fields and woods that make up this funny old island."

"This funny old island": as a phrase it was hardly equipped for the propaganda war against Hitler's trumpeted concepts of *Vaterland, Lebensraum, Grossraum,* and the like; but British quirks proved vital weapons in Ealing's war, enabling the expression of the indomitable national spirit. With the threat of Hitler removed, the eccentricities could flourish for their own sake; under Ealing's auspices, the funny old island grew funnier and older as the years went on. Characters in *Passport to Pimlico* (1949) gathered together to break away from Whitehall's austerity measures and become an independent state, although by the time of *The Titfield Thunderbolt* (1953), the nation's rebellious itch could only produce a battle to save a local branch railway line. As the fifties advanced, Ealing's funny old island became positively decrepit. Comedies repeatedly revolved around vintage objects, institutions, and characters: an old cargo boat in Mackendrick's *The Maggie* (1954), carrying furniture to an American's holiday home; an old lodging house and a wildly dotty landlady in his *Ladykillers* (1955; p. 64), conspiring to defeat Alec Guinness's band of criminals.

The habit spread outside Ealing. Group 3, a company set up with Balcon as chairman (1951–54) and intended to produce low-budget features using new talent, generated a trickle of mild comedies, in which quirky residents of far-flung locations clashed with officialdom. Henry Cornelius found great success outside Ealing with *Genevieve* (1954), structured round the annual vintage car race from London to Brighton. The Ealing comedies of penetrating satire and real cinematic cut and thrust—Hamer's *Kind Hearts and Coronets* (1949; p. 63) and Mackendrick's *The Man in the White Suit* (1951; p. 62)—exerted regrettably little influence.

Ironically, it was with these modest-budget comedies that Balcon finally achieved what Gaumont-British and Rank had struggled for so painfully and expensively: a decent foothold in the American market. Some adjustments were made to the export prints: early scenes in *Passport to Pimlico* were curtailed to speed up the exposition. "The Americans are impatient by nature. They are used to having their characters introduced quickly,"[15] wrote Michael Truman in *Film Industry* after a session in the United States reediting Ealing product. Truman also reported that the Scots accents of *Whisky Galore!* (retitled *Tight Little Island* for U.S. release) fell more easily on the American ear than the Englishman's slurs and mumbles. Along with the comedies, Frend's film of Nicholas Monsarrat's novel *The*

Cruel Sea (1952) and Watt's African adventures, *Where No Vultures Fly* (1951) and *West of Zanzibar* (1954), enjoyed limited but successful American circuit releases.

Ealing comedies of the fifties not only celebrated venerable institutions; they were also made by one. Under Balcon's stewardship the studio had developed its own idiosyncracies and codes of practice. The form and detail of the various film projects were thrashed out at regular meetings of key personnel at the famous Round Table in the company directors' dining room off the main studio canteen. Hal Mason, the production manager, would then prepare a blueprint for the films, outlining the deployment of manpower, floor space, props and sets; in a small studio, working with modest resources and a constant production line, a strict schedule was essential. With the film before the cameras, there would be daily viewings of rushes by Balcon, Mason, and the appropriate editor; at lunchtime the film unit itself would often gather to look over the material.

Throughout, Balcon operated as an impresario rather than a creative producer on the order of Val Lewton or David O. Selznick; there was no direct input into the scripts, no snatching of the director's megaphone on the studio floor. Continuing the practice of his early years at Ealing, Balcon gathered talents together, paired them off (generally in director-producer teams), encouraged them to generate their own projects and let them proceed—if not in perfect peace, then in reasonable tranquillity. Balcon's management was far from impersonal, however. During a lecture at the British Film Institute's summer school in 1945, he talked in general terms about a producer's methods in choosing colleagues. Film employees, he said, "must be chosen not only for their technical efficiency, but for their sympathy with the producer's point of view and ideas, and, of course, he must choose people with whose work he himself is in sympathy."[16]

His personal stake in Ealing's production varied, and is difficult to determine exactly. The comedies, certainly, were no particular obsession: Balcon's declared preferences were for serious stories of quiet, manly endeavor, such as *Scott of the Antarctic* and *The Cruel Sea,* or for the emotional traumas of mother and child—"a theme close to my heart," he admitted in his autobiography, "and which, I recognise, was a recurring one in Ealing films."[17]

The theme dominates *The Divided Heart* (1954), where a child's mother and foster mother fight for their rights in postwar Germany. Yet despite the characters' inner turbulence, *The Divided Heart* bears a cool surface. Crichton's direction is clinically exact; the two mothers (played by Cornell Borchers and Yvonne Mitchell) assume the posture rather than substance of grief and heartbreak, which for Ealing, and Balcon, was easier to handle than the messy, living reality. Kenneth Tynan reported in a 1955 interview that Balcon had qualms about the script of *The Divided Heart* because "it invaded territories of emotion where he felt uneasy."[18] This was the film whose theme he later claimed was close to his heart!

Sex, too, received circumspect treatment. Why were there not more feminine pulchritude and intimations of desire in Ealing films, Balcon was asked by *Picture Post* magazine. "I don't know why not," he replied, "but our

Ealing Round Table, ca. 1951. Left: Basil Dearden, Charles Frend, Michael Truman, Dr. Francis Koval, unidentified man, H. E. Alexander, Baynham Honri. Center: Miss Slater, Hal Mason, Michael Balcon, Charles Crichton, Margaret Harper Nelson. Right: Margaret Harper Nelson, W. P. Lipscomb, Michael Relph, Robert Hamer, Sidney Cole

minds just don't seem to run in that direction. Maybe I ought to see a psychiatrist."[19] For Balcon it had always been so: the costumes Jessie Matthews wore in her thirties musicals caused misgivings, particularly a cat suit in *It's Love Again* (1936), which seemed no costume at all—just an extra layer of skin, covered with silver spangles.

Balcon's cautious attitude to affairs of the human body permeated all aspects of Ealing production. Subjects that touched on "delicate" areas would scarcely be considered; Robert Hamer made predictably little headway, after *Kind Hearts and Coronets,* with a cherished subject set in the West Indies with a high sexual content. Even unprovocative films were censored, sometimes in absurdly discreet ways: during production of the wartime fantasy *The Halfway House* (1944), Balcon ordered a retake of one location shot at a railway station platform, to avoid the sight of the gent's lavatory.

Balcon's filtering processes helped give Ealing's mature films a shared style and tone. Family resemblances also appear in the films because the same family made them—the same informal repertory company of performers and the same band of directors, writers, and technicians. While Balcon's old company Gainsborough spent the forties building up the star appeal of Margaret Lockwood, Stewart Granger, and James Mason, Balcon satisfied himself with a pliable stock company of character players (Jack Warner, Gladys Henson, Gordon Jackson, Mervyn Johns, and Ralph Michael), topped off with the occasional luminous lead; Googie Withers, strong and vibrant, appeared in five films between 1944 and 1947. The

comedies developed their own personnel—Alec Guinness, Stanley Holloway, Cecil Parker, Joan Greenwood. Guinness, to be sure, grew to star status, both at home and abroad, but he was a star without a face, or at least without a single face; his personality became submerged in brilliant character impersonations, from the mild-mannered bank clerk of *The Lavender Hill Mob* and the toothy master criminal of *The Ladykillers* to the eight-strong d'Ascoyne family (all ages and sexes) in *Kind Hearts and Coronets* (p. 14).

Various possible reasons lie behind Balcon's avoidance of star names and his cultivation of group vehicles. Working with modest resources, even with Rank's financial cushion, he simply could not afford star names specially hired for single productions. After battling with Jack Hulbert, George Arliss, and the like at Gaumont-British, he also felt no need for star temperaments. Balcon lacked the gregariousness, the personal flamboyance, of such impresarios as Alexander Korda, and often found it hard to perform the producer's customary job of fraternizing with actors, establishing contacts, and oiling the publicity machine at social functions.

Instead of shaping Ealing films round star personalities, Balcon chose to work them up from stories, largely original. Several comedies, for instance, grew from stray ideas by T. E. B. Clarke. A newspaper item about Princess Juliana of the Netherlands giving birth in Ottawa, Canada, was spun into *Passport to Pimlico.* Research work for a serious drama, *Pool of London* (1951), combined with the chance discovery of a miniature Eiffel Tower, produced the germ of *The Lavender Hill Mob.*

When Clarke first intimated that *Pool of London* was turning into a comedy, Balcon exploded, calmed down, weighed the possibilities for a separate comedy film, made space in the schedules, shifted personnel, and allowed *Pool of London* to continue its serious way with another scriptwriter. Here is another aspect of Ealing's team spirit: Balcon gladly gave proven members of his studio room to maneuver. He never forced uncongenial projects on them, and tried himself to be accommodating. When Watt and Frend, for instance, felt like attempting something lighthearted after a heavy dose of drama, comedy material was obligingly found, though neither of the results—Watt's *Fiddlers Three* (1944) nor Frend's *A Run for Your Money* (1949)— was very successful.

The Ealing team spirit had another side: while Balcon allowed considerable freedom within Ealing, he was much less indulgent when his staff suggested working outside the studio, where financial rewards were generally greater. Employees at Ealing were kept on modest yearly salaries, with no financial stake in the films themselves. This caused some frustration and bitterness; Hamer struggled free after *His Excellency* in 1952 (though he renewed his association with Balcon later); Cornelius also left, after a bumpy ride with *Passport to Pimlico*.

Balcon clung so tenaciously to his team partly because he regarded them as his own people, his own

The Divided Heart, 1954, Charles Crichton (Armin Dahlen, Michel Ray, Cornell Borchers)

The Ladykillers, 1955, Alexander Mackendrick (Alec Guinness, Danny Green)

Mervyn Johns in *Pink String and Sealing Wax,* 1945, Robert Hamer

cockeyed reflection of British life grew less viable, even as a cozy, nostalgic fantasy. During those years the face of Britain finally removed its postwar frown; the last remnants of wartime rationing vanished in July 1954, and as the country grew toward full employment, the working public spent their wage packets on new items: television sets, washing machines, and American imports such as nylon shirts and do-it-yourself kits. This was a Britain that Balcon and Ealing found hard to respond to. While the country sprouted suburbs and housing developments, Ealing still celebrated village life or London suburbs with a village feeling. While chain stores such as Marks and Spencer's or Woolworth's became focal points in the daily round, Ealing films continued to promote corner shops and small family businesses. To those unhappy with the growing uniformity and materialism of British life, Ealing offered a brief reassurance that "this funny old island" still existed, but the reassurance grew increasingly weaker.

Ealing's problems in adjusting to the fifties were exacerbated by the company's worsening financial position. The industrialist Stephen Courtauld, who had supported the studio since the ATP period, left England for health reasons in 1952. For survival Balcon negotiated a large loan from the National Film Finance Corporation (NFFC), of which he was an honorary adviser (though he quickly resigned his position). Ultimately, the NFFC loan could only be paid off completely by the sale of Ealing assets—and the most profitable asset was the studio itself. The buyer, in October 1955, was BBC Television. It paid £300,000, and arranged for the erection of a commemorative plaque with a characteristic inscription written by Balcon: "Here during a quarter of a century were made many films projecting Britain and the British character."

It was a difficult time for everyone, not simply because of the pain in pulling up roots from Ealing's compact buildings, beehives, rose garden, and Red Lion pub. Employees felt dissatisfaction over the way the sale was managed and the lack of prior warning. Mackendrick only found out by reading the morning paper on his way to work; at the studio, the work force received the news from the studio manager rather than Balcon himself. There were also purely financial grouses: while Balcon and the other Ealing shareholders benefited from the sale, the work force felt themselves left high and dry.

Yet Balcon was anxious to keep his team—and the team spirit—intact. A new base formed at the Boreham Wood studio of M-G-M British after a plan for production at Pinewood fell through (the prickly association with Rank collapsed at the same time). Balcon duly altered the company title to suit his new

creation. In the press battles of 1940 about Hollywood "deserters," he had written revealingly how the offending Hitchcock was "promoted from department to department." At Ealing, the continuity of employment was remarkable; most of the directing team with whom Balcon fought the Second World War—Frend, Dearden, Crichton, Watt—was still with him when Ealing collapsed at the end of the fifties. The "new" people who began directing in the last years—Leslie Norman, Michael Truman, Seth Holt—had all been working in lesser capacities for a decade or more, as editors, writers, or associate producers. In this matter, Ealing was really like a fairy-tale castle, with a drawbridge and moat: those inside could rarely venture outside, and those outside were rarely requested in.

The system brought a degree of artistic freedom, confidence, and personal security; it also encouraged complacency and an ostrich attitude to the industry and the world at large. As the fifties advanced, Ealing's location: Ealing Studios became Ealing Films.

Balcon looked to the future by looking backward: "There we shall go on making dramas with a documentary background and comedies about ordinary people with the stray eccentric among them—films about day-dreamers, mild anarchists, little men who long to kick the boss in the teeth."[20] In fact he looked even further back than this brief list of early fifties trends indicates: the most lavish Ealing film made at Boreham Wood was Leslie Norman's *Dunkirk* (1958), which tried to turn the clock back to the British cinema's finest hour. In place of the fighting spirit that animated Balcon's earlier war films, *Dunkirk* viewed its subject with a downcast heart. "What a shambles we've made of the whole rotten affair," says Bernard Lee's journalist, a Jeremiah in a duffle coat, surveying the soldiers awaiting evacuation on the beach. The criticism of woolly British government remains the most interesting aspect of a tired, melancholy, dutiful film.

There was, however, one sign of fresh energy in *Nowhere to Go* (1958; p. 71), the first film directed by Seth Holt after lengthy Ealing experience as a producer and editor. It was also the first film to use the writing talents of Kenneth Tynan, employed as script editor for Ealing Films, though his recommendations were renowned for being regularly turned down by Balcon. Holt consciously designed this icy, cynical, and elliptical thriller as "the least Ealing film ever made,"[21] but it came far too late in Ealing's history to change the brand image.

After three years and six films, Balcon and Ealing Films became submerged in another bout of asset selling. The Associated British Picture Corporation (ABPC) offered to buy the assets of all Ealing companies; Balcon accepted "after much heart-searching."[22] At first there was talk of production continuing under ABPC, but only the film currently in progress, Watt's Sydney-based thriller *The Siege of Pinchgut* (1959; p. 71), was completed. For this work, Balcon moved house yet again, to ABPC's Elstree Studios, close to Boreham Wood. But after the completion of *Pinchgut* there was nothing; Ealing's charmed life was over.

Yet Balcon continued to cherish the methods and ethos of Ealing. Four months before the release of *The Siege of Pinchgut*, Balcon became chairman of a new filmmaking group, Bryanston. "We are not an arty crafty organization," he declared, "but we do want to tackle original and unusual subjects of international importance. We are now in a position whereby, working through a small selection panel, we can give a producer financial backing to make these subjects."[23]

"International importance": the phrase suggests that Balcon was reversing his goals and aiming for the stars. This was not so. Though Bryanston's association with the Woodfall group produced films that established a new image for British cinema—*The Entertainer* (1960), *Saturday Night and Sunday Morning* (1960), *A Taste of Honey* (1961), *The Loneliness of the Long Distance Runner* (1962)—the bulk of Bryanston's product remained distinctly modest. There were pocket comedies about charladies (*Ladies Who Do,* 1963) and honeymooners (*Double Bunk,* 1961); dramas and thrillers about tough East End schools (*Spare the Rod,* 1961), an army payroll robbery (*A Prize of Arms,* 1962), and airline pilots (*Cone of Silence,* 1960). Many were designed as supporting features.

Former Ealing personnel found a welcome in the Bryanston framework: Crichton, Frend, Mackendrick, Dearden, Relph, Danischewsky, Norman, Truman. Ealing's old doorman even performed the same duties at Bryanston's London office. Bryanston functioned, however, as a servicing body rather than a production center; the network of family relationships that bound the Ealing work force together no longer operated. After some thirty films, Bryanston succumbed to financial problems of its own and was sold to the television company, Associated Rediffusion.

Part of the problem lay in the restrictive methods of Britain's cinema circuits, always disinclined to book independent films. Another lay in the Woodfall film *Tom Jones.* "No doubt *Tom Jones* is engraved on my heart,"[24] Balcon wrote in his autobiography; for the project was snapped up by United Artists after Bryanston watched the estimated budget soar beyond its own reach. The shift to United Artists had far-

Sammy Going South, 1963, Alexander Mackendrick (Edward G. Robinson, Fergus McClelland)

reaching consequences. *Tom Jones* generated a financial bonanza; American companies poured their dollars into British productions, offering deals far more tempting to filmmakers than modest outfits such as Bryanston could ever hope to match. The indigenous British film Balcon had promoted was pushed into the background.

At the time of the *Tom Jones* submission, Bryanston's resources were already heavily committed to Balcon's own production, *Sammy Going South* (1963), based on W. H. Canaway's novel about an orphan traveling through Africa, directed by Mackendrick with a leisurely pace but great insight into the workings of a child's mind. This proved to be Balcon's last direct involvement with the creative side of filmmaking; during his frustrating years as chairman of British Lion, from 1964 to 1966, his time and energy were taken up with administration and boardroom skirmishes.

Inactive in the industry throughout the seventies, Balcon continued to bang the drum for British cinema past and present until his death in 1977. He bemoaned the lack of opportunities given to young filmmakers; he raged against Melvin Frank's proposal to remake *Kind Hearts and Coronets*. One may guess his reaction to the British cinema's current high profile: pleasure, pride, and a sharp entreaty to keep the flag flying.

Notes

1. Review of *The Lodger* in *The Bioscope* (London), vol. 68, no. 1040 (Sept. 16, 1926), p. 39.
2. Michael Balcon, "Sincerity Will Make the Film English," *The Era* (London), Nov. 11, 1931, p. 10.
3. Michael Balcon, "My Hollywood Star Captures," *Film Weekly* (London), vol. 15, no. 379 (Jan. 18, 1936), p. 8.
4. Quoted from "Balcon and the Stars," in Monja Danischewsky, ed., *Michael Balcon's 25 Years in Films* (London: World Film Publications, 1947), p. 54.
5. Michael Balcon, *Michael Balcon Presents . . . A Lifetime of Films* (London: Hutchinson, 1969), p. 66.
6. Michael Balcon, "Putting the *Real* Britain on the Screen," *Evening News* (London), Oct. 1, 1936, p. 11.
7. Quoted in Richard Haestier, "Producer's Faith in British Pictures," *Star* (London), July 11, 1938.
8. From an interview by Molly Hobman, "Mr. Balcon's Film Plans," *Birmingham Gazette,* July 23, 1938.
9. Michael Balcon, "Realism or Tinsel?," reprinted in Danischewsky, *op. cit.*, p. 71.
10. Quoted in "How Films Can Help Us to Win," *Evening News* (London), Sept. 8, 1939.
11. Michael Balcon, *Sunday Despatch* (London), Aug. 25, 1940.
12. Alfred Hitchcock, *New York World-Telegram,* Aug. 27, 1940.
13. Michael Balcon in an interview with John Ellis, in Geoff Brown, ed., *Der Produzent: Michael Balcon und der englische Film* (Berlin: Verlag Volker Spiess, 1981), p. 39.
14. Michael Balcon, "Let British Films Be Ambassadors to the World," *Kinematograph Weekly* (London), vol. 335, no. 1969 (Jan. 11, 1945), p. 31.
15. Michael Truman, "Cutting British Films for the United States," *Film Industry* (London), vol. 7, no. 61 (Nov. 17, 1949), p. 8.
16. Michael Balcon, *The Producer* (London: British Film Institute, 1945).
17. Balcon, *A Lifetime of Films,* p. 181.
18. Kenneth Tynan, "Ealing's Way of Life," *Films and Filming* (London), vol. 2, no. 3 (Dec. 1955), p. 10.
19. Quoted in Robert Muller, "What Happens to the Starlets?" *Picture Post* (London), Oct. 8, 1955, p. 16.
20. Michael Balcon, "Let's Stop This Moaning about British Films," *Daily Mail* (London), March 14, 1956.
21. From an interview by Kevin Gough-Yates in *Screen* (London), vol. 10, no. 6 (Nov.-Dec. 1969), p. 9.
22. Balcon, *A Lifetime of Films,* p. 189.
23. Quoted in John Vincent, "British Producers Search for Freedom," *Films and Filming* (London), vol. 5, no. 9 (June 1959), p. 28.
24. Balcon, *A Lifetime of Films,* p. 198.

Passport to Pimlico, 1949, Henry Cornelius (Frederick Piper,
Hermione Baddeley, Philip Stainton, Raymond Huntley)

Michael Balcon and the Idea of a National Cinema

Laurence Kardish

WE ALL DO IT: in discussing films, sooner or later we all refer to national origin. We cannot easily get away from the idea of national characteristics and ascribe them as readily to the works of art and industry, as most films are, as we do to individuals. Why we persist in this discourse suggests that the imprint of national bias runs deep, and that characterization by nationality somehow "works." We presume, or pretend to presume, our audience knows what we mean when we say something or someone is American or British. We know we mean something *more* than geographic location, but that unsaid *more* implies ascription by nationality to be an oratorical strategy.

Designation by nationality carries emotional weight and is almost never disinterested. When we refer to another nationality, the reference may imply a criticism: when we refer to our own, however, the reference functions like a call. Nationality objectifies the "we," reinforces our being, puts another name to our existence, protects our ontology, makes us belong, and gives that belonging a continuity. Whoever calls us by our rightful name has the right to pat our collective back, to castigate or scold us; some atavistic pride obliges us to rally round. Which brings us to Michael Balcon and the idea of a national cinema.

Michael Balcon was one of the most respected and influential men in the history of British cinema. His reputation derives not merely from his association with some 350 films—in itself a substantial contribution to the entire body of British filmmaking—but also from the fifty years he spent as the vigorous, indefatigable champion of British cinema and films. Here a distinction is in order.

British cinema comprises the whole vertical industry; the emphasis is economic. British cinema has as much to do with how films are produced, distributed, and exhibited as with the process of filmmaking itself. British films are what the industry is all about, the product of endeavor and the work that provides the forces with a teleology. Out of British cinema emerge British films. This seems like a truism; but if by British films something indige-

nous is meant, then it is not. Balcon's activity in his half-century as filmmaker and celebrant of Britain may be seen as, first, establishing a continuity for British filmmaking and, later, giving the idea of a national cinema some meaning beyond geography.

Balcon was tireless in promoting British cinema. His earliest association with the business was as a Midlands distributor of, among others, Tarzan and Harold Lloyd films. A film distributor in Britain theoretically need not distribute British films, but a producer in Britain would of geographic necessity make a British film. In shifting from distribution to production when the majority of films in British theaters were American, Balcon thus could not avoid the issue of nationalism. He bore the idea of a national cinema as an escutcheon to attract attention to his films, to get them exhibited, and to have his investment returned. The call for a national cinema was a tool of the market, a reasonable, spontaneous, and efficacious weapon against restrictive business practices, including the tendency to play it safe by showing American films.

In his autobiography, published in 1969, Balcon wrote: "The [First World] War had virtually killed off British production"; America, in turn, moved in with "all the films that British cinemas required," maintaining an economic stranglehold on those theaters through "blind" and "block" booking, which required exhibitors to contract films sight unseen and in bulk.[1] This grip was further tightened when American producers, who had already recouped their investment at home, were able to undersell British filmmakers obliged to make back their money in the contained British and surprisingly meager Dominions markets.

The idea of a national cinema—how can a country continue to make films if it has no system to show them?—may have been articulated out of financial necessity, but the cry was also emotionally informed.

Born in 1896 into a "respectable but impoverished"[2] Jewish family in Birmingham, Balcon was a first-generation Englishman who believed in manifesting his "faith in the country which in the last century had provided sanctuary for [his] forebears."[3] Balcon's works reaffirmed a nation that not only provided a haven but permitted opportunities for a respectable family to rise out of impoverishment. If this sounds familiar, Balcon's zeal for Britain bears comparison to the sentiments of first-generation North American film executives Harry Cohn, Marcus Loew, David O. Selznick, and the Warner brothers who, with the exception of Selznick, were also born into impoverished families. This ardor bears relevance to what would become first virtues and then limitations of Balcon's Ealing films.

Before leaving school at seventeen, Balcon was already devoted to the popular new entertainment and art form, the movies. He remained in Birmingham as assistant to the Dunlop Rubber Company's managing director. Not particularly happy in industry, he quit tire manufacturing, and with the encouragement of his friend Victor Saville became a film distributor and later a filmmaker. If industry depressed him, what was he doing substituting one business for another? As historian Rachael Low has noted, the "film industry was not yet bound by tradition and class barriers."[4] Qualifications for entry were vision, daring, and knowing where to find capital. It was an industry for which Balcon had much natural enthusiasm.

In 1923, when Balcon and Saville made their first feature film, *Woman to Woman,* directed by the already veteran Graham Cutts, the stars of the British screen (excepting Betty Balfour and Alma Taylor) were from Hollywood. To secure financing and possible entree to the United States market, the hopeful filmmakers hired the American actress Betty Compson. While demonstrating that his idea of a national cinema was not xenophobic, Balcon also started two new British actors on their careers, Clive Brook, as leading man, and Victor McLaglen, in a very small part.

Woman to Woman appears to have been lost. Its 1929 sound remake starring Betty Compson, whose return performance is diminished by her voice, has been preserved. The later version is of interest as much for being Saville's first all-talking feature as for its social implications. Balcon's first feature adopted what had already become discernible patterns of British filmmaking. *Woman to Woman* was based on a moderately successful play, and many of its performers, Clive Brook included, were from the West End. Its sentiment was melodramatic, and its subtext, louder than the story, was about class. Its plot device was amnesia, a condition the British aristocracy in purple fiction suffers with the frequency of a common cold. *Woman to Woman* was orthodox and a commercial success. Even though his next film was a resounding failure, and the following one "may never have been shown at all,"[5] Balcon had established himself.

Woman to Woman, 1923, Graham Cutts (Betty Compson, Clive Brook)

Woman to Woman, 1929, Victor Saville (Betty Compson, George Barraud)

Balcon's fourth film, *The Passionate Adventure* (1924), was made in part with money from the Lewis J. Selznick Company, then in receivership in America. Again, Cutts directed; an American (Alice Joyce) played the lead, and Brook and McLaglen were also featured. With *The Passionate Adventure* came the public appearance of Balcon's company name, "Gainsborough Pictures." This choice was brilliant for an industry not yet constrained by class but already desirous of it. Gainsborough's portraits and landscapes are part of British patrimony, and with three syllables Balcon accorded his films an instant status and swift legitimacy at home, while abroad a Gainsborough picture would be identified by educated people as British and, at the very least, well-made.

Recognizing the need for a steady production schedule if the industry were to mature, Balcon bought Islington, the facility where his first films had been shot. Originally built as a power station for an underground railway, Islington had been renovated by Famous Players-Lasky (Paramount), the American company that had leased Balcon the studio. With Islington came a small staff, including a young title designer and "general handyman,"[6] Alfred Hitchcock, whom Balcon had had the good sense in 1923 to make Cutts's assistant on *Woman to Woman*.

By the time Gainsborough acquired Islington in 1925, Cutts as premier director resented Hitchcock's ability and rise. Although Cutts's satisfactory version of Ivor Novello's play *The Rat*, starring Novello and Mae Marsh, was one of the popular films of 1925, so estranged was Cutts that he almost subverted Balcon's strategy for the development of an industry.

Balcon intended to promote "people of unusual promise" from within his organization—after a period of apprenticeship.[7] Hitchcock, his first graduate, had been assigned to make two films in Germany co-produced by Gainsborough and Emelka, a Munich studio. Hitchcock returned in 1926 to direct his first London-made feature, *The Lodger: A Story of the London Fog* (p. 18). Cutts disparaged it as opaque, and C. M. Woolf, Gainsborough's distributor, sufficiently convinced, held the tonal film from release. Balcon countered by engaging Ivor Montagu, a fellow founder of the Film Society in London, to help Hitchcock restructure the film. Intertitles were reduced by one-third; a few scenes were reshot. Early in 1927, *The Lodger* opened to much acclaim, vindicating Hitchcock and Balcon. Hitchcock remained with Gainsborough, however, for only two more films, *Downhill* and *Easy Virtue* (both 1927), while Cutts and Novello followed *The Rat* with two sequels: *The Triumph of the Rat* (1926) and *The Return of the Rat* (1929).

By 1927 Balcon had produced at Islington a small but consistent body of British features by British directors adapted from British sources and starring a majority of British performers. Yet exhibitors continued to treat British films without hospitality. Balcon, in the teeth of American competition, decided to take political action; allied with the Federation of British Industries, he convinced Parliament that governmental encouragement was necessary to compel British cinemas to play British films. The Cinematograph Films Act was passed in 1927 and took effect January 1, 1928. The Quota Act, as it immediately became known, restricted blind and block booking, and required theaters to show a minimum percentage of British films, ranging from at least 5 percent in 1928 to 20 percent in 1936.[8]

Having helped clear the ground for an expanding industry, Balcon could focus on what it was that made a British film essentially British. In a 1931 article attempting to define or prescribe the distinctive nature of British films, Balcon referred to "native simplicity and sincerity."[9] Simplicity perhaps referred to the modest circumstances of filmmaking in Britain, but if sincerity had to do with "making pictures which express England," then Britain, according to Gainsborough, enjoyed the same reality as Ruritania. Sincerity was defined negatively, in opposition to American "co-ed pictures and portentous gangster epics." Ambiguity is for the most part absent from Balcon's canon; he mistrusted works that fascinated and repelled at the same time, and may have been reacting to contemporary releases such as *Little Caesar* and *Public Enemy,* American films that extolled villainy by its dramatic portrayal, disclaimers notwithstanding. Implicit in the idea of native sincerity is the restricting of topics to native subjects, and presumably Balcon did not see co-eds and gangsters as part of Britain's social topography.

This topography was hardly delineated at Islington, but there were exceptions, and *Blighty* (1927) is one of the very few films that attempted to reflect contemporary society. Based on an original story by Ivor Montagu, *Blighty* was directed by another member of the Film Society, Adrian Brunel, who had been making short and feature-length films for ten years. *Blighty,* wrote Balcon, "was about the realization that the outbreak of the First World War was the end of an era, and more, perhaps most, important, it suggested the breaking down of class barriers, a process which has been continued very slowly from that time."[10] Webster's New World Dictionary defines "blighty" as British slang for "England; home," and the household of the aristocratic Villiers family is a metaphor for Britain during and after the First World War. When war is declared, the Villiers's son and chauffeur volunteer for service. In Europe the son meets a country girl (Nadia Sibirskaïa): he is killed and she gives birth to their child. The chauffeur receives a blighty wound and is sent home, decorated for bravery. He marries the Villiers's daughter. The foreign wife of the late Villiers Junior is located: after the slightest hesitation, the family embraces the humble daughter-in-law and grandchild. Still, the fracturing of class seems too swift and easy to be honest, and *Blighty* emerges more as a liberal wish in the right direction than as a historical statement. *Blighty* does anticipate an Ealing theme that would recur dur-

Blighty, 1927, Adrian Brunel (Godfrey Winn, Nadia Sibirskaïa)

Hindle Wakes, 1931, Victor
Saville (Edmund Gwenn,
Sybil Thorndike, Belle
Chrystall)

ing and after the next war: members of a circumscribed group, here the aristocratic Villiers household, forgo differences under stress and unite to overcome adversity; in crisis, a cohesive social unit obtains.

The film is significant for more than its text and intention, however. Newsreel footage of battle and victory punctuates the narrative and gives authenticity to the story. Actuality does not arrest the action but contributes to its development. Balcon would increasingly use documentary in situating fiction, an approach evident in Victor Saville's *Hindle Wakes* (1931), one of the most cogent films Balcon produced. Unlike other Gainsboroughs in that it is tough and unsentimental, and unlike other Balcons in that its attitude is feminist, *Hindle Wakes* is quite possibly a masterpiece. The action begins with an opening montage of seemingly unrehearsed candid shots of workers in the mills of the Lancashire town of Hindle. The mills are closing down as everyone prepares to take their holidays, or "wakes." Mary Heathcote (Belle Chrystall) is about to spend her vacation by the seaside—or so her parents think. The screenplay, by Saville and Angus

MacPhail, adapted from the Stanley Houghton play, translates Mary's subsequent misadventure into a tough-minded and incisive drama about class, property, marriage, and the making of difficult choices.

As movies began to speak, and Balcon continued to ponder the special aspects of British film, "a suitable standard of English"[11] became part of his formulation. *Hindle Wakes* was neither Balcon's nor Saville's first all-talking feature (that was *Woman to Woman,* 1929), but it was an early and assured one. Its language, if not always "suitable," is expressive and appropriate to character and situation. What is said in *Hindle Wakes* and how it is said reflect both class and sex. Aural variations shade the film as much as the saturine light that inflects it.

To establish his independence, Saville had quit the Balcon-Cutts partnership in 1924 when Gainsborough was set up. Then, having produced six films and directed three features, he returned to Gainsborough in 1929 as director of *Woman to Woman* redux. His work for Balcon between 1929 and 1936 is as rich as that of any *auteur* in British cinema. His textured compositions raise the banal narratives of the Edna Best-Herbert

Rome Express, 1932, Walter
Forde (Eliot Makeham,
Cedric Hardwicke,
Conrad Veidt)

Marshall romances *Michael and Mary* (1931)[12] and *The Faithful Heart* (1932) to high melodrama. His first musical, the daffy and delirious *Sunshine Susie* (1931), was a remake of the German *Die Privatsekretärin,* and starred its lead, Renate Müller, as the insouciant Susie opposite a raffish Jack Hulbert. In 1933 alone, Saville fashioned three different and distinguished works. His shadowed but good-natured version of J. B. Priestley's popular novel *The Good Companions* (referring to a group of itinerant players whose bumpy fellowship anticipates Ealing-depicted communities) was the first talking film to be viewed by the King and Queen of England in

Friday the Thirteenth, 1933, Victor Saville (Ralph Richardson, unidentified player, Donald Calthrop, Jessie Matthews)

public and starred, among others, Jessie Matthews and John Gielgud. *Friday the Thirteenth,* sporting almost the entire Gainsborough acting company, including Matthews and Ralph Richardson as romantic opposites, comprised several stories, some of "extravagant levity," others of "half-hearted seriousness,"[13] connected by a clever narrative device and a consistently winsome tone. *I Was a Spy,* if not always believable, was a smooth, suspenseful history of a Belgian woman (Madeleine Carroll) who during the First World War became one of the Allies' greatest spies. *Evergreen* (with songs by Rodgers and Hart), British cinema's most celebrated musical comedy until 1968's *Oliver!,* and *Evensong,* the moving biography of a fictitious diva (Evelyn Laye), followed in 1934. Jessie Matthews, who played both mother and daughter in *Evergreen,* played at being a man in Saville's *First a Girl* (1935, p. 23), a fluid version of the 1933 German film *Viktor und Viktoria.*

Gainsborough went public in 1928, and the principals of Gaumont-British, a wholly British-owned company, provided major capital for Balcon's company. Although Gainsborough's formal association with Gaumont began at that time, it was not until three years later that Balcon, still producing out of Islington, also took over production for Gaumont-British at its recently modernized Shepherd's Bush studio. "The combined potential of the two studios... was at least eighteen films a year."[14] Thus began not only five years of grinding work but a period in which Balcon, employing hundreds of skilled workmen, would demonstrate the industry's contribution to the national economy.

Rome Express (1932, Walter Forde), Balcon's initial production at Gaumont-British, was his most elaborate to date. Handsome, trivial, and entertaining, it signaled the hundred-odd films Balcon and his colleagues would complete through 1937. Sidney Gilliat, who had been writing for the cinema since 1928, received his first on-screen credit with *Rome Express.* It was also the first British film for German actor Conrad Veidt, who would later appear in other Gaumont films, including *I Was a Spy* (1933), *Jew Süss* (1934, after which he could not return home), *The Passing of the Third Floor Back* (1935), and *King of the Damned* (1935).

Using the advanced technical resources of Shepherd's Bush, Forde, who during the twenties had made a number of silent comedies in which he also starred, directed *Rome Express* with a fine pace and visual punch. The streamlined comedy-thriller is populated with international stereotypes who respond too wittily ever to give offense. Although the plot is complex, it unravels at full speed as the train rushes to its destination under the steam of tracking cameras and breezy back projection. *Rome Express* is tremendously assured.

*The Man Who Knew Too
Much,* 1934, Alfred Hitch-
cock (Frank Vosper, Leslie
Banks, Nova Pilbeam,
Peter Lorre)

Jessie Matthews and Victor
Saville on the set of *It's
Love Again,* 1936

Jew Süss, 1934, Lothar Mendes (Conrad Veidt, Cedric Hardwicke)

The 39 Steps, 1935, Alfred Hitchcock (Madeleine Carroll, Robert Donat)

Balcon's Gaumont-British films at Shepherd's Bush were British in execution but transoceanic in intention. They were cosmopolitan and reflected little of the reality that lay beyond the studio walls. As a body, the films could be compared favorably to RKO's films of the thirties—smooth, fluid when not ponderous, intelligent even when broad, elegant but not lavish, glamorous and often choreographed to an infectious syncopation. In his autobiography, Balcon divided his Gaumont-British and Gainsborough work into six noncomprehensive categories (the examples selected are mine):[15]

1. Hitchcock films: *Waltzes from Vienna* (1934), *The Man Who Knew Too Much* (1934), *The 39 Steps* (1935), *The Secret Agent* (1936), and *Sabotage* (1936; p. 25).
2. The Jessie Matthews musical films: among others, the three directed by Saville: *Evergreen* (1934), *First a Girl* (1935; p. 23), and *It's Love Again* (1936).
3. The Anglo-German films: these include *F.P. 1* (1933, Karl Hartl), *The Only Girl* (1933, Friedrich Hollaender), and *My Heart Is Calling* (1935, Carmine Gallone), with, respectively, Conrad Veidt, Lilian Harvey, and Jan Kiepura.
4. Comedies, particularly those of Jack Hulbert, Cicely Courtneidge, and Tom Walls. Hulbert appeared in *Bulldog Jack* (1935, Forde), Cicely Courtneidge in *Me and Marlborough* (1935, Saville), and they appeared together in, at Gainsborough, *The Ghost Train* (1931, Forde), and *Jack's the Boy* (1932, Forde). Walls directed and starred in filmed versions of

the Ben Travers Aldwych farces, including *A Cuckoo in the Nest* (1933; p. 21), *Turkey Time* (1933), and *A Cup of Kindness* (1934).

5. The George Arliss films: *The Iron Duke* (1934, Saville), *The Guv'nor* (1935, Milton Rosmer), *East Meets West* (1936, Herbert Mason), and *His Lordship* (1936, Mason).

6. The "epics" made with an eye on the American market: *Jew Süss* (1934, Lothar Mendes), *The Tunnel* (1935, Maurice Elvey; p. 20), *Rhodes of Africa* (1936, Berthold Viertel, starring Walter Huston as Rhodes), and *King Solomon's Mines* (1937, Robert Stevenson).

Missing from Balcon's list is an underappreciated staple of British film, the Gothic melodrama, represented by *The Ghoul* (1933, T. Hayes Hunter, with Boris Karloff), *The Clairvoyant* (1935, Maurice Elvey, with Claude Rains and Fay Wray), and *The Man Who Changed His Mind* (1936, Robert Stevenson, with Karloff and Anna Lee). This omission is curious considering Balcon would produce at Ealing *Dead of Night* (1945; p. 33), one of the great supernatural films of all time.

There are certain tendencies, and perhaps even traditions, that inform British filmmaking. None of these is peculiar to British film, but the admixture is. The coalescence of tendencies and traditions can probably never be defined with any precision, but patterns can be discerned. This approach does not attempt to prescribe what it is that makes a film British; it merely suggests a way to study a field of film. Of these tendencies, although they are not Balcon's idea, several may be noted which help locate Balcon's work in the history of British film. Among them are a bias toward the written word performed, a respect for literary sources and the dramaturgy of the theater; a bent toward Romanticism, often manifesting itself in melodrama; an enthusiasm for the clean vulgarity and irrepressible vitality of the music hall; and an inclination to position fiction realistically. With few exceptions, this last propensity was not evident at Gaumont-British. Yet it is the foundation for Balcon's policy at Ealing: but before there was Ealing there was Balcon meeting Flaherty.

In 1931, at "one or other of the pubs where film men foregather to talk about films," John Grierson introduced Balcon to Robert Flaherty, whom Grierson had dubbed "father of the documentary film"; according to Balcon, Flaherty "had arrived in London after several years of unequal struggle with Hollywood."[16] Having this in common, Balcon listened raptly as Flaherty described the Aran Islands, which neither man had yet seen. Straightaway Balcon offered Flaherty £10,000 of Gaumont-British money to record "the struggle for life of the Aran Islanders" on their barren, treeless rocks off Ireland's Galway coast. Enthusiasm for Flaherty's work does not adequately explain why Balcon, usually cautious, acted so swiftly and with such commitment.

Man of Aran, 1934,
Robert Flaherty

Perhaps he wanted to show that where Hollywood would not support "a great man, an original[,] a man of genius," Britain could. Or suspicious of public-sector filmmaking, Balcon may have wanted to entice Flaherty away from Grierson's government-sponsored projects and into the private sector. Or he may have wanted the indomitability of an unknown group in a far-flung corner of Britain recorded with the heroic pictorialism for which Flaherty was famous.

Man of Aran (1934), otherwise known as "Balcon's Folly," emerged as much a piece of romantic fiction as a historical recreation. Real people in a real place carried on several activities—some were quotidian and actual, others quite unnatural. The prodigious climax was a shark hunt which, although breathtaking, was not something the islanders did in the normal course of events—sharks had quit Aran's waters some years earlier. *Man of Aran* is an aesthetic work of landscape; Balcon was proud of the film, but even though it had a profitable run on Broadway and won the Mussolini Gold Cup at the first Venice Film Festival (1934), the producer would never again make a film in which narrative was subordinate to the way things appear.

Part of Balcon's "grinding schedule" at Gaumont-British required trips to the States in search of Amer-

ican stars to make his films more attractive and marketable abroad. These visits, reluctantly made, confirmed Balcon's "growing conviction that a film to be international must be thoroughly national in the first instance."[17] Gaumont's budget could not afford top American stars, who were in any case under long-term contracts with the major Hollywood studios. What Gaumont could afford were performers who were not particularly marketable and whose presence was often curious in a film "largely British in conception."

Balcon first met Louis B. Mayer, head of Metro-Goldwyn-Mayer, on one of these scouting missions. On a later trip Balcon showed him the handsome *Tudor Rose,* whose low cost so impressed Mayer that he immediately cabled London with instructions to hire everyone associated with the production. A modest historical drama directed, said Balcon, "with great skill and feeling by one of our rising young men, Robert Stevenson,"[18] *Tudor Rose* was about the ill-fated Lady Jane Grey who, as the American title indicates, was "Nine Days a Queen." *Tudor Rose* was released in August 1936, the same year in which Gaumont-British, exhausted by financial crises exacerbated by principal stockholders, proclaimed its virtual abandonment of feature production. In November Balcon asked to be

Bulldog Jack, 1935, Walter
Forde (Jack Hulbert)

Tudor Rose, 1936, Robert Stevenson (Nova Pilbeam)

released from his contract, and a few weeks later M-G-M announced that Balcon was to head up its new British operation at Denham.

There was nothing inconsistent with Balcon's plans for a national cinema in going to work for M-G-M. The filmmaker envisioned "the real working partnership" between Britain and Hollywood to be one in which the latter would supply the former the financial backing (without which no industry is possible), the global distribution network, and "when suitable," the stars.[19] It was too good to be true.

The fiercely independent Balcon believed M-G-M had "explicitly offered [him] autonomy,"[20] and this is what he accepted. Balcon was put in charge of production at M-G-M British Studio Limited and made a member of its Board of Directors. His contract could have run for seven years but was abrogated by mutual consent after eighteen of the unhappiest months of the producer's life. During this time three properties were chosen, *A Yank at Oxford, The Citadel,* and *Goodbye, Mr. Chips,* and only the first was completed during Balcon's tenure.

Balcon and M-G-M concurred on the choice of Jack Conway, "a thoroughly capable and experienced M-G-M man,"[21] as director for *Yank* and on the signing of Robert Taylor for the hero. After this Balcon's latitude for free judgment was restricted. Insisting on changes in Sidney Gilliat's screenplay, the West Coast assigned writers who were neither needed nor wanted, including, to Balcon's embarrassment, a depressed F. Scott Fitzgerald. Other than its purported Oxford location, the eccentricity of the professorial staff, and the wit of the dialogue (particularly the banter between the Yank and his tutors), precious little about *Yank* could be thought British. What was most unlike M-G-M, how-

ever, was the second feminine lead, Elsa Craddock (Vivien Leigh). Elsa is a seductress of students, an adulteress of extraordinary temerity. She is a character absolutely unknown in American films of the mid-thirties (and missing from Ealing films of the forties and fifties); rather than being punished for her transgressions, as would have happened in Code-dominated America,[22] Elsa is only exiled to Aldershot, whose principal residents are military. One cannot help but think that Elsa's fate (which is awarded to no other Balcon heroine) may very well be the producer's sly revenge on those who broke the promise of autonomy.

No longer a callow upstart from the Midlands, Balcon, as Rachael Low observed, "had traveled far.... The acquaintance of people from a higher social class also enlarged his horizons; he himself described in his autobiography how meeting Lord Lee of Fareham opened his eyes to a different way of life, and the solid civilised home of the country gentleman was to attract him."[23] To Balcon's dismay, being a gentleman counted for nothing at M-G-M British in areas that concerned a gentleman most—giving one's word and taking responsibility. Balcon discovered not only that if he wanted independence as head of production he would be deprived of work, but that no one would acknowledge the diminution of his role. Thus by the time *Yank* was completed Balcon was no longer supervising production on M-G-M's next British film, *The Citadel*: he was house pariah. Demanding to be released from his contract, Balcon's solicitor wrote to M-G-M's attorneys: "As your clients are fully aware, Mr. Balcon has no duties whatsoever to perform other than to sit down in

A Yank at Oxford, 1938, Jack Conway (Vivien Leigh, Maureen O'Sullivan)

Ealing Studios

the happiest and most rewarding period of my working life."[25]

What Balcon moved into late in 1938 was a six-acre studio in a leafy residential area (not quite suburban) within reach of central London by public transport. Abutting undramatically onto a village green, the complex came with a slogan inscribed in large letters on one of its walls, "The Studio with the Team Spirit." Among others, the team included Basil Dearden, once Dean's assistant; Wilfrid Shingleton, an art director; Ronald Neame, a cameraman; and Formby, the singing comedian from Lancashire. With Balcon came a number of loyal and able colleagues from both Gaumont-British and M-G-M, including Angus MacPhail; the screenwriter Pen Tennyson, who had been a junior assistant since 1932; Robert Stevenson, who directed *The Ware Case*; Michael Relph, an assistant production designer; and Gilliat, whose screenplay for *A Yank at Oxford* was, after all the other drafts, the version more than less used.

His M-G-M education still stinging, Balcon made it possible for his creative people to work without interference at Ealing. His policy was rewarded with great loyalty, and it became rare for filmmakers trained at Mr. Balcon's Academy for Young Gentlemen[26] to leave Ealing. Production conferences were held regularly and frequently. At these Round Tables, as he called them, each unit would present a progress report on its project, and future Ealings would be discussed: Balcon would preside over these meetings "like a buoyant and pugnacious housemaster."[27] Directly accountable to Ealing's Board of Directors for production, Balcon had ultimate authority in deciding what was made at Ealing and who would make it. It was not an authority exercised capriciously. The consensus of his associates was of cardinal importance, and once a decision was made, responsibility was immediately delegated. Michael Relph wrote:[28]

The development of projects and the production of individual films was in the hands of two-men teams comprising a director and associate producer, later accorded the title of producer. Balcon, as studio chief, was of course in overall control—at first with the "Producer" title on all films, and later with "A Michael Balcon Production" credit. The creative responsibility for individual films, however, lay with these producer-director teams and it was in their composition that Balcon's flair as an impresario was of vital influence.

The "how" of making films at Ealing was congruent with the narrative description of many Ealing films. Working together, the recurrent Ealing theme, was irresistible as the country prepared for war. Although entertainment was still of paramount consideration in the making of theatrical films, Balcon believed there now existed the moral imperative of timeliness. Pictures dealing "with problems" would occupy the Ealing

his office and do nothing. It is only on rare occasions that Mr. Balcon has any conversation with any of the executives of the company of which he is a Director."[24]

As brief and frustrating as it was, Balcon's M-G-M sojourn was also an instructive lesson on how not to run a studio. Fiat was not congruent with Balcon's sensibility, and if M-G-M's way of making films was American, it was a process alien to Balcon. At Ealing he would structure a cabinet system that was as British as the films it made.

Upon release from his M-G-M contract in 1938, Balcon realigned himself with Walter Forde, producing *The Gaunt Stranger*. For this morose Edgar Wallace thriller the sound stages of Associated Talking Pictures were used. Located at Ealing, ATP had been established in 1931 by Basil Dean, one of the leading impresarios and major theater producers of his time. In 1929 Dean had decided to make motion pictures his principal interest, and Stephen Courtauld of the famous textile family had helped finance the building of a studio.

By 1937, ATP's in-house production schedule was spotty and excepting the comedies of the two popular working-class performers George Formby and Gracie Fields (soon to leave the studio), the films made at Ealing scarcely returned their investments. The stages were available for hire. While completing his second film at Ealing, *The Ware Case* (1938), Balcon was "invited to join the boards of the Ealing group of companies with control, subject to the board, of the production programme"; so began, wrote Balcon, "what proved to be, despite an intervening world war,

schedule and these would be "documentary in approach."[29]

There Ain't No Justice (1939), Balcon's first film as Ealing's production chief, was as signal for Ealing as *Rome Express,* his first film at Shepherd's Bush, had been for Gaumont-British. Pen Tennyson, like Hitchcock and Stevenson before him, was promoted up from the floor to direct. Over the next decade, he would be followed by Henry Cornelius, Charles Crichton, Basil Dearden, Charles Frend, Robert Hamer, and Alexander Mackendrick. Even though racketeering in boxing was not a burning issue in 1939, *There Ain't No Justice* was Ealing's inaugural "problem" film. When it was first proposed by Tennyson, Balcon found the narrative unimpressive but the story "wonderfully authentic" in its "atmosphere" and "honest and realistic" in its "portrayal of the life of a Cockney family."[30] *There Ain't No Justice* is not so much documentary as it is veristic. "Authentic," "honest," and "realistic" in this instance do not mean it was shot close to the source, the East End of London, but refer to the modesty and natural development of the action.

Balcon never fully articulated what the "documentary approach" was, but he did attach importance to it. Identifying it as "the greatest single influence on British film production," he also thought it was *not* "to be lightly attached to films of a specific, factual type; it is an attitude of mind towards filmmaking."[31] Earlier, Balcon had been enthusiastic about Flaherty's works, in part because they were about ordinary people coping with the extraordinary situation of their everyday lives. In *Nanook of the North* (1922) and *Man of Aran* (1934), the drama of the common man was his struggle with the landscape; man and nature were adversaries. What Balcon extracted from Flaherty was his interest in ordinary people in extraordinary moments. Where Balcon parted company with Flaherty was in seeing those extraordinary moments as exceptional and not a daily or chronic aspect of life. Balcon's people inhabit a benign territory, and if their community is endangered, it remains so only until a spoiler can be identified and something done about it. So it is with *There Ain't No Justice.* The Cockneys' neighborhood is warm and cozy. The sudden presence of gangsters disturbs life's equanimity, but concerted action solves the problem.

Balcon believed that the influence of the documentary movement "helped to establish a national style,"[32] and if it did develop at Ealing, the contribution from 1939 of Alberto Cavalcanti, a Brazilian-born filmmaker, was as important as anyone's to that development. Cavalcanti studied architecture in Switzerland before moving to Paris, where he designed sets for the French avant-garde and in 1926 made *Rien que les heures,* a seminal work of impressionist cinema. Reality was Cavalcanti's raw material. He was not a mere cataloger

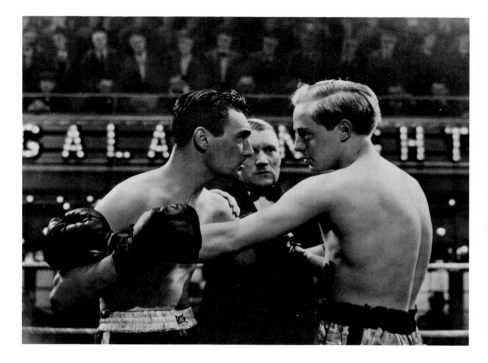

of appearances. Sensitive to the designs found in the material of everyday life, keen to the way in which disparate images work together and lose their discreteness in the mind's eye as they follow one another rapidly in film, Cavalcanti was a master plastic artist.

Like Flaherty, Cavalcanti had been invited to London by Grierson, and between 1934 and 1939 he directed or supervised some of the most acclaimed films sponsored by the General Post Office (GPO) production unit. They included *Pett and Pott* (1934), *Rainbow Dance* (1936, Len Lye), and *Night Mail* (1936, Basil Wright and Harry Watt). Mobilization drained Ealing of personnel, and Balcon, determined to continue production unabated, was obliged to locate other staff. Cavalcanti, just over forty, was not willing to be naturalized and so could not become production chief of the GPO, a Government unit. He was unhappy and looking for a job when approached by Balcon. Established at Ealing, Cavalcanti made one of the most revealing wartime films, *Went the Day Well?* (1942; pp. 31, 56), and one of cinema's spookiest, *Dead of Night* ("The Ventriloquist's Dummy" episode, 1945); he also trained a generation of Young Gentleman Filmmakers.

The Proud Valley (1940), Tennyson's second film, is a quantum jump in both issue and documentary approach for Ealing. Exterior shooting locates the somber coal town where the original script called for the miners to defy management by reopening and communally working a closed pit. Never comfortable with the original ending, Balcon had persuaded himself that the writer/director's being the great-grandson of the poet laureate would be taken into account if the film

There Ain't No Justice, 1939, Pen Tennyson (Michael Hogarth, Jimmy Hanley)

were criticized. Barely a week after shooting began, Britain was at war, and Balcon thought it neither tactful nor helpful to end the film with a violation of authority, no matter how progressive or reasonable that violation might be. The film ends instead with an expression of solidarity, which Balcon thought fit in with the national mood. While concerted action became an Ealing password, nowhere in the Ealing oeuvre would private property be expropriated for the public good.

Despite its rousing climax, *The Proud Valley* got a muted reception. Its star, Paul Robeson, whose David Goliath is inhumanly good and at odds with the otherwise realistic tone of the film, commented on the "imperialistic ambitions of the Allies"[33] when he returned to America. This so angered Lord Beaverbrook, the press magnate, that he instructed his newspapers to ignore the film entirely. Balcon thought *The Proud Valley* good national propaganda and was disturbed that the pique of one man could inhibit the war effort.

He felt bested not only by Beaverbrook but by Whitehall. Balcon had penned a memo on the contribution of cinema to the national effort as war seemed imminent. The receipt of the letter was acknowledged by the Government but nothing came of it. When war was declared, cinemas were shut down briefly, for fear of their being Luftwaffe targets; ultimately the Government decided that occasional relaxation took precedence over fears for public safety. The film industry, however, was threatened with closure as being an unnecessary diversion of personnel and *matériel*. Balcon and his colleagues pointed out to the Government that open cinemas had to find films to play; and if British studios were closed, American films would once again fill the theaters. This argument was persuasive. The Quota Laws were maintained, and with the need for instructional and propaganda films, production was actually encouraged.

Nationalization of the cinema became an issue. It was proposed not as a means of controlling the flow of ideas during war but as a cure for the recurring ills of the industry. Balcon, a mild and benign capitalist and a lifelong foe of bureaucracy, was appalled by the notion. His response is insufficiently argued but curious. He found fault not with the manner in which films were distributed and exhibited, but with the extravagant way in which they were made. Balcon's answer to nationalization was to do what he had begun to do at Ealing—make films "in our idiom" and have them budgeted for "home and Empire"; in 1935 he had observed that "Americans...have a warm and somewhat sentimental feeling towards Britain...our city scenes and countryside fascinate [them], our accent, if not affected, pleases [them]."[34] What Americans don't like, Balcon now argued, were "poor imitations" of their own idiom, films of "hard technical perfection."[35] Unvarnished in appearance, Ealing films were resolutely earnest.

Balcon insisted that in addition to its own idiom, Britain had another advantage over American films (or at least American films made between 1939 and 1941): its "distance to the creative stimulus...[which was] the palpable threat of extinction."[36] An advantage of dubious merit, but it does indicate how involved Balcon and Ealing were with the war. Believing "the most democratic nation in a time of crisis will subject itself to regimentation for the common good," so Balcon regimented Ealing.[37] The studio fulfilled the Ministry of Information's quota for direct propaganda films and without solicitation supplied a number of others for theaters, including *Yellow Caesar* (1941, Cavalcanti) on the nature of fascism; *Find, Fix and Strike* (1942, Compton Bennett) about strategy; and *Trois Chansons de Résistance* (1943, Dearden). With these works Balcon proved that no ministerial film plan was needed to make producers behave patriotically, nor was it necessary to establish an official unit to make propaganda and information films. The private sector, under contract, could do the job.

Balcon considered entertainment "badly needed"[38] and "important from the point of view of morale"[39] during the war. Indeed, he characterized some of Ealing's wartime films as "non-propaganda escapist comedies";[40] however, of the eight films made starring the popular performers George Formby and Will Hay, only two, *Turned Out Nice Again* (1941, Marcel Varnel) and *My Learned Friend* (1943, Hay and Dearden),

*The Proud Valley, 1940,
Pen Tennyson (Clifford
Evans, Simon Lack, Paul
Robeson, Charles
Williams, Jack Jones)*

respectively, were devoted to something other than doing battle with inept Nazis or fifth columnists. Most Ealing entertainments came in the guise of indirect propaganda, attesting to the exhilaration and efficacy of working together, and included *Convoy* (1940, Tennyson's last film; p. 29), *The Big Blockade* (1942, Charles Frend's first feature), *The Foreman Went to France* (1942, Frend/Cavalcanti; p. 58), *Nine Men* (1943, Harry Watt), and *San Demetrio London* (1943, Frend; p. 30).

All these works contained footage of actuality, but an effective balance between documentary and story elements was not achieved at once. Balcon faults *Convoy* for having too much story "at the expense of realism."[41] His comment has nothing to do with the ratio of actual combat to studio footage but rather with the narrative's failure to be informed by the documentary approach as he interpreted it. For Balcon, documentary tended toward verism, and *Convoy's* major plot development had to do with the sudden dropping in on the officers' bridge of a woman with a history. Although *Convoy* was basically restricted to a single class, the other narratives were not, and the constituents of their fighting groups represented all classes and geographic areas of

Britain. Their stories unfolded naturally, without melodramatic contrivance, and the documentary footage reinforced the credibility of the action.

The Next of Kin (1942; p. 30) was an outright propaganda film. Unusual for an Ealing in that its director, Thorold Dickinson, was brought in for a single specific project and that it was financed in part by the War Office, originally *The Next of Kin* was to be a dramatization of the effects of "careless talk" by members of the Services. However, Dickinson understood the problem to be not just a military one: the public was also responsible for breaches of security. The scenes of soldiers and war workers being indiscreet were theatrical and contrived, replete with shadows and dramatic angles, and not at all documentary in nature; but the casualties of careless talk, the victims of a supposedly unexpected attack, now anticipated by a prepared enemy, were powerfully and graphically shown in a canny intercutting of both simulated and actual combat footage. The problem with authenticity is that it tends to be sobering, which may not be the effect propaganda wants. The climax, which gives the film's title its poignancy, was so harrowing that the

Went the Day Well?, 1942, Alberto Cavalcanti (Muriel George, Patricia Hayes)

Nine Men, 1943, Harry Watt (Grant Sutherland, Jack Lambert)

Prime Minister, Winston Churchill, contemplated holding this cautionary tale from release for fear it would cause alarm, despondency, and sorrow. He permitted arbitration by military jury, however, and it ruled in favor of the film's release. *The Next of Kin* was a popular and critical success. The same could not be said of Ealing's other 1942 fable for home-front vigilance, Cavalcanti's *Went the Day Well?* "Oddly enough," Balcon wrote in 1975, "it's never been recognised as an important British film. I think it was."[42]

The film describes forty-eight hours in the life of a quaint but exemplary Gloucestershire village called Bramley End, located somewhere off the main road. In two days a detachment of German soldiers, disguised and trained to behave as members of the British army, billets itself in the village, takes over communications, and isolates the village from the rest of the United Kingdom. In a narrative that is prototypical science fiction, the newcomers are discovered to be aliens, and their murderous nature is revealed. The Germans kill some inhabitants and wound others: they are then defeated by villagers who have gone through a mutation from being of "the kindest character" to "absolute monsters."[43] James Agee in reviewing the film (released in the United States as *48 Hours*) noted that Bramley was populated by "remarkably lifelike, charming dolls... instead of characters," but admired the relating of the villagers "to their houses, their town, their tender lucid countryside."[44] What the perceptive Agee recognized in 1944, five years before "Ealing comedy" became a generic expression in America, were two Ealing hallmarks: landscape (recalling Balcon's observation that "our city scenes and countryside fascinate

[the American]") and types (in Agee's words, "the soberer and self-congratulatory grandnieces and nephews of Gilbert and Sullivan").

Agee applauded "the cold-blooded revenge" that constitutes the climactic moment of the film as "good and terrible to see," while critic Elizabeth Sussex found the avenging "devastating."[45] Both are right. The behavior exhibited by the population of Bramley is not what one would expect from people of the kindest character. *Went the Day Well?* opens on a graveyard. The tombstones are for German soldiers who have died away from home. With this introduction the audience might reasonably expect a flashback drama of apostasy, but it gets nothing of the sort. Having murdered the vicar and the telephone operator, having assassinated the entire home guard, and having been ready to shoot five children, the Germans are given a proper burial by the much-abused townsfolk. How quickly decency returns; how chilling that is. The gracious behavior of the villagers is supranatural. The recognition that the butchers now have unknown mourners of their own grieving at home is considerate, and that amiable recognition is part and parcel of Balcon's Britain.

In his autobiography, Balcon describes a wartime reminiscence with the illuminating chronology that the event happened after "one of the earliest German air raids on London" but *before* "any great state of anti-German feeling, as the raids had not yet developed on a large scale..."[46] The observation that a single blitz was insufficient to raise the wrath of the British people is in keeping with the absence of fury at Ealing. When there is anger expressed in an Ealing film—and it is infrequent—it is usually manifested by women, and then only after the passion has been mediated by deliberation and the emotion turned to ice. Witness Nora (Valerie Taylor) executing the traitorous squire (Leslie Banks) in *Went the Day Well?* Ealing's wartime films are pacific at heart.

In 1943 Harry Watt left the Crown Film Unit and followed Cavalcanti to Ealing Studios, "where they were beginning," Watt later wrote, "partly due to [Cavalcanti's] influence, to make the fine realist films... that were to give [Ealing] such a distinguished record."[47] Watt, who had made, among other strong nonfiction films, the popular *Target for To-night* (1941), an understated account of a British raid on German positions, directed the leanest, simplest, and most paradigmatic of Ealing's wartime narratives, *Nine Men* (1943). The opening shots romantically and poetically present boot-camp maneuvers: this exercise in military lyricism is cut short by an officer explaining "Umpity-Poo" to his trainees. *Un petit peu* is that "little extra," the cooperative spirit that liberated some of the nine soldiers from a state of siege in North Africa. With a small stretch of sand in South Wales effectively masquerading as the Libyan desert, *Nine Men* presented the clearest articulation of national unity: the fighters, diversely accented, are regular chaps, and the signification of their group is obvious. The "Umpity-Poo" flashback, the film's adventure part, is taut and unadorned, proceeding as if covered by a dauntless correspondent.

Nine Men may have been fiction appearing as reportage, but actual newspaper stories inspired *The Foreman Went to France* (1942) and *San Demetrio London* (1943). Both told of nonmilitary personnel performing heroically. In *San Demetrio* the crew of a tanker nearly cut in half by the Germans reboard the vessel, bring her back to port, and receive unexpected remuneration for their efforts; in *The Foreman* a "works manager" penetrates just-occupied France to recover a vital piece of machinery. The crew of the *San Demetrio* is not an invention, but *The Foreman's* writers improvised a plucky team around their hero. Helping the foreman are a good-natured Scot (played by Ealing's resident "Geordie," Gordon Jackson), a cheerful Cockney (Tommy Trinder), and an intense American (Constance Cummings). Action may have been initiated by an individual, but its successful execution required the group.

Balcon and Cavalcanti together designed a national style in response to crisis. It was a style in which function (text) was served by form (appearance), and in which landscape energized fiction. Would this architectonic whole be appropriate in time of peace? Balcon determined that it should. But what happens to the idea of communal activity, no matter how realistic in setting, when the threat to existence is no longer palpable? *Johnny Frenchman* (1945), completed just before the war's end, provides the answer—the message mellows and the work risks being silly. The film has none of the earnestness of earlier Ealings; it features Cornish and Breton fishermen, traditional rivals, who unite in frustrating the Germans, but their collaboration is feisty and jocular. Although the location exteriors—the moody skies of Cornwall, the damp port town of Mevagissey—threaten seriousness, the surfeit of type and the realistic aspect of the outdoor shooting do not work in harmony.

Johnny Frenchman is like an Ealing comedy before its time, although its tone may not have been meant to be so benevolent. Since it was made when victory was imminent, perhaps its goodnaturedness could not be avoided; its avuncularity should more likely be attributed to T. E. B. ("Tibby") Clarke, whose first solo feature screenwriting credit it was. His next would be on the "first" Ealing comedy, *Hue and Cry* (1947; p. 60), followed by several others: *Passport to Pimlico* (1949; p. 60), *The Magnet* (1950), *The Lavender Hill Mob* (1951; p. 16), *The Titfield Thunderbolt* (1952), and the last, *Barnacle Bill* (1957).

The Foreman Went to France, 1942, Charles Frend (Tommy Trinder, Clifford Evans, Constance Cummings, Gordon Jackson)

Ealing comedy means more than a comedy made at Ealing. It is not a burlesque like the loony *Fiddlers Three* (1944), a musical fantasy concocted by the otherwise realist filmmaker Harry Watt. It does not denote the films made as vehicles for music hall performers, such as Formby and Hay; as popular and funny as *Turned Out Nice Again* (1941) and *The Goose Steps Out* (1942) were, they are not "Ealing comedies." Whatever an Ealing comedy was, it was not a musical. Ealing comedies received critical acclaim at home and were popular abroad. Ealing's "other" comedies were disdained by critics at home and their humor, being regional, was considered unexportable abroad. Also, with one possible exception, Ealing comedies are postwar.

Dubbed by Kenneth Tynan "the regimental mascot of the British cinema," the Ealing comedy interpreted "a national way of life and [took] as [its] general theme the extraordinary and resilient British coping with a series of perfectly alarming situations."[48] The earliest alarming situation appeared in 1939 in what Charles Barr has identified as the happy ancestor to the generic Ealings, Walter Forde's *Cheer Boys Cheer*. Ironside, an enormously large and totally mechanized urban brewery (whose product has had the taste "rationalized" out of it) presents Greenleaf, a father-and-daughter-run brewery, pastorally located, with a perfectly alarming situation: Ironside wants to absorb Greenleaf. Greenleaf resists. Ironside's owner, a corporate Führer, charges his acquisitive son with doing Greenleaf in. A romantic attachment deflects Ironside's expansion, and Greenleaf continues to make the ale that "makes you cry." Greenleaf's employees, loyal, eccentric, and seen by Ironside as "a bunch of village idiots," constitute the prototype for the communities that would later inhabit Ealing comedies. *Cheer Boys Cheer* differs from the postwar comedies in its caesurae where the narrative stops and the comedians who make up Greenleaf's dotty staff do their routines. Ealing comedies were "good stories in their own right," wrote Balcon, and most sported original screenplays. Their action was fueled by "the mild anarchy . . . in the air." Balcon explained: "The country was tired with regulations and regimentation," and the comedies sided with the light-hearted rebels. "The comedies reflected the country's moods, social conditions and aspirations."[49]

The anarchy was mild and the rebels giddy. The comedies may have mocked the vagaries of the British, but they did not question basic British institutions such as the monarchy, the police, and the military, all of which Balcon held in great affection. Nor were social or political assumptions argued. As Tynan noted, the men Balcon chose to train, promote, and retain were mostly middle class, "politically . . . liberal," and "socially . . . Bohemian."[50] They may have seen themselves at society's edge, but their rebellion was limited by either themselves or their employer to the safe and easy targets of bureaucracy and greed.

One senses that not every one at the Round Table supported Balcon's policy of bloodlessness. "They're all the same capitalist bunch," the American says in *The Foreman Went to France,* as she berates the financial backers of the French fascists, "scared to death of communism and just waiting to sell their country to the highest bidder." The Island publican in *Whisky Galore!*

(1949), angered by his sudden loss of business, betrays his neighbors by revealing the whereabouts of the hidden whiskey to the customs men. In such Ealing films of the forties a leftist current can be discerned straining to become more pronounced. It is not allowed out and by the fifties has dried up.

Besides an irreverence of spirit, the comedies also shared a certain look inherited from wartime verism. Before plot came setting: location determined what would happen throughout. *Hue and Cry* (1947), directed by Crichton, is played with bravado in a London half-devastated by the Blitz. Urban spaces opened wide by bombings provide the Blood and Thunder Boys with an expanse to run and feel the exuberance of the unconstrained. The city's new topography invested this robust tale of amateur sleuthing and junior derring-do with a veracity and immediacy. The dense and fluid opening moments of *Passport to Pimlico* (1949; p. 42), among Cornelius's best work, and the mock documentary introduction to the island of Todday in *Whisky Galore!* (a miniparody of *Man of Aran*), locate the narratives precisely and authentically. This strategy tends to play down the absurdity of what will follow; it understates the events and pretends that the mild anarchy pervading these comedies is unexceptional after all. Perhaps this accounts for the serene brouhaha of Ealing's comedies.

The limits of acceptable protest are sketched mirthfully in *Passport to Pimlico*. Pimlico, a residential area of London, is discovered to have been deeded centuries ago to the duchy of Burgundy: geographically in London, Pimlico becomes the resurrected remnant of a medieval Gallic kingdom. "It's just because we are English we are sticking to our rights to be Burgundians," shouts the very sensible Mrs. Pemberton (Betty Warren) in Ealing's clearest articulation of British eccentricity. Irregularity does have its boundaries, though. Burgundians or not, being English means keeping order, and neo-Burgundians, enthusiastic though they are over the inapplicability of British rationing rules in Burgundy, also fear the withdrawal of the metropolitan police. They do not want their streets turned into a "spiv's paradise" nor to be "murdered in their beds."

In *Whisky Galore!* the Todday Islanders, having rescued more whiskey from a grounded freighter than rationing permitted, are obliged to hide the cases of alcohol. Although they regard their booty as "the elixir of life" itself, the Toddayities do not openly defy His Majesty's Laws. Publicly they abide, privately they imbibe. There is something disturbing about the silence of this communal circumvention, but *Whisky Galore!* was not a cynical comedy.

Ealing's most engaged film, at least in any sustained sense, is *The Man in the White Suit* (1952). The hapless inventor (Alec Guinness) of an indestructible fabric

Cheer Boys Cheer, 1939, Walter Forde (Graham Moffatt, Nova Pilbeam, Moore Marriott, Jimmy O'Dea [second from right], with unidentified players)

Hue and Cry, 1947, Charles Crichton (Harry Fowler)

Passport to Pimlico, 1949, Henry Cornelius (un-identified player, Barbara Murray)

Whisky Galore!, 1949,
Alexander Mackendrick
(Morland Graham,
John Gregson)

finds, much to his surprise, that he is considered an adversary by both management and labor of an enormous textile factory, whose plant looks modern but whose operation is reactionary. A satire that was never more than droll, *The Man in the White Suit* sets up an ingenious and exquisite situation, and neatly avoids resolution by stopping the narrative dead in its tracks.

To Balcon's annoyance, Americans thought of Ealing comedies as Alec Guinness comedies. Although Guinness was absent from four key films, *Hue and Cry, Passport to Pimlico, Whisky Galore!* and *The Titfield Thunderbolt,* they had good reason to think so. Guinness looked as ordinary as the films themselves. He was part of the topography, the way the land lay—common, familiar, nothing special. Guinness's appearance and the appearance of an Ealing film fit. But appearances are deceiving. Guinness was a chameleon. As mundane as was his presence, so was his body expressive. With the most subtle gestures, he created characters that were both unassuming and extraordinary. Despite the energy released during the course of an Ealing comedy, Guinness's are some of the most subdued comic films in cinema. His characters implode.

Although there are signature moments in Ealing films, the studio style predominated—unobtrusive, modest, and quite adequate. Mackendrick (*Whisky Galore!, The Man in the White Suit, The Ladykillers*) and Cornelius (*Passport to Pimlico*) were able to temper the visual blandness of most Ealing productions, but a homogeneity settles over the work of Crichton, Dearden, and Frend. The first features of Robert

Hamer, *Pink String and Sealing Wax* (1945), *It Always Rains on Sunday (*1947), and *Kind Hearts and Coronets* (1949), are marked by plays of light and shadow, careful composition, telling angles and considered camera movement. Balcon thought Hamer "one of the most remarkable of the young men I gathered around me at Ealing";[51] judging from the films cited, he was also the most subversive. Mathematician, poet, and film editor, Hamer, who Balcon also thought "engaged on a process of self-destruction," was given his first opportunity to direct in 1945 with "The Haunted Mirror" episode (p. 33) in the spectral *Dead of Night* (whose structural antecedent was the effective *Friday the Thirteenth,* p. 47, produced by Balcon twelve years earlier). What is of interest here and in the three following works is the sardonic view of a key British (and American) institution, the family. To Hamer the family is a noxious response to sexuality: it constrains. Its sole virtue is its ability to confer privilege, and this has nothing to do with togetherness and everything to do with inheritance.

If Hamer were self-destructive, he would have welcomed the frustration of working for Balcon. Balcon required the status quo to be preserved to the end of an Ealing film; yet all the signals in the first hour of any Hamer film indicate that this must not be. The narratives in *Pink String and Sealing Wax* and *It Always Rains on Sunday* are caustic and throbbing (as are the performances of Googie Withers in each); the endings, however, are paltry and unlikely. They do not flow from the preceding action but seem imposed by a sensibility more in agreement with Hollywood's Production Code than with the producer who once allowed the adulteress of *A Yank at Oxford* (p. 52) the sunset of an officers' club. The beleaguered families in Hamer's first features are either bullied or cramped. Each experiences trauma; yet despite the emotional pain, the family emerges as if nothing significant had happened.

The one film in which Hamer kept the narrative trajectory sharp was the sublime *Kind Hearts and Coronets* (1949). *Kind Hearts* is a typical Ealing comedy *only* in that a problem is defined and solved: how one Louis Mazzini (Dennis Price) is to take his place as a d'Ascoyne. High in sensibility and lacking in sentiment, Mazzini, wronged by his relatives, considers the d'Ascoyne title his right and due. Mazzini becomes a d'Ascoyne brilliantly: by becoming the family's sole survivor. Of the eight d'Ascoynes—all played by Alec Guinness (p. 14)—standing between Mazzini and the title, six are assassinated by the pretender to the coronet, one dies of natural causes, and one from stupidity. Although Balcon's heroes tend to be foggy if not amateurish, Mazzini moves with too much consideration and care to be endearing. He is neither affable nor

neighborly: he is suave and he works alone. He does not bumble, but in joyous reaction to an unexpected piece of good news he does make a mistake which provides the cinema with one of its nearly perfect endings.

Hamer does not situate Mazzini in reality but in an imagined crystal of privilege made manifest. Artifice and elegance, never high on Ealing's agenda, permeate the film from set design through dialogue. The world Mazzini aspires to is halcyon and idealized. Those who are about to vacate it are foolish, self-interested, and unappreciative of it. Mazzini uses English not only to demonstrate superiority and court his noble victims but to tell his tale with such grace and wit as to elicit from his uncertain audience a cool assent. It is ironic that although Balcon had earlier identified the suitable use of English as something which might distinguish British films from American ones, language was never used with such exquisite precision as in this most uncharacteristic of Balcon's Ealings.

Monja Danischewsky, Balcon's clever and peppy publicity man, attached the slogan "the Ealing film that begs to differ" to Crichton's *Hue and Cry*. The phrase was appropriate in 1947, but by the time *The Titfield Thunderbolt* (1952, Crichton) appeared, what Ealing comedies differed with was reality. In an increasingly

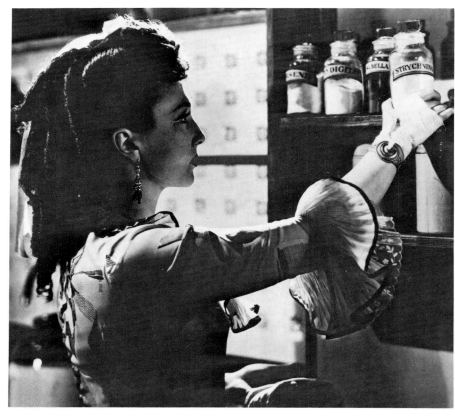

Opposite: *The Man in the White Suit,* 1951, Alexander Mackendrick (Alec Guinness)

It Always Rains on Sunday, 1947, Robert Hamer (Googie Withers, Patricia Plunkett, Edward Chapman, David Lines, Susan Shaw)

Opposite: *Pink String and Sealing Wax,* 1945, Robert Hamer (Googie Withers)

Kind Hearts and Coronets, 1949, Robert Hamer (Dennis Price, Alec Guinness)

divided nation a pervasive geniality was more an Ealing construct than a fact of life. The manufacture of a false homogeneity required situations that became increasingly exaggerated and grotesque. For all its authentic West Country location, Titfield might just as well be Brigadoon. Its inhabitants are all purposely quaint, and each is occupied with a peculiar but harmless avocation: When the introduction of a bus threatens the closure of their small branch railway, the Titfielders, some of whom love their antiquated train and some of whom prefer that Titfield remain in the previous century (first buses, then "zebra crossings"), rescue their line. In accomplishing this the lengths to which they go are so absurd that the audience, incapable of even beginning to believe what is going on, remains disengaged.

The Ladykillers (1955, Mackendrick), adapted by American expatriate William Rose from his black dream, is a bizarre comedy that does not go off the tracks. The vampirish Dr. Marcus (Alec Guinness) and his fuzzy gang of crooks (in the guise of chamber musicians) descend on a boardinghouse run under the slight but unwavering hand of a septuagenarian, Louisa Wilberforce (Katie Johnson). She may be a respectable petite bourgeoise, but she is not priggish. She is kindly and maternal, and the gang members literally die to do her in. Unlike Mazzini, whose killings are allowed to happen almost expeditiously, the rogues in *The Ladykillers* fumble their way to their own deaths. Not quite competent (but neither incompetent) they are genetically Greenleaf. Louisa Wilberforce, the landlady, triumphs by being British (and Victorian) to her very core. Proper manners remain invincible. Naughty without ever being wicked, *The Ladykillers* was Ealing's last successful conceit.

It was not only Ealing comedies that reflected Britain quaintly. An excellent natural illustration of cozy familiarity and soothing insularity may be found in *Painted Boats* (1945, Crichton). A paean to the country's canal workers, *Painted Boats* starred Britain's "tender, lucid countryside" as it paid homage to the nation's waterway transporters. At the time the film was made, goods were moved through a network of man-made and privately financed canals: navigating these cuts were houseboats owned and operated by individual families. Each vessel was brightly and distinctively painted for identification and decoration. Each family/crew knew the others: together they constituted a self-contained unit whose members lived and "worked with their own" and who kept *matériel* afloat during the war. Wanting to salute the transporters and recognizing the importance of the groups as both emblem and metaphor, Balcon determined Ealing should prepare a suitable encomium. Given the intimate relationship of the workers to landscape, the decision to shoot most of

the film on location was sensible. Although *Painted Boats* was professionally cast, it was to look like a documentary, and it does. There was little dialogue but enough narration and recitative to carry not only the two converging stories but to capsize them. For all its sunlight and pleasantly riparian view, *Painted Boats* does not trust its images: it is a delicate work that cracks under too much wordage. In both its ambition and the context of Balcon's Britain, however, *Painted Boats* remains of particular interest.

Another idealistic representation appears in *The Captive Heart* (1946, Dearden). Shot in part in a former POW camp in Germany, *The Captive Heart* smartly contrasts the English village from which Celia Mitchell

Painted Boats, 1945, Charles Crichton

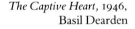

(Rachel Kempson) writes to the man she believes to be her husband (Michael Redgrave) with the yard in which that man is imprisoned. The captured British soldiers have improvised their area of confinement into a garden suburb. The barracks are made to seem like detached and tattily decorated cottages. Each residence appears to have a garden plot; flowers are grown. Men lounge about with pipe and paper. There is no village green but there is a playing field—the spirit is unconquerable.

How much was myth? A contemporary of Balcon, the critic G. Campbell Dixon, wrote that "of all our film producers Mickey Balcon is the most English, judged by the spirit and style and content of his pictures. Does this seem odd to say of a man proud of his Jewish race and faith? I don't really see why.... Nobody ever made a more English film than *The Captive Heart,* where the pace is deliberately allowed to drag—partly to suggest the slow tempo of prison life, of course, but more fundamentally because the English are the most patient race in Europe."[52] This quote comes three years *after* Agee spotted Ealing's "self-satirizing and self-congratulatory" characters.

Another Dearden film, *The Blue Lamp,* was an enormously popular 1950 police drama that spawned a long-running television series. A youthful Dirk Bogarde plays a brutal and psychotic delinquent who murders a policeman (Jack Warner) on the eve of retirement. Like other Ealings, *The Blue Lamp* was shot in part on the streets and in part in the studio where the sets were modeled after particular locations. Its form is diaristic, "slice of life," and its observation of the everyday routine of Scotland Yard and of police stations means to be documentary. "As usual with Ealing pictures," Frank Enley wrote in a perceptive and angry review for *Sight and Sound,* "great pains have been taken to present a respectable surface"—one too respectable to be honest.[53]

Enley makes much of the reaction of Mrs. Dixon (Gladys Henson) to the news that her policeman husband has died. Of the flowers she is holding at the time she says: "I must put these in water." Enley compares this modest response to the manner in which "direct and unforced" grief was expressed in the recently released American film *The Naked City* (1948, Jules Dassin). Mrs. Dixon's quiet reaction was required by "a myth of national proportion." Enley observed that in Britain "it was not unheard of for women to weep at a time of bereavement." The myth, however, insists that the British are brave:

... that is, they face tragedy without ever showing emotion. Sang-froid unites all classes but apart from this there's a sharp division. The upper classes are usually dignified in their

everyday lives, while the lower classes are eccentric (vocabulary, costumes, ideas of entertainment) and therefore comical. The chief emotional overtone of all this, it seems to me, is complacency; and complacency is the enemy of good art—of truthful perception and valid sympathy.[54]

Though his comments were not directed at Ealing so much as at the assumptions of contemporary British filmmakers, Enley's points do help explain the flatness of many Ealing films in the fifties.

Dearden, Enley noted, directed *The Blue Lamp* with his "usual polish and competence: the surface is impeccable and the centre dead." The same could not be said of Dearden's next film, *Pool of London* (1951), whose location comprised the busy docks and tenebrous warehouses of London portside and whose several merging narratives involved sailors, customs officers, smugglers, and river police. The romance in *Pool of London* between a black seaman and a local girl may be tentative and poignant but it is not dead at the center. There is no pandering to type and less assurance about they way things work. *Pool of London,* if not critical, is certainly aware that social problems obtain, and is a vigorous and gritty work.

Between 1945 and 1952, four directors, Crichton, Dearden, Frend, and Hamer, directed twenty-six films for Ealing. In 1952 Lindsay Anderson wrote about the production of *Secret People* (1952, Thorold Dickinson) in his book *Making a Film*. He observed that while Balcon had structured Ealing so that there would be a

continuity of production, the system was not without liabilities. When a "small nucleus of writers and technicians under regular contract" worked together for any length of time their films would evidence a "familiarity of tone" and a "recognisable bias in approach to subjects, characterisation and treatment"; Anderson predicted that there was a point where "consistency declines into sameness." So when Thorold Dickinson returned to Ealing to direct his own screenplay, his appearance was welcomed as a "stranger bride in a family tending towards inbreeding."[55]

Secret People did nothing to alter the "recognisable biases" at Ealing, which by 1952 were entrenched. A work that first appeared to be about violence as a questionable means of effecting substantive political change became a melodrama about its unacceptability. It presented a totalitarian government of an unnamed country which eliminates its democratic opposition. Some rebels escape to join exiles already in London; initially these refugees have the viewers' sympathy. When the rebels, however, plan to assassinate a visiting representative of the hated regime, the audience is asked to disapprove. What if, the film asks, a civilian is harmed? Which is, of course, what happens. As it charts the tribulations of Maria Brent (Valentina Cortese), a refugee whose life is marred with coincidence, the film is more personalized than I have indicated but Maria's story is too awkward to be of interest. Like other Ealings, *Secret People* is original; unlike them, its

Left: *Pool of London,* 1951, Basil Dearden

Right: *The Blue Lamp,* 1950, Basil Dearden (Jimmy Hanley, Dirk Bogarde, Peggy Evans)

narrative goes haywire, and suffers many climaxes, none of which is satisfactory.

In spite of his "almost atavistic dislike of . . . monopoly," in 1944 Balcon aligned Ealing with the Rank Organisation. Ealing had a studio, but it did not have cinemas. Most theaters were owned by one of two combines, one of which was Rank, and both of which, being vertical, made films. Ealing, therefore, was at "a grave disadvantage" until it joined Rank, whereupon Ealing became a "favored nation" within the organization, enjoying complete production autonomy and independence, favorable distribution terms, and a "50% contribution toward each film Ealing made."[56] Ealing films were to be financed with British capital for distribution and exhibition in Great Britain by British interests.

Ealing's alignment with Rank was soon followed by the end of war, and Balcon, not usually given to public jubilation, announced that British films could become "Ambassadors to the World . . . projecting . . . the true Briton." Somehow "the true Briton" was to reflect "a complete picture" of the nation, a difficult task given that Britain was "a leader in Social Reform . . . a patron [of the arts] . . . a questing explorer, adventurer and trader . . . the home of great industry and craftsmanship . . . a mighty military power."[57] This hyperbole hardly seems compatible with Ealing's unassuming posture. Fortunately Balcon, with few exceptions, did not follow through on his rhetoric, and Britain's best ambassadors became Ealing's own comedies.

Encouraged by Rank to be more ambitious, Ealing made forays into the lush terrain of historical reconstruction, and they were somewhat peculiar. Ealing's earliest "prestige" picture, its first release in color, was an expensive flop, and no wonder, with a title like *Saraband for Dead Lovers* (1948, Dearden). Based loosely on history, this intelligent melodrama was more interested in how the corridors of power were traversed than in the meager comings and goings of the young lovers thwarted by the imperialistic ambitions of the House of

Saraband for Dead Lovers, 1948, Basil Dearden (Beatrice Varley, Flora Robson)

Hanover. The lovers, played by Joan Greenwood and Stewart Granger, are treated diffidently, and whatever passion they occasionally manifest holds no candle to the repressed sexuality—the only kind known at Ealing—of Flora Robson, who smolders throughout. Considering Balcon's earlier rhapsodizing about Britain, it is odd that the villains, who are the most compelling characters in the film, include the Electress Sophia (played by a full-bodied Françoise Rosay) and her appalling son George (Peter Bull), the future king of England. *Saraband,* shot in part in Prague, is a handsome film, and its saturated colors are appropriately dark. However, it is chamber *guignol*: if it was meant to be an epic, it is definitely Ealing-size.

This is not true of *Scott of the Antarctic* (1948), which was made in part on location, and has a track amplified by the symphonic score of Ralph Vaughan Williams. At first *Scott* seems a curious choice to illustrate Britain as a questing explorer, but it is not. A line from *Whisky Galore!* is pertinent: "We play the game for the sake of the game. Other nations play to win." Although Scott arrives at the South Pole after Amundsen, that is not the point: being second is not a failure. What was inspiring was the adventure itself and how it was undertaken. Scott's final diary entries are quoted, and they serve as the moral center of the film: "We took risks . . . [but] things have come out against us and we have no cause for complaint. . . . Had I lived I should have had a tale to tell of the hardihood, endurance and courage of my companions which would have stirred the heart of every Englishman."

The film, while eliciting admiration for Scott and his crew, never lets the audience forget the ill-fated nature of the expedition. It is dour. The narrative requires Scott (John Mills) to be both boyish in enthusiasm and inflexible in action. In preparing for the voyage he makes a decision that dooms him. While the Norwegian explorer brought "dogs, dogs, dogs"—four hundred of them—to Antarctica, Scott brought not only dogs and ponies but motorized vehicles that froze. Amundsen had advised the Englishman that mechanical devices could not be eaten. The implication disgusted Scott; playing the game requires behavior that is proper and that excludes eating one's companions. That Scott died "only eleven miles from store a-plenty" is solemnly noted but not developed for its ironic implications. The film recognizes the hero's imperfect nature yet does *not* treat him ambivalently or ambiguously. That is *Scott's* glory.

Scott of the Antarctic and *The Cruel Sea* (1952, Frend) were two of Balcon's favorite films, and like *San Demetrio London* and *Nine Men,* they deal with men bonded in situations of crisis. In *The Cruel Sea,* "the heroines," intones the narrator, "are the ships," one of

The Cruel Sea, 1952, Charles Frend (Donald Sinden, Jack Hawkins)

which goes down. The villain is not the German Navy (in Ealing's few postwar films, locating the enemy is no simple matter) but the sea itself; cruel as it is, made crueler by man. At the beginning the film is announced as a romance, and not unlike *Scott,* it is about the getting on with it, which in this case means being ever vigilant in the protection of convoys. Determination, hardihood, and perseverance, Scott's qualities, are characteristics of Erickson (Jack Hawkins), captain first of the *Compass Rose,* later of the *Saltash Castle,* as seen by his protégé, the young Lieutenant Lockhart (Donald Sinden), Ealing's idea of an ingenue. The apprenticeship of Lockhart to Erickson is as personal as *The Cruel Sea* becomes. As Lockhart explains to a picnic date, his relationship with his superior is "about the only type war allows you." During its 126-minute running time, *The Cruel Sea* does have incident, often quite dramatic, but it has less action than an American counterpart would have had. *The Cruel Sea* is patient; the film recognizes that waiting was part of the maritime theater. *The Cruel Sea* concludes with an effective understatement by Lockhart. In five years of duty, only two U-boats were sunk; that "seemed a lot at the time."

In surveying Balcon's history films, from *Balaclava* (1930) to *Dunkirk* (1958), it appears that the producer found it immodest to isolate unqualified British victories for his subjects. The one time he did, the achieve-

ment was set halfway round the world in Australia and was occasioned by a threat which never materialized. Balcon regarded Watt's sinewy *The Overlanders* (1946) as the "first and only British Western."[58] Actually this Western is less British than it is Empire; and it is mostly Ealing, in that it follows the familiar line of ordinary individuals banding together once they realize concerted action is necessary. Anticipating Japanese invasion of the Northern Territory, ranchers, settlers, and cowboys hurriedly drive a hundred thousand head of cattle, potential food for the enemy, two thousand miles to the south. Based on actual incident, the adventure was shot on location with a cast of actors (including a laconic Chips Rafferty) and nonprofessionals. The unfamiliar topography arrests the eye, and the footage of the drive is bold and exciting.

Ealing Studios comprised physical plant and personnel. Stephen Courtauld, who had remained a principal backer of the studio since 1931, retired to Rhodesia in 1952, and the entire indebtedness of the property fell to Balcon and his associate of long standing, Reginald Baker, Ealing's manager. The studio had never been adequately capitalized, and even Balcon's association with Rank could not diminish the financial burden he inherited. Part of this was met with a loan from the National Film Finance Corporation (from whose

The Overlanders, 1946,
Harry Watt

board Balcon resigned), but a "hard core of the capital amount"[59] had to be met with the sale of the studio and its equipment to the British Broadcasting Corporation in 1955.

Balcon then thought to move personnel and policy to Pinewood Studios, where the Rank Organisation was building new stages. However, Rank was not prepared to let Ealing have the exclusive and autonomous use of any of its stages, and with the final film made at Ealing, *The Long Arm* (1956, Frend), Ealing and Rank dissolved their arrangement for joint distribution of Ealing films. In 1956 Ealing was groundsless.

Arthur Loew, then president of M-G-M and an old colleague of Balcon's, invited Ealing to continue production at its British facility, now at Boreham Wood. Loew, however, left the company in a bitter stockholders' fight soon after Balcon started working, and for the three years of his contract Balcon once again "had little or no personal contact with the management team"[60] at M-G-M.

The penultimate Ealing, and the last one at M-G-M, was "the least Ealing film ever made."[61] Seth Holt's appropriately titled *Nowhere to Go* (1958) receives no mention in Balcon's autobiography and points in a direction Balcon would hesitate to follow. *Nowhere to Go* is Ealing in its location work, including various British landscapes (London and Wales), but modern in its jaunty pessimism and fractured narrative. An attractive delinquent (George Nader) is the not unsympathetic protagonist; the film's style is jagged and jazzy, and its subtext is alienation—a novel subject for a studio where identity never seemed to be a question.

Nowhere to Go was surely one of the earliest theatrical films to be influenced by Free Cinema, that loose assemblage of nonfiction filmmakers pronounced a movement in 1956. Balcon was chairman of the BFI Experimental Film Fund, which underwrote some of the works of Free Cinema, and he most certainly would have known the initial films of Lindsay Anderson, Karel Reisz, and Tony Richardson. It is likely Balcon shared the discovery of these films with his own staff, including Holt, who had been an Ealing editor, then the producer on *The Ladykillers.* The lyricism, the open-ended quality, and the candid nature of observation that characterize Free Cinema were so strong and fresh that they percolated through Ealing.

In the midfifties, Balcon may have resisted reflecting the fractious spirit of the times, but in his last two

Ealings it certainly made itself felt. The hero of *Nowhere to Go* is confused and disaffected; Matt Kirk (Aldo Ray) of *The Siege of Pinchgut* (1959), a one-time criminal, begins by protesting his innocence on a recent charge and ends by threatening to blow up Sydney Harbor if he is not given a retrial. A bloody confrontation is forced when mediation might have resolved the stand-off, and the audience at last sees the authorities ambivalently. Violence, *Secret People* taught, was not an acceptable way of settling disputes, and yet in *The Siege of Pinchgut* the behavior of the police, one of Ealing's most cherished institutions, may be duplicitous.

With the dispersal of Ealing's assets, in 1959 Balcon and several other independent producers set up Bryanston, a cooperative for which Balcon served "in a part-time capacity" as chairman until its assets were sold in 1965. Balcon produced one film for Bryanston, the brutal and picaresque *Sammy Going South* (1963, Mackendrick; p. 40) in which those virtues so admired by Balcon in Captains Scott and Erickson are found in a ten-year-old orphan, Sammy, who walks two thousand miles across Africa from Port Saïd to Durban in search of a putative aunt.

In 1964 Balcon was invited to become chairman of

Top: *Nowhere to Go*, 1958, Seth Holt (George Nader)

Right: *The Siege of Pinchgut*, 1959, Harry Watt (Aldo Ray, Heather Sears)

British Lion, which owned Shepperton Studios, considered a glamorous ward of Government. Balcon, believing British Lion to be a species of public property, hoped to make the studio a rallying point for independent British producers, and drew up a production schedule that included ten to fifteen features a year in alliance with the New York distributor/exhibitor Walter Reade. However, it soon became clear that his appointment was titular, and disappointed, he resigned in 1966. But at seventy he did not retire from filmmaking completely.

Balcon, whose initiative had been "crucial and timely"[62] in the establishment of the British Film Institute Experimental Film Fund in 1951, remained its chairperson through 1972. By this time the Fund had not only developed into the BFI Production Board (1966), but had financially assisted some eighty-five British films, including early works by the following directors: Lindsay Anderson (*O Dreamland,* 1953), Nick Broomfield (*Who Cares?,* 1971), Kevin Brownlow (*Nine, Dalmuir West,* 1968), Jack Gold (*The Visit,* 1959), Tony Richardson and Karel Reisz (*Momma Don't Allow,* 1956), Ken Russell (*Amelia and the Angel,* 1958), Ridley Scott (*Boy and Bicycle,* 1965), and Peter Watkins (*Dust Fever,* 1962).

Toward the end of his life, Balcon observed from his home in Upper Parrock, Sussex, that the British film industry was once again operating for the most part with speculative capital from the United States. Believing that international productions "lead to the most stringent restrictions of creativity," and fearing "mid-Atlantic mutations,"[63] Balcon continued to hope the American idiom would not "destroy all sense of consistent or distinctive style in pictures made in British studios."[64] His idea of a national cinema was basically one of a national style of filmmaking. It had taken him almost twenty years to determine a recognizably indig-

Momma Don't Allow, 1956, Karel Reisz and Tony Richardson

enous style at Ealing, and it was a vital achievement. Although in the end Balcon's films had lost their pertinence, he had by now helped found what grew into the BFI Production Board to encourage a future generation of British filmmakers. It was Sir Michael's insurance that the consistent and distinctive style of British films would not predecease him.

Notes

1. Michael Balcon, *Michael Balcon Presents . . . A Lifetime of Films* (London: Hutchinson, 1969), pp. 12–13.
2. *Ibid.,* p. 2.
3. *Ibid.,* p. 53.
4. Quoted from the original English typescript for Rachael Low, "Die Anfange: Gainsborough und Gaumont-British," in Geoff Brown, ed., *Der Produzent: Michael Balcon und der englische Film* (Berlin: Verlag Volker Spiess, 1981), p. 45.
5. *Ibid.,* p. 47.
6. Balcon, *A Lifetime of Films,* p. 18.
7. *Ibid.,* p. 26.
8. Statistics found in Ernest Betts, *The Film Business: A History of British Cinema, 1896–1972* (London: Allen and Unwin, 1973), p. 82.
9. Michael Balcon, "Sincerity Will Make the Film English," *The Era* (London), Nov. 11, 1931, p. 10.
10. Balcon, *A Lifetime of Films,* p. 25.
11. Balcon, "Sincerity Will Make the Film English," *op. cit.,* p. 10.
12. At least *Michael and Mary*'s first half is of interest. Informed by a cinematic sensibility, it moves in and out of several sets and ranges over several periods of time. The second half takes place within a single protracted evening in a drawing room; at best, its direction is undistinguished.
13. From a review of *Friday the Thirteenth* by Mordaunt Hall, *The New York Times,* May 15, 1934, p. 18, col. 1.
14. Balcon, *A Lifetime of Films,* pp. 57–58.
15. *Ibid.,* pp. 62, 63.
16. *Ibid.,* pp. 68–70.
17. *Ibid.,* p. 61.
18. *Ibid.,* pp. 107–8.
19. *Ibid.,* p. 100.
20. *Ibid.,* p. 101.
21. *Ibid.,* p. 102.
22. To avoid legislative censorship, the Motion Picture Producers and Distributors of America established in 1934 a code of censorship and an administrative office (popularly

called the Hays Office after the long-term president, Will H. Hays) to regulate the content of their films. Subscription to the code was not required by law, but since the studios owned the great majority of theaters, virtually every American feature-length film made between 1934 and 1953 was submitted and modified until approved.

23. Low, "Die Anfange," p. 59.
24. Arthur Benjamin in a letter to M-G-M, April 28, 1938, Balcon Collection, BFI, London.
25. Balcon, *A Lifetime of Films*, pp. 120–21.
26. The expression was invented by Monja Danischewsky, whose memoirs *White Russian, Red Face* (London: Gollancz, 1966) contained a chapter on Mr. Balcon's Academy.
27. Kenneth Tynan, "Ealing's Way of Life," *Films and Filming* (London), vol. 2, no. 3 (Dec. 1955), p. 10.
28. Michael Relph, "Ealing and After," *Sight and Sound* (London), vol. 47, no. 1 (Winter 1977–78), p. 11.
29. Balcon, *A Lifetime of Films*, p. 130.
30. *Ibid.*, p. 123.
31. *Ibid.*, p. 130.
32. *Ibid.*
33. *Ibid.*, p. 127.
34. Balcon, "Putting the New British Talkie on the Map in the States," *Daily Film Renter* (London), vol. 8, no. 2441 (Jan. 1, 1935).
35. Michael Balcon, "Rationalise!" *Sight and Sound* (London), vol. 9, no. 36 (Winter 1940–41), pp. 62–63.
36. Michael Balcon, "The British Film during the War," *Penguin Film Review* (London), no. 1 (Aug. 1946), pp. 69–71.
37. *Ibid.*, 71.
38. Balcon, *A Lifetime of Films*, p. 132.
39. Balcon, "The British Film during the War," p. 71.
40. *Ibid.*
41. Michael Balcon, "Realism or Tinsel?"; reprinted in Monja Danischewsky, ed., *Michael Balcon's 25 Years in Film* (London: World Film Publications, 1947), p. 71.
42. Quoted by Elizabeth Sussex, "Cavalcanti in England," *Sight*

and Sound (London), vol. 44, no. 4 (Autumn 1975), p. 209.
43. Cavalcanti, quoted by Sussex, *ibid.*, p. 210.
44. Review of *48 Hours, The Nation*, July 15, 1944; reprinted in *Agee on Film* (Boston: Beacon Press, 1964), p. 104.
45. Sussex, p. 209.
46. Balcon, *A Lifetime of Films*, p. 145.
47. Harry Watt, *Don't Look at the Camera* (New York: St. Martin's Press, 1974), p. 185.
48. Kenneth Tynan, "Ealing: The Studio in Suburbia," *Films and Filming* (London), vol. 2, no. 2 (Nov. 1955), p. 4.
49. Balcon, *A Lifetime of Films*, pp. 159, 158.
50. Tynan, "Ealing's Way of Life," p. 10.
51. Balcon, *A Lifetime of Films*, pp. 162–63.
52. G. Campbell Dixon, "A Film Critic Reviews a Producer," in Danischewsky, ed., *Michael Balcon's 25 Years in Films*, p. 41.
53. Frank Enley, "The Blue Lamp," *Sight and Sound* (London), vol. 19, no. 2 (April 1950), pp. 76–78.
54. *Ibid.*, p. 78.
55. Lindsay Anderson, *Making a Film: The Story of "Secret People"* (London: Allen and Unwin Ltd., 1952), p. 14; reprinted in series "Garland Classics of Film Literature" (New York and London: Garland Publishing, 1977).
56. Balcon, *A Lifetime of Films*, pp. 152–55.
57. Michael Balcon, "Let British Films Be Ambassadors to the World,"*Kinematograph Weekly* (London), vol. 335, no. 1969 (Jan. 11, 1945), p. 31.
58. Balcon, *A Lifetime of Films*, p. 150.
59. *Ibid.*, p. 183.
60. *Ibid.*, p. 187.
61. Seth Holt, interview in *Screen* (London), Nov.–Dec. 1969, p. 9; quoted in *Der Produzent*, p. 139.
62. Peter Sainsbury, "The Financial Base of Independent Film Production in the U.K.," *Screen* (London), vol. 22, no. 1 (1981), p. 45.
63. Quoted in "Balcon's Testament," *Sight and Sound* (London), vol. 47, no. 2 (Spring 1978), p. 68.
64. Balcon, *A Lifetime of Films*, p. 210.

Kind Hearts and Coronets, 1949, Robert Hamer
(Dennis Price)

Chronology

Catherine A. Surowiec

KEY TO ABBREVIATIONS			
	d: director	BN: British National	ITC: Independent Television Corp.
	p: producer	CAPAD: Co-operative Association of Producers and Distributors	M-G-M: Metro-Goldwyn-Mayer
			MOI: Ministry of Information
	Film companies:	Col.: Columbia	NFFC: National Film Finance Corp.
	ABPC: Associated British Pictures Corp.	Crown: Crown Film Unit	Par.: Paramount Pictures
	AFM: Allied Film Makers	EMB: Empire Marketing Board Film Unit	Pascal: Gabriel Pascal Productions
	AIP: American International Pictures		Python: Python Productions
	ATP: Associated Talking Pictures	EMI: Electrical and Musical Industries	Rock: Rock Studios (Joe Rock)
	ATV: Associated Television Corp.	FN: First National Pictures	Sheffield: Sheffield Photo Co.
	B & D: British & Dominions	G-B: Gaumont-British	Smith: George Albert Smith Films
	BFM: British Film Makers	G-B I: Gaumont-British Instructional	UA: United Artists
	BHE: British Home Entertainments	GPO: General Post Office Film Unit	United Kingdom: United Kingdom Photoplays
	BIF: British Instructional Films	Hepworth: Hepworth Co. (pre-1919); Hepworth Picture Plays (post-1919)	
	BIP: British International Pictures		Urban: Charles Urban Trading Co.
	BL: British Lion	IA: Independent Artists	WB: Warner Brothers
	BLPA: British Lion Production Assets	IP: Independent Producers	

	Selected Historical and Cultural Events, including Radio and Television	Balcon and the British Film Industry	Selected British Films
1889		William Friese-Greene patents motion-picture camera	
1896	London *Daily Mail* begins publication *The Grand Duke,* last Gilbert & Sullivan operetta, premieres Lit: *Jude the Obscure* (Hardy)	Lumières's first program in Britain, Polytechnic Hall, Regent St., London, includes *Sortie des usines Lumière, L'Arroseur arrosé* Birt Acres demonstrates camera and projector, Royal Photographic Society, London; later in year, presents first royal film performance for Prince of Wales R. W. Paul exhibits films to paying audience, Olympia and Alhambra music halls, London First official film of Queen Victoria, Balmoral Castle Birth of Reginald Baker, Michael Elias Balcon (Birmingham), John Baxter, Maurice Ostrer	*Persimmon's Derby* (d/p: Paul) *The Soldier's Courtship* (d/p: Paul)
1897	Queen Victoria's Diamond Jubilee Royal Automobile Club founded, London Sir Henry Tate donates Tate Gallery to British people Lit: *Captains Courageous* (Kipling), *Dracula* (Stoker), *The Invisible Man* (Wells)	Queen Victoria's Diamond Jubilee filmed by R. W. Paul and others Cecil Hepworth writes *Animated Photography: The A.B.C. of the Cinematograph,* first book on film Am. producer Charles Urban founds Warwick Trading Co. Birth of Alberto Cavalcanti, Maurice Elvey, Victor Saville (Birmingham)	
1898	Th: *Caesar and Cleopatra* (Shaw) Lit: *The War of the Worlds* (Wells), *Wessex Poems* (Hardy)	Gaumont Co., Britain, organized by A. C. Bromhead and T. A. Welsh Hepworth makes first film, *Express*	*The Corsican Brothers* (d/p: Smith)

	Selected Historical and Cultural Events, including Radio and Television	Balcon and the British Film Industry	Selected British Films
1898, continued	Death of Lewis Carroll, William Gladstone	*Trains in a Railway Cutting, Surrey* Birth of Gracie Fields, Walter Forde, John Grierson	
1899	Boer War (–1902) London borough councils established Birth of Noël Coward	Newsreel coverage of Boer War "Brighton School": G. A. Smith, James Williamson, Esme Collings, et al. R. W. Paul opens indoor studio, Muswell Hill, London Birth of Alfred Hitchcock	*Country Life* series (d/p: Williamson) *Henley Regatta* films (d/p: Hepworth; d/p: Williamson)
1900	Labour Party founded; first Secretary, James Ramsay MacDonald Birth of Lady Elizabeth Bowes-Lyon, the future Queen Mother Commonwealth of Australia created London *Daily Express* begins publication Lit: *Lord Jim* (Conrad) Death of John Ruskin, Sir Arthur Sullivan, Oscar Wilde	Birth of Edward Black (Birmingham)	*Army Life, or How Soldiers Are Made* series (d/p: Paul) *Attack on a China Mission* (d/p: Williamson) *Grandma's Reading Glass* (d: Smith, p: Warwick) *How It Feels to Be Run Over* (d/p: Hepworth)
1901	Death of Queen Victoria; Edward VII succeeds to throne Music: *Pomp and Circumstance no. 1* (Elgar) Th: *Quality Street* (Barrie)	Birth of Len Lye	*The Big Swallow* (d/p: Williamson) *Fire!* (d/p: Williamson) *Funeral of Queen Victoria* (d/p: Hepworth)
1902	Arthur Balfour (Conservative) becomes Prime Minister King Edward VII establishes Order of Merit *Times Literary Supplement* (London) begins publication Th: *The Admirable Crichton* (Barrie) Lit: *The Four Feathers* (Mason), *The Hound of the Baskervilles* (Conan Doyle), *The Tale of Peter Rabbit* (Potter) Birth of William Walton Death of Samuel Butler, Cecil Rhodes	Will Barker Film Co. begins prod. at Ealing Birth of Anthony Asquith, Emeric Pressburger, Ralph Richardson	*The Call to Arms* (d/p: Hepworth) *Coronation of Edward VII* (d/p: Hepworth; d/p: Williamson) *The Soldier's Return* (d/p: Williamson)
1903	Emmeline Pankhurst founds National Women's Social and Political Union Royal Naval College founded, Dartmouth First motor taxis in London Th: *Man and Superman* (Shaw) Lit: *The Way of All Flesh* (Butler, posth.) Birth of Kenneth Clark, Cyril Connolly, George Orwell, Evelyn Waugh	Pathé founds London branch Urban founds Charles Urban Trading Co. Birth of Ian Dalrymple, Thorold Dickinson, Angus MacPhail	*Alice in Wonderland* (d/p: Hepworth) *Borneo* series (d: Lomas, p: Urban) *The Delhi Durbar* (d/p: Paul) *Natural History* series (d: Martin-Duncan, p: Urban) *Progress of the Race* (d/p: Hepworth) *Unseen World* series (d: Martin-Duncan, p: Urban) *Voyage of the "Arctic," or How Capt. Kettle Discovered the North Pole* (d/p: Paul)
1904	Russo-Japanese War begins (–1905) London Symphony Orch. gives first concert Abbey Theatre founded, Dublin Th: *Peter Pan* (Barrie), *Riders to the Sea* (Synge) Birth of Cecil Beaton, Cecil Day-Lewis, Graham Greene, Christopher Isherwood, Nancy Mitford	Clarendon Film Co. builds elaborate studio, Croydon: two stages, glass-roofed, plus three-acre lot with artificial lake Birth of George Formby, John Gielgud, Ivor Montagu, Anna Neagle	*Coaling a Battleship at Nagasaki* (d/p: Hepworth) *Man the Lifeboat* series (p: Gaumont)
1905	Sir Henry Campbell-Bannerman (Liberal) becomes Prime Minister Sinn Fein Party founded by Irish nationalists, Dublin First motorbuses and Piccadilly and	Biograph Cinema (orig. Bioscope) opens, Victoria, London Birth of Muriel Box, David Macdonald, Michael Powell, Robert Stevenson	*The Aliens' Invasion* (d/p: Hepworth) *A Den of Thieves* (d/p: Hepworth) *Falsely Accused* (d: Fitzhamon, p: Hepworth) *The Life of Charles Peace* (d: Haggar,

	Selected Historical and Cultural Events, including Radio and Television	Balcon and the British Film Industry	Selected British Films
1905, continued	Bakerloo underground lines open, London Th: *Major Barbara* (Shaw) Lit: *Kipps* (Wells), *The Scarlet Pimpernel* (Orczy)		p: Sheffield) *Rescued by Rover* (d: Fitzhamon and Hepworth (?), p: Hepworth)
1906	Rolls-Royce Ltd. founded by Henry Royce and Charles Rolls "Everyman's Library" series begins publication Lit: *The Four Just Men* (Wallace); *The Man of Property,* first *Forsyte Saga* novel (Galsworthy) Birth of Samuel Beckett	G. A. Smith and Charles Urban patent Kinemacolor, first commercially successful color process *The Hand of the Artist* (d: W. R. Booth), Britain's first animated film Electrical engineer Eugene Lauste patents sound-on-film recording process Daily Bioscope, continuous newsreel cinema, opens, Bishopsgate, London Hale's Tours (travelogues projected in mock railway coach), Oxford St., London Birth of Carol Reed, Harry Watt	*The Curate's Dilemma* (d/p: Paul) *Dick Turpin's Ride to York* (d: Fitzhamon, p: Hepworth) *The ? Motorist* (d: Booth, p: Paul)
1907	Boy Scouts founded by Lord Baden-Powell Rudyard Kipling wins Nobel Prize for Literature Th: *Playboy of the Western World* (Synge) Lit: *The Secret Agent* (Conrad) Birth of W. H. Auden, Daphne du Maurier, Christopher Fry	Barker builds stage at Ealing Hepworth develops Vivaphone sound-recording system *Kinematograph Weekly,* trade paper, founded Birth of T. E. B. Clarke, John Croydon, Humphrey Jennings, Frank Launder, Jessie Matthews, Laurence Olivier, Paul Rotha, Basil Wright	*That Fatal Sneeze* (d: Fitzhamon, p: Hepworth) *The Water Babies* (d: Stow, p: Clarendon) *When the Devil Drives* (d: Booth, p: Urban)
1908	H. H. Asquith (Liberal) becomes Prime Minister; David Lloyd George, Chancellor of the Exchequer Borstal System (reform schools) started Port of London Authority founded Isadora Duncan becomes popular interpreter of the dance Lit: *The Old Wives' Tale* (Bennett), *A Room with a View* (Forster), *The Wind in the Willows* (Grahame) Birth of Ian Fleming	*A Visit to the Seaside* (d: G. A. Smith, p: Natural Colour Kinematograph Co.), first color film Gaumont Film Co. holds first trade show; exhibitors preview films for booking purposes U.S. imposes duty on film imports; Brit. film exports drop Birth of Sidney Cole, Sidney Gilliat, David Lean, John Mills, Michael Redgrave	*John Gilpin's Ride* (d/p: Hepworth) *Romeo and Juliet* (p: Gaumont)
1909	Aviator Louis Blériot flies across English Channel in 37 min. Old-age pensions introduced London hairdressers give first permanent waves Music: *Fantasia on a Theme of Thomas Tallis* (Vaughan Williams) Birth of Malcolm Lowry, Stephen Spender Death of George Meredith, Florence Nightingale, J. M. Synge	First Cinematograph Films Act; deals with theater safety regulations Brit.-produced films account for ca. 15 percent of theatrical programming Graham Cutts enters films as exhibitor, Newcastle-on-Tyne Birth of Charles Frend, Joseph Losey, James Mason	*The Airship Destroyer* (d: Paul?/Urban?, p: Warwick) *The Mystery of Edwin Drood* (d: Gilbert, p: Gaumont)
1910	Death of King Edward VII; George V succeeds to throne Union of South Africa created Scott leaves on expedition to South Pole Dr. H. H. Crippen, wife poisoner, executed 122,000 telephones in use in Britain Arthur Evans completes excavation of Knossos, Crete Roger Fry organizes first Post-Impressionist exhibition, London	Weekly newsreels: Pathé Louis Levy becomes silent film accompanist; joins Balcon as mus. dir., 1929 Birth of Charles Crichton	*East Lynne* (p: Precision)

	Selected Historical and Cultural Events, including Radio and Television	Balcon and the British Film Industry	Selected British Films
1911	Coronation of King George V Ramsay MacDonald becomes Chairman of Labour Party Lloyd George introduces National Health Insurance Bill London *Daily Herald* begins publication Birth of Randolph Churchill, William Golding, Terence Rattigan Death of W. S. Gilbert	*Lt. Daring* (p: British & Colonial Kinematograph Co.), first of series Birth of Monja Danischewsky, Basil Dearden, Robert Hamer, Muir Mathieson	*Henry VIII* (d/p: Barker) *Pirates of 1920* (p: Cricks & Martin) *Richard III* (p: Benson) *Tatters: A Tale of the Slums* (d: Coleby, p: Cricks & Martin)
1912	Labor unrest: strikes by coal miners, transport workers, London longshoremen General Post Office (GPO) takes over British telephone system Scott second explorer to reach South Pole; members of expedition perish S.S. *Titanic* (Cunard Line) sinks on maiden voyage after colliding with iceberg First Royal Command Variety Performance, Palace Theatre, London Charlie Chaplin and Stan Laurel leave for U.S. with Karno music-hall troupe	Board of Film Censors est.; sets two ratings: U (Universal) and A (Adult) First film in "Pimple" comedy series (–1922), starring Fred Evans (p: Folly Films) Birth of Alexander Mackendrick, Penrose Tennyson	*Oliver Twist* (d: Bentley, p: Hepworth) *Saved by Fire!* (p: Clarendon)
1913	Suffragette demonstrations in London Robert Bridges becomes Poet Laureate (–1930) *New Statesman* (London) founded by Sidney and Beatrice Webb Music: *Falstaff* (Elgar) Irene and Vernon Castle make Broadway debut in *The Sunshine Girl* Th: *Pygmalion* (Shaw) Lit: *Sons and Lovers* (Lawrence) Birth of Benjamin Britten	London Film Co. opens Twickenham Studios George Pearson makes first film, *The Fool* Adrian Brunel and Maurice Elvey enter films Birth of John and Roy Boulting, Henry Cornelius	*The Battle of Waterloo* (d: Weston, p: British & Colonial) *David Copperfield* (d: Bentley, p: Hepworth) *East Lynne* (d: Haldane, p: Barker) *Hamlet* (d: Plumb, p: Hepworth) *Ivanhoe* (d: F. and W. Melville, p: Zenith) *A Message from Mars* (d: Waller, p: United Kingdom/Urban) *Sixty Years a Queen* (d: Barker and Smith, p: Barker)
1914	Britain declares war on Germany; World War I begins (–1918) Irish Home Rule Act passed but suspended for duration of war First C. B. Cochran revue, *Odds and Ends,* London Music: Song "Tipperary" popularized by Jack Judge, music-hall comedian Lit: *Dubliners* (Joyce) Birth of Dylan Thomas	Neptune Film Co. builds Boreham Wood Studios Birth of Alec Guinness	*A Study in Scarlet* (d: Pearson, p: Samuelson)
1915	Gallipoli campaign: disastrous British landings; German U-boat sinks *Lusitania;* zeppelin raids on British cities Music: Ivor Novello writes "Keep the Home Fires Burning" Lit: *Of Human Bondage* (Maugham), *The Thirty-nine Steps* (Buchan)	Gaumont builds studio at Shepherd's Bush Kinematograph Renters' Society organized Alexander Korda becomes producer/dir., UFA, Berlin Lupino Lane makes *Nipper's Busy Holiday* (p: John Bull), first of "Nipper" comedy series Birth of Dennis Price, Michael Relph	*The Bottle* (d/p: Hepworth) *My Old Dutch* (d: Trimble, p: Turner)
1916	David Lloyd George (Coalition) becomes Prime Minister Easter Rebellion, Dublin Military conscription (men ages 18–41) begins; tanks first used by British T. E. Lawrence appointed British liaison officer to Faisal's army	First Royal Command Performance of feature film, Hepworth's *Comin' Thro' the Rye,* Marlborough House Entertainment Tax added to cinema admissions Film prod. declines during war Victor Saville enters films as salesman	*The Battle of the Somme* (d: Malins and McDowell, p: Brit. Topical Committee for War Films) *Milestones* (d: Bentley, p: Samuelson) *Ultus: The Man from the Dead* (d: Pearson, p: Gaumont)

	Selected Historical and Cultural Events, including Radio and Television	Balcon and the British Film Industry	Selected British Films
1916, continued	"Summertime" (daylight-saving time) introduced Th: *The Bing Boys Are Here,* wartime revue; *Chu-Chin-Chow,* musical (Norton and Asche); *Hobson's Choice* (Brighouse) Lit: *A Portrait of the Artist as a Young Man* (Joyce), *Women in Love* (Lawrence, pub. 1921) Death of Lord Kitchener	and theater mgr. Birth of Trevor Howard	
1917	Royal family renounces German names and titles; becomes House of Windsor Gen. Allenby takes over British command in Palestine Air attacks on Britain Order of the British Empire created Imperial War Museum (London) founded; will open 1936 Chaplin's yearly salary in U.S. reaches $1 million Th: *Heartbreak House* (Shaw)	War Office allows D. W. Griffith to shoot scenes for *Hearts of the World* on location at front, France Dept. of Information founded; dir.: John Buchan All-star *Masks and Faces* (d: Fred Paul, p: Ideal) produced to promote Brit. films, raise funds for Royal Academy of Dramatic Art Natl. Council of Public Morals establishes commission to investigate film Birth of Valerie Hobson, Googie Withers	*Justice* (d: Elvey, p: Ideal)
1918	Armistice R.A.F. supersedes Royal Flying Corps British govt. abandons Home Rule for Ireland Women (with property) over 30 granted right to vote Education Act raises leaving-school age to 14 Worldwide influenza epidemic (by 1920, ca. 22 million dead) Lit: *Eminent Victorians* (Strachey), *Ulysses* (Joyce, pub. 1922)	Thomas Welsh and George Pearson found Welsh-Pearson; studio at Craven Park Dept. of Information reorganized as Ministry of Information; Minister: Lord Beaverbrook Death of Birt Acres	*The Better 'Ole* (d: Pearson, p: Welsh-Pearson) *Dombey and Son* (d: Elvey, p: Ideal) *Hindle Wakes* (d: Elvey, p: Diamond-Super)
1919	Versailles Peace Conference Housing Act provides for subsidy of public housing Irish Republican Army formed Gold standard suspended Lady Nancy Astor first woman elected to House of Commons (–1945) Lit: *The Moon and Sixpence* (Maugham), *The Story of Dr. Dolittle* (Lofting)	Balcon and Saville found Victory Motion Pictures, Birmingham; Oscar Deutsch, Chairman H. Bruce Woolfe founds British Instructional Films (BIF), Elstree British Lion (BL) opens studio, Boreham Wood Herbert Wilcox enters films, works for Astra Films rentals	
1920	League of Nations founded Conference of San Remo gives Britain Palestine mandate Communist Pact of Great Britain formed Black & Tans sent to Ireland Govt. of Ireland Act provides separate Parliaments for Northern and Southern Ireland First women accepted in degree programs at Oxford Marconi opens first public broadcasting station, Wittle Th: Basil Dean founds ReandeaN, theatrical prod. co.; first hit, *The Skin Game* (Galsworthy) Lit: *Outline of History* (Wells)	Paramount British opens Famous Players studio, Islington; Hitchcock hired as title writer, designer, George Gunn as engineer Herbert Wilcox and Graham Cutts found Graham-Wilcox Prods. Birth of Dirk Bogarde	*Alf's Button* (d/p: Hepworth) *At the Villa Rose* (d: Elvey, p: Stoll) *Helen of Four Gates* (d/p: Hepworth) *Nothing Else Matters* (d: Pearson, p: Welsh-Pearson) *Wuthering Heights* (d: Bramble, p: Ideal)

	Selected Historical and Cultural Events, including Radio and Television	Balcon and the British Film Industry	Selected British Films
1921	Depression Winston Churchill becomes Colonial Secretary Southern Ireland separated from Great Britain; becomes Irish Free State (–1937) Dr. Marie Stopes opens first family-planning clinic British Broadcasting Co. founded; becomes British Broadcasting Corp., 1927 Duke of Westminster sells Gainsborough's *Blue Boy* and Reynolds's *Mrs. Siddons* to Am. collector Collis P. Huntington for £200,000 Th: Pierrot revue *The Co-optimists* opens, London (–1930); *The Green Goddess* (Archer) Lit: *The Analysis of Mind* (Russell)	Harold Boxall becomes studio mgr., Islington; later Gainsborough general mgr. (1924–36), Gaumont-British mgr. (1931–36) Betty Balfour becomes star in *Squibs* (d: Pearson, p: Welsh-Pearson) Walter Forde débuts in "Walter" comedy shorts (d: James B. Sloan, p: British Super Comedies) British Natl. Film League founded to promote native film industry Louis Levy becomes mus. dir. at Shepherd's Bush Pavilion; develops theme songs for silent films Death of William Friese-Greene	*The Battle of Jutland* (d: Woolfe, p: BIF) *The Old Curiosity Shop* (d: Bentley, p: Welsh-Pearson) *Tansy* (d/p: Hepworth)
1922	Andrew Bonar Law (Conservative) becomes Prime Minister Unemployment Insurance Act goes into effect BBC begins broadcasting, Marconi House, London Lord Carnarvon and Howard Carter discover Tutankhamen's tomb, Egypt Lit: *The Forsyte Saga* completed (Galsworthy), *Jacob's Room* (Woolf), *The Waste Land* (Eliot)	Gaumont Co. becomes independent Brit. distrib. Herbert Wilcox produces first film, *The Wonderful Story* (d: Cutts, p: Graham-Wilcox Co.) J. Stuart Blackton directs and produces *The Glorious Adventure* in Prizmacolor Press photographer Bernard Knowles becomes asst. cameraman at Islington	*Squibs Wins the Calcutta Sweep* (d: Pearson, p: Welsh-Pearson)
1923	Stanley Baldwin (Conservative) becomes Prime Minister Prewar gold standard restored George, Duke of York (future King George VI), weds Lady Elizabeth Bowes-Lyon London *Radio Times* begins publication Royal Fine Arts Commission formed; advises on public bldgs. and memorials Music: "Façade," work for two reciters and chamber ensemble (Walton) Th: *London Calling* (Coward) Lit: *The Inimitable Jeeves* (Wodehouse)	Balcon produces first film, *Woman to Woman* (d: Cutts, p: Balcon-Saville-Freedman); premieres following year; among greatest commercial successes of 1920s Birth of Lindsay Anderson, Richard Attenborough, Seth Holt	*Comin' Thro' the Rye* (d/p: Hepworth) *Love, Life and Laughter* (d: Pearson, p: Welsh-Pearson) *The Man without Desire* (d: Brunel, p: Atlas Biocraft) *Mist in the Valley* (d/p: Hepworth) *Paddy the Next Best Thing* (d: Cutts, p: Graham-Wilcox) *The Prodigal Son* (d: Coleby, p: Stoll)
1924	Ramsay MacDonald, first Labour Prime Minister, succeeded by Baldwin British Imperial Airways begins operations Th: *Charlot's Revue*, New York, makes international stars of Lillie, Lawrence, and Buchanan; *Juno and the Paycock* (O'Casey); *The Vortex* (Coward) Lit: *The Constant Nymph* (Kennedy), *A Passage to India* (Forster) Death of Joseph Conrad	Balcon and Cutts found Gainsborough Pictures, buy Islington studios from Famous Players; purchase negotiated by Reginald Baker Balcon weds Aileen Leatherman Film-industry crisis: "Black November"; studios shut down for one month Films made in Britain: 34; British Films Week est. to bolster sinking industry; exhibitors asked to show Brit. films exclusively one wk. per yr. Hepworth Co. fails; studios sold to Archibald Nettlefold Betty Balfour and Alma Taylor head *Daily News* poll of favorite stars	*Reveille* (d: Pearson, p: Welsh-Pearson)
1925	G. B. Shaw wins Nobel Prize for Literature	Hitchcock directs first feature, *The Pleasure Garden*	*The Rat* (d: Cutts, p: Gainsborough)

	Selected Historical and Cultural Events, including Radio and Television	Balcon and the British Film Industry	Selected British Films
1925, continued	Th: *The Ghost Train* (Ridley) Lit: *The Informer* (O'Flaherty), *The Painted Veil* (Maugham) Birth of Peter Brook	Films made in Britain: 23; 95 percent of Brit. screen time filled by Am. movies Film Society founded in London by Iris Barry, Montagu, Brunel, MacPhail, Asquith, Walter Mycroft, Sidney Bernstein, Shaw, Wells, Ellen Terry, et al.; Kinema Club, Cambridge, and others follow DeForest Phonofilms (sound shorts) made and exhibited in Britain (–1926) Birth of Jill Balcon, Richard Burton, Peter Sellers	
1926	Birth of Princess Elizabeth (future Queen Elizabeth II) General strike, result of coal lockout, lasts nine days Sean O'Casey emigrates to England Th: *The Plough and the Stars* (O'Casey) Lit: *The Ringer* (Wallace), *Winnie-the-Pooh* (Milne)	Balcon and Carlyle Blackwell organize Piccadilly Pictures; first feature, *Blighty* (d: Brunel), released 1928 *The Lodger* establishes Hitchcock as major dir. Wilcox and J. D. Williams found British National (BN) studios at Elstree; first prod., *Madame Pompadour* (d: Wilcox) Feature films made in Britain: 26 Birth of Karel Reisz, John Schlesinger	*Boadicea* (d: Hill, p: BIF) *The Flag Lieutenant* (d: Elvey, p: Astra-Natl.) *The Little People* (d: Pearson, p: Welsh-Pearson) *Mademoiselle from Armentières* (d: Elvey, p: Gaumont) *Nell Gwynne* (d: Wilcox, p: BN/W. M. Prods.) *The Triumph of the Rat* (d: Cutts, p: Gainsborough)
1927	Automatic telephone service instituted in London, radio telephone service between Britain and Australia John Logie Baird demonstrates color television, Glasgow Cartoonist David Low joins staff of London *Evening Standard* (–1950); creates Colonel Blimp Th: *One Damned Thing after Another,* Cochran revue (Rodgers and Hart) Lit: *Cambridge Hist. of Eng. Lit.* (15 vols., completed; begun 1907), *To the Lighthouse* (Woolf)	Gaumont-British Picture Corp. (G-B) formed; absorbs Woolf & Freedman distribution co., Ostrer bros. cinema chains, and Ideal Films renting co.; based at Bromheads's Gaumont Co. studios, Shepherd's Bush Cinematograph Films Act ("Quota Act") passed: requires exhibition of incremental percentage of Brit. films over next decade; results in "quota quickies"; restricts blind and block booking of films John Maxwell founds British International Pictures (BIP); takes over BN studios, Elstree Wilcox founds British & Dominions Film Corp. (B & D); studios at Elstree British Lion Corp. (BL) opens studio at Beaconsfield; owns film rights to Edgar Wallace crime novels Hitchcock leaves Gainsborough to join BIP (–1932) Ian Dalrymple joins Balcon as ed., Gainsborough (–1935) Saville directs first film, *The Arcadians* (p: Gaumont) *Close Up,* critical review, founded by Macpherson and Bryher (–1933)	*The Battles of the Coronel and Falkland Islands* (d: Summers, p: BIF-Brit. Projects) *Confetti* (d: Cutts, p: FN/Pathé) *Downhill* (d: Hitchcock, p: Gainsborough) *Easy Virtue* (d: Hitchcock, p: Gainsborough) *Hindle Wakes* (d: Elvey, p: Gaumont) *The Ring* (d: Hitchcock, p: BIP) *Tiptoes* (d: Wilcox, p: BN)
1928	Teleprinters and teletypewriters in wide use in Britain, U.S., and Germany Women over 21 given vote Th: *This Year of Grace,* revue (Coward) Lit: *Decline and Fall* (E. Waugh), *Lady Chatterley's Lover* (Lawrence), *Orlando* (Woolf) Death of Thomas Hardy, Emmeline Pankhurst, Ellen Terry	Gainsborough Pictures Ltd. founded by Balcon, Maurice Ostrer, and C. M. Woolf, capitalized by G-B; lease G-B studios at Lime Grove, Shepherd's Bush Angus MacPhail joins Balcon as scenarist, Gainsborough (–1936) BIF opens new studios at Welwyn City U.K. premiere of Warners talkie *The Jazz Singer,* Piccadilly Theatre, London (September 27) Associated British Cinemas Ltd. (ABC)	*Champagne* (d: Hitchcock, p: BIP) *The Constant Nymph* (d: Brunel, p: Gainsborough) *Dawn* (d: Wilcox, p: B & D) *The First Born* (d: Mander, p: Gainsborough/Mander Prod. Synd.) *H. G. Wells Comedies* series: *Bluebottles, The Tonic, Daydreams* (d: Montagu, p: Angle Pictures) *Moulin Rouge* (d: Dupont, p: BIP) *Shooting Stars* (d: Bramble and Asquith, p: BIF)

	Selected Historical and Cultural Events, including Radio and Television	Balcon and the British Film Industry	Selected British Films
1928, continued		cinema circuit founded Birth of Stanley Kubrick, Tony Richardson, Nicolas Roeg	*Tesha* (d: Saville, p: BIP/Burlington) *Underground* (d: Asquith, p: BIF) *The Vortex* (d: Brunel, p: Gainsborough) *Wait and See* (d: Forde, p: Nettlefold)
1929	Great Depression begins Ramsay MacDonald (Labour) becomes Prime Minister Music: *Bittersweet,* operetta (Coward); *Wake Up and Dream,* revue (Porter) Th: *Journey's End* (Sherriff) Lit: *The Good Companions* (Priestley), *Marriage and Morals* (B. Russell) Birth of John Osborne Death of Lily Langtry	Balcon and electrician George Gunn visit U.S., order sound equipment for Islington studios; Balcon produces last silent films, with synchronized scores Louis Levy becomes Gainsborough/G-B mus. dir. (–1937) Gainsborough produces first sound features, *Woman to Woman* (d: Saville) and, the next year, *Journey's End* (d: Whale), at Tiffany-Stahl, Hollywood Saville rejoins Balcon, as dir. (–1936) Ostrer bros. negotiate sale of G-B stock to William Fox (U.S.); Board of Trade intervenes, preventing foreign national's gaining controlling interest in company John Grierson founds Empire Marketing Board (EMB) Film Unit (–1933), forerunner of General Post Office (GPO) Film Unit Basil Dean founds Associated Talking Pictures (ATP); Reginald Baker on admin. bd. *Blackmail* (d: Hitchcock, p: BIP), first successful commercial talkie made in Britain	*Atlantic* (d: Dupont, p: BIP) *Drifters* (d: Grierson, p: EMB) *High Treason* (d: Elvey, p: Gaumont) *The Informer* (d: Robison, p: BIP) *Juno and the Paycock* (d: Hitchcock, p: BIP) *Kitty* (d: Saville, p: BIP/Burlington) *The Manxman* (d: Hitchcock, p: BIP) *Piccadilly* (d: Dupont, p: BIP) *Tusalava* (d: Lye, p: Film Society) *Would You Believe It?* (d: Forde, p: Nettlefold)
1930	Birth of Princess Margaret Picture telegraphy begins between Britain and Germany Amy Johnson flies solo from London to Australia in 19½ days BBC Symphony Orch. founded; Sir Adrian Boult, Dir. John Masefield becomes Poet Laureate (–1967) Th: *Private Lives* (Coward) Lit: *Poems* (Auden) Birth of Harold Pinter Death of Sir Arthur Conan Doyle, D. H. Lawrence	Fire destroys Gainsborough's Islington studios; filming of first Gainsborough talkie in Britain, *Symphony in Two Flats* (d: Gundrey), completed at BIP, Elstree Wilcox produces films of Ben Travers Aldwych Theatre farces	*Balaclava* (d: Elvey, p: Gainsborough) *A Cottage on Dartmoor* (d: Asquith, p: BIF) *Elstree Calling* (d: Brunel, Charlot, Hitchcock, Hulbert, and Murray, p: BIP) *Murder* (d: Hitchcock, p: BIP) *Rookery Nook* (d: Walls and Haskins, p: B & D) *Young Woodley* (d: Bentley, p: BIP)
1931	Financial crisis: gold standard abandoned; value of pound sterling drops. Labour govt. replaced by emergency "National" govt.; Ramsay MacDonald remains Prime Minister (Coalition, –1935) Statute of Westminster passed; regulates status of Dominions in British Commonwealth of Nations (Australia, Canada, Ireland, New Zealand, Union of South Africa, United Kingdom) King George V installs 2-millionth British telephone, Buckingham Palace Lilian Baylis founds Sadler's Wells Opera, London; becomes English National Opera, 1974 Th: *Cavalcade* (Coward) Death of Arnold Bennett, Sir Thomas	Walter Forde joins Balcon, as dir. (–1935); first Gainsborough film, *Third Time Lucky* BL and Gainsborough sign contract to co-produce Wallace films at Beaconsfield studio; first prod., *The Ringer* (d: Forde) G-B assumes full control of Gainsborough; Balcon in charge of prod. at G-B, Shepherd's Bush, and Gainsborough, Islington, suffers nervous breakdown late in yr., recovers over next six months Alex Vetchinsky, trained architect, joins Balcon as designer for *Michael and Mary* (d: Saville) Angus MacPhail becomes story sup. at G-B (–1937) German cameraman Mutz Greenbaum	*The Ghost Train* (d: Forde, p: Gainsborough) *Hindle Wakes* (d: Saville, p: Gainsborough) *Rich and Strange* (d: Hitchcock, p: BIP) *Service for Ladies* (d: A. Korda, p: Par. Brit.) *Sunshine Susie* (d: Saville, p: Gainsborough) *Tell England* (d: Asquith and Barkas, p: BIF)

	Selected Historical and Cultural Events, including Radio and Television	Balcon and the British Film Industry	Selected British Films
1931, continued	Lipton, Dame Nellie Melba	(Max Greene) emigrates to England, joins Balcon as cinematographer; first film, *Hindle Wakes* (d: Saville) ATP Studios built at Ealing, West London Stephen Courtauld, textile magnate, joins ATP board; supports Ealing until retirement, 1952 Alexander Korda arrives in Britain; works for Paramount British Film debut of Gracie Fields, in *Sally in Our Alley* (d: Elvey, p: ATP) Birth of Jonathan Balcon	
1932	Eamon de Valéra elected President of Irish Free State Sir Oswald Mosley founds British Union of Fascists (banned 1940) Unemployment rate reaches 22.5 percent BBC opens Broadcasting House, London; takes over television research from Baird Co. Actor Tom Walls's horse April the Fifth wins Derby Comedy team The Crazy Gang debuts at London Palladium Shakespeare Memorial Theatre opens, Stratford-upon-Avon London Philharmonic Orch. founded, Sir Thomas Beecham, Dir. John Galsworthy wins Nobel Prize for Literature Lit: *Brave New World* (Aldous Huxley) Death of Kenneth Grahame, Lady Gregory, Lytton Strachey, Edgar Wallace	*Sight and Sound,* film quarterly, founded by the British Institute of Adult Education; Institute publishes report "The Film in National Life," recommending est. of Film Institute Sunday Entertainments Act passed; establishes Cinematograph Fund, permits Sunday film exhibition at local discretion, with share of proceeds to Cinematograph Fund & charity; exhibitors fill Sunday programs with Brit. and Am. B-movies, quota quickies, and revivals A. Korda founds London Films; produces and directs *Wedding Rehearsal,* released 1933 Associated British Film Distributors (ABFD) formed to handle ATP (later Ealing) product (–1941) Shepherd's Bush expands to four stages; first prod., *Rome Express* (d: Forde); first solo screenplay credit for Sidney Gilliat (hired by Balcon 1931) Robert Stevenson joins Balcon as screenwriter for *The Faithful Heart* (d: Saville) Penrose Tennyson joins Balcon as junior asst.; first project, *The Good Companions* Michael Relph hired by Balcon as asst. art dir. at G-B; becomes full art dir., then assoc. producer (1940s) Alfred Junge emigrates to Britain, becomes art dir. and sup. of G-B art dept., Shepherd's Bush (–1937) John Croydon becomes asst. studio mgr., G-B (–1935) Isidore Ostrer announces G-B–UFA co-prod. plan; G-B to distribute English-language versions made in Germany Muir Mathieson becomes asst. mus. dir. for Korda's London Films; later becomes mus. dir. Wilcox produces and directs *Goodnight Vienna,* first starring vehicle for Anna Neagle Birth of Richard Lester	*Dance Pretty Lady* (d: Asquith, p: BIF) *Jack's the Boy* (d: Forde, p: Gainsborough) *The Lodger* (d: Elvey, p. Twickenham) *Number Seventeen* (d: Hitchcock, p: BIP)
1933	London Transport Board est. Th: *Laburnum Grove* (Priestley) Lit: *Down and Out in Paris and London* (Orwell), *Lost Horizon* (Hilton),	British Film Institute (BFI) founded; financed by Cinematograph Fund (Sunday admissions levy); Chairman of Advisory Council: John Buchan;	*Bittersweet* (d: Wilcox, p: B & D) *Doss House* (d: Baxter, p: Sound City) *The Fire Raisers* (d: Powell, p: G-B) *Friday the Thirteenth* (d: Saville,

	Selected Historical and Cultural Events, including Radio and Television	Balcon and the British Film Industry	Selected British Films
1933, continued	*Murder Must Advertise* (Sayers), *The Shape of Things to Come* (Wells) Death of John Galsworthy, Henry Royce	C. M. Woolf on Board of Governors Grierson forms GPO Film Unit; joined by Basil Wright, Arthur Elton, Edgar Anstey BIP reorganized as Associated British Pictures Corp. (ABPC), at Elstree *The Private Life of Henry VIII* (d: A. Korda, p: London Films), first British international financial success; beginning of three-year boom in Brit. prod. Shepperton Studios opened at Littlewood Park Films produced in Britain: over 200 Ostrer bros. reorganize and enlarge G-B: two studios, over 300 cinemas, film labs, printers, newsreels, educational films, and equipment companies; Balcon signs five-year contract Charles Frend joins G-B as ed. (–1937) King George V and Queen Mary attend first Charity Matinee Royal Film Performance of talking picture, *The Good Companions,* New Victoria Cinema Association of Cinematograph Technicians, first film trade union, begins to organize prod. workers at G-B studios, Shepherd's Bush; contract negotiated 1936 Board of Film Censors adds H (Horrific) category; prohibits admission to children under 16 J. Arthur Rank enters distribution with Methodist religious films Death of James Williamson	p: Gainsborough) *The Ghoul* (d: Hunter, p: G-B) *The Good Companions* (d: Saville, p: G-B) *I Was a Spy* (d: Saville, p: G-B) *Industrial Britain* (d: Grierson and Flaherty, p: EMB) *90° South* (d/p: Ponting; filmed 1911–12)
1934	Road Traffic Act introduces driving tests S.S. *Queen Mary* (Cunard Line) launched Gordonstoun School founded Glyndebourne Opera Festival founded by John Christie Gielgud's production of *Hamlet,* New Theatre, London Music: *Conversation Piece,* operetta (Coward) Lit: *Claudius the God* and *I, Claudius* (Graves), *Goodbye, Mr. Chips* (Hilton) Death of Frederick Delius, Sir Gerald du Maurier, Sir Edward Elgar, Gustav Holst, Sir Arthur Wing Pinero	Rank forms British National Films; first prod., *The Turn of the Tide* (d: Walker), released 1935 Humphrey Jennings, Len Lye join GPO Film Unit Cavalcanti becomes producer/dir. at GPO Film Unit Film debut of Will Hay, in *Those Were the Days* (d: Bentley, p: BIP) Sound-film debut of George Formby, in *Boots! Boots!* (d: Tracy, p: Blakeley's Prods.) Marcel Varnel emigrates to Britain Ernest Irving becomes mus. dir. for ATP (later Ealing) Hitchcock signs contract with G-B *Monthly Film Bulletin* (BFI) begins publication	*Chu-Chin-Chow* (d: Forde, p: Gainsborough) *Evergreen* (d: Saville, p: G-B) *The Iron Duke* (d: Saville, p: G-B) *Jew Süss* (d: Mendes, p: G-B) *Man of Aran* (d: Flaherty, p: Gainsborough) *Nell Gwyn* (d: Wilcox, p: B & D) *The Private Life of Don Juan* (d: A. Korda, p: London Films) *Radio Parade of 1935* (d: Woods, p: BIP) *Red Ensign* (d: Powell, p: G-B) *The Rise of Catherine the Great* (d: Czinner, p: London Films) *Say It with Flowers* (d: Baxter, p: Real Art) *The Scarlet Pimpernel* (d: Young, p: London Films) *Sing as We Go!* (d: Dean, p: ATP) *Tell Me If It Hurts* (d/p: Massingham) *Those Were the Days* (d: Bentley, p: BIP) *Waltzes from Vienna* (d: Hitchcock, p: Tom Arnold Prods.)
1935	King George V's Silver Jubilee Stanley Baldwin (Coalition) becomes Prime Minister Mosley addresses Fascist mass meetings London publisher Victor Gollancz	National Film Library (later National Film Archive) opens at BFI, London; Ernest Lindgren, Dir. (–1973) C. M. Woolf leaves G-B; Mark Ostrer becomes chairman and managing dir.	*Boys Will Be Boys* (d: Beaudine, p: Gainsborough) *Bulldog Jack* (d: Forde, p: G-B) *Coalface* (d: Cavalcanti, p: GPO) *Escape Me Never* (d: Czinner, p: B & D)

	Selected Historical and Cultural Events, including Radio and Television	Balcon and the British Film Industry	Selected British Films
1935, continued	founds Left Book Club Th: *Murder in the Cathedral* (Eliot), *Night Must Fall* (Williams) Lit: *The Stars Look Down* (Cronin) Death of T. E. Lawrence	Woolf and Rank found General Film Distributors Pinewood Studios open; Rank, chairman Warner Bros. begins production at Teddington studios A. Korda becomes member of United Artists (Chaplin, Fairbanks, Pickford, and Goldwyn); arranges U.S. distrib. for London Films; builds Denham Studios (−1936, designed by Gropius and Fry); first prod. at new studio, *Rembrandt,* released 1936 Henry Cornelius, Charles Crichton, and Robert Hamer join London Films' editing dept. John Croydon becomes studio mgr., Gainsborough and G-B (−1936)	*The Face of Britain* (d: Rotha, p: G-B I) *First a Girl* (d: Saville, p: G-B) *Forever England* (d: Forde, p: G-B) *The Ghost Goes West* (d: Clair, p: London Films) *Housing Problems* (d: Anstey and Elton, p: Brit. Comm. Gas Assn.) *Midshipman Easy* (d: Reed, p: ATP) *No Limit* (d: Banks, p: ATP) *The Phantom Light* (d: Powell, p: Gainsborough) *Sanders of the River* (d: Z. Korda, p: London Films) *Shipyard* (d: Rotha, p: G-B I) *Song of Ceylon* (d: Wright, p: Ceylon Tea Propaganda Bd./GPO/New Era) *The 39 Steps* (d: Hitchcock, p: G-B) *The Tunnel* (d: Elvey, p: G-B)
1936	Death of King George V; Edward VIII succeeds to throne, abdicates in December; George VI succeeds to throne Crystal Palace destroyed by fire Penguin Books founded by Allen Lane TV: BBC London inaugurates regular television service (daily, but limited hrs.), with high-definition (405-line) transmission Th: *French without Tears* (Rattigan) Lit: *South Riding* (Winifred Holtby, posth.) Death of G. K. Chesterton, A. E. Housman, Rudyard Kipling	Natl. Film Library presents first public screening, Polytechnic Hall, Regent St., commemorating 40th anniversary of Lumières's first British screenings Boom year for film prod.; much expansion and foreign investment Technicolor opens labs in London Forde leaves G-B, signs with Max Schach's Capitol Films Launder and Gilliat's first script collaboration, *Seven Sinners* (d: de Courville, p: G-B) Balcon to Hollywood; Black and Gilliat take charge of Gainsborough during his six-month absence; produce *Tudor Rose* (d: Stevenson) Balcon leaves G-B, signs two-yr. contract with M-G-M British as head of production Edward Black succeeds Balcon as head of production at Gainsborough (−1945) Moyne Committee (govt.-sponsored) evaluates industry needs for new Cinematograph Act; suggests quality tests for quota quickies (instead, cost test instituted); also proposes govt. film-financing agency (not instituted)	*And So to Work* (d/p: Massingham) *As You Like It* (d: Czinner, p: Inter-Allied) *Colour Box* (d: Lye, p: GPO) *It's Love Again* (d: Saville, p: G-B) *Laburnum Grove* (d: Reed, p: ATP) *The Man Who Changed His Mind* (d: Stevenson, p: Gainsborough) *Night Mail* (d: Wright and Watt, p: GPO) *Rainbow Dance* (d: Lye, p: GPO) *Rhodes of Africa* (d: Viertel, p: G-B) *The Robber Symphony* (d: Feher, p: Concordia) *Sabotage* (d: Hitchcock, p: G-B) *Secret Agent* (d: Hitchcock, p: G-B) *Things to Come* (d: Menzies, p: London Films)
1937	Coronation of King George VI; radio broadcast of ceremony first international program heard in U.S. Neville Chamberlain (Coalition) becomes Prime Minister Irish Free State becomes Eire (−1949); Prime Minister, Eamon De Valéra Duke of Windsor marries Mrs. Wallis Simpson, France Mass Observation, contemporary anthropology project set up to study daily life; est. by Humphrey Jennings, Tom Harrisson, and Charles Madge Billy Butlin opens first commercial holiday camp in Britain Lit: *The Citadel* (Cronin), *The Road to Wigan Pier* (Orwell) Death of Sir James M. Barrie	Filippo Del Giudice founds Two Cities Films John and Roy Boulting found Charter Films Erich Pommer and Charles Laughton found Mayflower Pictures (−1940) Film-industry crisis. Korda introduces pay cuts at London Films; Twickenham Studios bankrupt; G-B closes Shepherd's Bush studios Korda abandons prod. of *I, Claudius* (d: Von Sternberg) *Wings of the Morning* (d: Schuster, p: New World/Fox British), first U.K. Technicolor feature Odeon Cinema Circuit, founded 1933 by Oscar Deutsch with 26 theaters, expands to 180	*Dark Journey* (d: Saville, p: Saville Prods./London Films) *The Edge of the World* (d: Powell, p: Rock) *Elephant Boy* (d: Flaherty and Z. Korda, p: London Films) *Fire over England* (d: Howard, p: Pendennis/London Films/UA) *Good Morning, Boys!* (d: Varnel, p: Gainsborough) *The High Command* (d: Dickinson, p: Fanfare) *King Solomon's Mines* (d: Stevenson, p: G-B) *The Man Who Could Work Miracles* (d: Mendes, p: London Films) *Oh, Mr. Porter!* (d: Varnel, p: Gainsborough) *O-kay for Sound* (d: Varnel,

	Selected Historical and Cultural Events, including Radio and Television	Balcon and the British Film Industry	Selected British Films
1937, continued			p: Gainsborough) *Storm in a Teacup* (d: Saville and Dalrymple, p: Saville Prods./London Films) *Victoria the Great* (d: Wilcox, p: Imperator) *Young and Innocent* (d: Hitchcock, p: G-B)
1938	Munich Conference gives Germany part of Czechoslovakia; politics of appeasement Gas masks issued to British civilians during Munich crisis; air-raid precautions introduced; Women's Voluntary Services founded by Lady Reading S.S. *Queen Elizabeth* (Cunard Line) launched Edward Hulton starts magazine *Picture Post* (London) Lupino Lane popularizes "Lambeth Walk" in stage show *Me and My Gal* Th: *The Corn Is Green* (Williams) Lit: *Brighton Rock* (Greene), *Rebecca* (du Maurier)	Cinematograph Films Act sets new, lower quota regulations; minimum cost level, scale of quota privileges based on prod. values, result in more foreign (especially U.S.) investment Balcon leaves M-G-M British; succeeded as head of production by Saville Co-operative Assn. of Producers and Distributors (CAPAD) formed by Ealing and Pinewood Studios; finances films with "national viewpoint"; Balcon produces *The Gaunt Stranger* (d: Forde) and *The Ware Case* (d: Stevenson) ATP reorganized as Ealing Studios; Balcon succeeds Basil Dean as head of production on invitation of Reginald Baker, admin. head of Ealing (with Balcon until 1958) Monja Danischewsky becomes publicity dir., Ealing (–1948) Basil Dearden becomes assoc. producer, Ealing International Federation of Film Archives (FIAF) formed by London, New York, Paris, and Berlin archives; holds first conference in New York in 1939	*Bank Holiday* (d: Reed, p: Gainsborough) *The Citadel* (d: Vidor, p: M-G-M Brit.) *The Drum* (d: Z. Korda, p: London Films) *Keep Smiling* (d: Banks, p: 20th Cent. Prods.) *The Lady Vanishes* (d: Hitchcock, p: Gainsborough) *North Sea* (d: Watt, p: GPO) *Pygmalion* (d: Asquith and Howard, p: Pascal) *Sixty Glorious Years* (d: Wilcox, p: Imperator) *South Riding* (d: Saville, p: Saville Prods./London Films) *They Drive by Night* (d: Woods, p: WB-FN) *This Man Is News* (d: Macdonald, p: Pinebrook) *Vessel of Wrath* (d: Pommer, p: Mayflower) *A Yank at Oxford* (d: Conway, p: M-G-M Brit.)
1939	King George VI and Queen Elizabeth visit U.S. Germany invades Poland; Britain and France declare war on Germany Women and children evacuated from London, Sept.; radar stations est. to warn of approaching enemy aircraft; military conscription for men ages 18–41 instituted; Basil Dean founds E.N.S.A. to provide entertainment for troops British Overseas Airways Corp. (BOAC) founded Anglo-Saxon burial ship excavated, Sutton Hoo, Suffolk Myra Hess organizes National Gallery lunchtime concerts Council for the Encouragement of Music and the Arts created by govt.; later becomes The Arts Council of Great Britain Music: *The Dancing Years,* operetta (Novello) Lit: *Finnegans Wake* (Joyce), *How Green Was My Valley* (Llewellyn), *Mrs. Miniver* (Struther) Death of W. B. Yeats	Angus MacPhail becomes story sup., Ealing (–1948) Saville to U.S. as producer (–1949) Hitchcock and Stevenson to U.S., under Selznick contract Rank gains control of Denham labs and studios from Korda Feature films produced in Britain: 96 All cinemas closed at outbreak of war; many reopen within wks., with restricted hrs.; some requisitioned; food stored at Pinewood and parts of Denham; Elstree requisitioned; ABPC moves to Welwyn Balcon campaigns against waiving quota in wartime; remains at 15 percent throughout war Wartime Ministry of Information (MOI) revived; Dir. of Films Division: Sir Joseph Ball, succeeded late in yr. by Sir Kenneth Clark, and in 1940 by Jack Beddington Ealing begins prod. of shorts on wartime topics Final screening of The Film Society, New Gallery Cinema, Regent St., features *Alexander Nevsky* (d: Eisenstein)	*Cheer Boys Cheer* (d: Forde, p: ATP/Ealing) *The Four Feathers* (d: Z. Korda, p: London Films) *The Four Just Men* (d: Forde, p: Ealing/CAPAD) *French without Tears* (d: Asquith, p: Two Cities) *A Girl Must Live* (d: Reed, p: Gainsborough) *Goodbye, Mr. Chips* (d: Wood, p: M-G-M Brit.) *The Lion Has Wings* (d: Powell, Brunel, and Hurst, p: London Films) *Nurse Edith Cavell* (d: Wilcox, p: Imperator) *Peace and Plenty* (d: Montagu, p: Progressive Film Inst.) *Shipyard Sally* (d: Banks, p: 20th Cent. Prods.) *Spare Time* (d: Jennings, p: GPO) *The Spy in Black* (d: Powell, p: Harefield) *The Stars Look Down* (d: Reed, p: Grafton) *Stolen Life* (d: Czinner, p: Orion Prods.) *There Ain't No Justice* (d: Tennyson, p: Ealing/CAPAD) *Trouble Brewing* (d: Kimmins, p: ATP/Ealing)

	Selected Historical and Cultural Events, including Radio and Television	Balcon and the British Film Industry	Selected British Films
1939, continued			*Young Man's Fancy* (d: Stevenson, p: Ealing/CAPAD)
1940	Winston Churchill (Coalition Conservative) becomes Prime Minister Dunkirk evacuation, May 26–June 4; 225,585 troops Home Guard formed; 250,000 enrolled within 24 hrs. London Blitz, Sept. 1940–Jan. 1941; large-scale air raids: 13,339 killed, 17,937 severely injured; Guildhall and eight Wren churches destroyed Battle of Britain; R.A.F. begins night bombing of Germany Coventry Cathedral destroyed Fascist leader Mosley imprisoned under Defence Regulations; released 1943 David Low's anti-Hitler cartoons, London *Evening Standard* Lit: *The Power and the Glory* (Greene) Death of John Buchan, Mrs. Patrick Campbell, Neville Chamberlain	A. Korda to U.S. (–1943) John Halas and Joy Batchelor found animation studio, Halas & Batchelor Cartoon Films Rank acquires controlling interest in G-B (251 cinemas) and Odeon (306 cinemas) circuits Feature films produced in Britain: 56 GPO Film Unit becomes Crown Film Unit, division of MOI Balcon hires Cavalcanti from Crown Film Unit; remains with Ealing until 1947 Forde leaves Ealing, last film for Balcon, *Sailors Three;* Dalrymple leaves Ealing, joins Crown Film Unit as producer Crichton joins Ealing as ed.; Croydon becomes prod. sup (–1943) Death of Oscar Deutsch, John Maxwell	*Conquest of the Air* (d: Z. Korda, Esway, Menzies, et al., p: London Films) *Contraband* (d: Powell, p: BN) *Convoy* (d: Tennyson, p: Ealing) *Gaslight* (d: Dickinson, p: BN) *Let George Do It!* (d: Varnel, p: ATP/Ealing) *London Can Take It* (d: Jennings and Watt, p: GPO) *Men of the Lightship* (d: Macdonald, p: GPO) *Night Train to Munich* (d: Reed, p: 20th Cent. Prods.) *Pastor Hall* (d: R. Boulting, p: Charter Films) *The Proud Valley* (d: Tennyson, p: Ealing/CAPAD) *Return to Yesterday* (d: Stevenson, p: Ealing/CAPAD) *The Thief of Bagdad* (d: Whelan, Powell, and Berger, p: London Films)
1941	Massive air raid, London, May 10–11; 1,436 killed, 1,732 injured; H.M.S. *Hood* sunk by Germans; *Bismarck* sunk by British Rationing "points system" introduced (–1950); utility clothing and furniture encouraged Lend-lease begins (–1945); Atlantic Charter announced; U.S. enters war Th: *Blithe Spirit* (Coward) Death of Lord Baden-Powell, Amy Johnson, James Joyce, Virginia Woolf	Approx. 170 cinemas closed because of bombings Feature films produced in Britain: 47 British Film Producers' Assn. formed WB invests in ABPC & its subsidiary, ABC cinema circuit Formby leaves Ealing for Columbia British; Will Hay becomes Ealing's top comedy star Hamer joins Ealing as ed. *Warsaw Concerto* composed by Richard Addinsell for *Dangerous Moonlight* (d: Hurst, p: RKO) Birth of David Puttnam Death of Pen Tennyson	*The Common Touch* (d: Baxter, p: BN) *Cottage to Let* (d: Asquith, p: Gainsborough) *49th Parallel* (d: Powell, p: Ortus) *The Ghost Train* (d: Forde, p: Gainsborough) *Kipps* (d: Reed, p: 20th Cent. Prods.) *Love on the Dole* (d: Baxter, p: BN) *Major Barbara* (d: French, Lean, and Pascal, p: Pascal) *"Pimpernel" Smith* (d: Howard, p: BN) *Ships with Wings* (d: Nolbandov, p: Ealing) *Target for To-night* (d: Watt, p: Crown) *Turned Out Nice Again* (d: Varnel, p: Ealing) *Yellow Caesar* (d: Cavalcanti, p: Ealing)
1942	Field Marshal Montgomery victor at El Alamein; Allies conquer North Africa Sir William Beveridge's Report on Social Security and National Insurance; proposes social insurance system, full employment, national health service, child allowances, and "new deal" in housing and education Tommy Handley's *ITMA [It's That Man Again]* most popular BBC radio feature (1939–49)	Balcon hires Harry Watt from Crown Film Unit; Michael Relph becomes chief art dir. Feature films produced in Britain: 46 Two Cities joins Rank Org. Powell and Pressburger form prod. co., The Archers; first film, *The Silver Fleet* (d: Sewell and Wellesley), released 1943 Independent Producers (IP) founded to handle business and legal matters for independents associated with Rank; includes The Archers, Leslie Howard, Gabriel Pascal, Launder and Gilliat, Cineguild (Lean, Neame, and Havelock-Allan), and Wessex Prods. (Ian Dalrymple) Death of Charles Urban, Arthur Woods, C. M. Woolf	*The First of the Few* (d: Howard, p: Misbourne/Brit. Aviation Pictures) *The Foreman Went to France* (d: Frend, p: Ealing) *In Which We Serve* (d: Coward and Lean, p: Two Cities) *Listen to Britain* (d: Jennings, p: Crown) *The Next of Kin* (d: Dickinson, p: Ealing) *One of Our Aircraft Is Missing* (d: Powell and Pressburger, p: BN) *Thunder Rock* (d: R. Boulting, p: Charter Films) *Went the Day Well?* (d: Cavalcanti, p: Ealing) *The Young Mr. Pitt* (d: Reed, p: 20th Cent. Prods.)
1943	Invasion of Italy; fall of Mussolini Th: *This Happy Breed* (Coward) Lit: *The Small Back Room* (Balchin)	Journalist T. E. B. Clarke joins Ealing as contract writer Hamer promoted to assoc. producer,	*The Demi-Paradise* (d: Asquith, p: Two Cities) *Desert Victory* (d: R. Boulting and

	Selected Historical and Cultural Events, including Radio and Television	Balcon and the British Film Industry	Selected British Films
1943, continued		Ealing Croydon promoted to assoc. producer, Ealing (–1947); Hal Mason succeeds him as prod. sup. Henry Cornelius joins Ealing as assoc. producer; hired from South African Propaganda Service Feature films produced in Britain: 51 A. Korda becomes head of production, M-G-M British (–1945) Churchill obstructs export of *The Life and Death of Colonel Blimp* (d: Powell and Pressburger, p: The Archers/London Films); film cut by third for U.S. release Death of Leslie Howard, R. W. Paul	Macdonald, p: Brit. Service Film Units) *Fires Were Started* (d: Jennings, p: Crown) *The Gentle Sex* (d: Howard and Elvey, p: Two Cities/Concana) *The Man in Grey* (d: Arliss, p: Gainsborough) *Nine Men* (d: Watt, p: Ealing) *San Demetrio London* (d: Frend, p: Ealing) *The Silent Village* (d: Jennings, p: Crown) *Tunisian Victory* (d: R. Boulting and Capra, p: Brit. & Am. Service Film Units) *We Dive at Dawn* (d: Asquith, p: Gainsborough) *World of Plenty* (d: Rotha, p: MOI)
1944	Allies capture Rome; D-Day: Normandy invasion; Battle of the Bulge: Germany launches last great offensive; heavy air raids on London, V-1 and V-2 rockets Women have assumed new role in country's civil defense, auxiliary services (ATS, WRNS, WAAFS), and specified industries. Of 17½ million women ages 14–64 in Britain, more than 7½ million engaged full-time; 900,000 employed part-time; countless others doing volunteer work Ministry of National Insurance est. Butler Education Act provides "free secondary education for all" First nonstop flight from London to Canada Olivier and Ralph Richardson become dirs. of Old Vic Co. Lit: *The Horse's Mouth* (Cary), *The Razor's Edge* (Maugham)	Balcon-Rank agreement: Rank to fund Ealing with prod. money (50 percent) and guarantee distribution throughout Britain; Rank stable of contract artists to be available upon request; prods. to be controlled by Ealing Rank org. forms Children's Entertainment Division; Mary Field, dir. Board of Trade's Cinematograph Films Council issues Palache Report, "Tendencies to Monopoly in the Cinematograph Film Industry," aimed at Rank empire; Rank owns 56 percent of all studio floor space in country Feature films produced in Britain: 38 Launder and Gilliat found Individual Pictures (–1950); first prod., *The Rake's Progress* (d: Gilliat), released 1945 Sidney Cole joins Ealing as assoc. producer; Seth Holt joins as asst. ed.; Michael Truman, as ed. and assoc. producer	*A Canterbury Tale* (d: Powell and Pressburger, p: Archers/IP) *Fanny by Gaslight* (d: Asquith, p: Gainsborough) *Madonna of the Seven Moons* (d: Crabtree, p: Gainsborough) *On Approval* (d: Brook, p: Brook/IP) *Our Country* (d: Eldridge, p: Strand) *Tawny Pipit* (d: Saunders and Miles, p: Two Cities) *This Happy Breed* (d: Lean, p: Cineguild) *The Way Ahead* (d: Reed, p: Two Cities) *Western Approaches* (d: Jackson, p: Crown)
1945	Germany surrenders in May; V-E Day. Japan surrenders in August; V-J Day Labour Party sweeps General Elections; Clement Attlee becomes Prime Minister Music: *Peter Grimes,* opera (Britten) Lit: *Animal Farm* (Orwell), *Brideshead Revisited* (E. Waugh) Death of David Lloyd George	Sydney Box succeeds Edward Black as head of production, Gainsborough MOI replaced by Central Office of Information Feature films produced in Britain: 44	*Blithe Spirit* (d: Lean and Coward, p: Cineguild/Two Cities) *Brief Encounter* (d: Lean, p: Cineguild/IP) *Dead of Night* (d: Cavalcanti, Crichton, Dearden, and Hamer, p: Ealing) *A Diary for Timothy* (d: Jennings, p: Crown) *Henry V* (d: Olivier, p: Two Cities) *I Know Where I'm Going* (d: Powell and Pressburger, p: Archers/IP) *Perfect Strangers* (d: A. Korda, p: M-G-M Brit./London Films) *Pink String and Sealing Wax* (d: Hamer, p: Ealing) *The Seventh Veil* (d: Bennett, p: Theatrecraft/Ortus) *The True Glory* (d: Reed and Kanin, p: Army Film Unit) *Waterloo Road* (d: Gilliat, p: Gainsborough) *The Way to the Stars* (d: Asquith, p. Two Cities) *The Wicked Lady* (d: Arliss, p: Gainsborough)

	Selected Historical and Cultural Events, including Radio and Television	Balcon and the British Film Industry	Selected British Films
1946	National Insurance and National Health Service Acts passed Bank of England, coal industry, and British air transport nationalized London Airport opens The Arts Council of Great Britain founded Music: *The Rape of Lucretia*, opera (Britten) Th: *The Winslow Boy* (Rattigan) Death of John Logie Baird, H. G. Wells	*The Overlanders* (d: Watt), first in series of Balcon/Ealing prods. shot in Australia Feature films produced in Britain: 44 Cinema attendance: 1.6 billion annually; 31 million weekly Rank launches *This Modern Age* (–1949), seeks to rival U.S. *March of Time* Baynham Honri becomes studio mgr., Ealing; Alexander Mackendrick joins Ealing as sketch artist; Relph promoted to producer/writer, forms partnership with Dearden British Kinematograph, Sound, & Television Society (BKSTS) (founded 1931) incorporated British Film Academy founded; David Lean, Chairman; Roger Manvell, Secretary-General *Penguin Film Review* (Roger Manvell, ed.) begins publication (–1949)	*Caesar and Cleopatra* (d: Pascal, p: Pascal Prods./IP) *The Captive Heart* (d: Dearden, p: Ealing) *Great Expectations* (d: Lean, p: Cineguild/IP) *Green for Danger* (d: Gilliat, p: Individual Pictures/IP) *I See a Dark Stranger* (d: Launder, p: Individual Pictures/IP) *London Town* (d/p: Ruggles) *A Matter of Life and Death* (d: Powell and Pressburger, p: Archers/IP) *The Years Between* (d: Bennett, p: S. Box)
1947	Princess Elizabeth weds Philip Mountbatten, Duke of Edinburgh Fuel crisis and severest winter since 1894 provoke austerity measures End of rule in India. Dominions of India and Pakistan created School-leaving age raised to 15 Alec Guinness emerges as new star at Old Vic, in *King Lear, Richard II* Lit: *Under the Volcano* (Lowry), *Whisky Galore* (Compton Mackenzie) Death of Henry Gordon Selfridge	Dalton Duty imposed on imported films; 75 percent tax leads to U.S. embargo; disastrous year for Brit. cinema; Rank and Korda suffer huge financial losses in 1948 Govt. raises exhibitors' quota of required screen time for Brit. films from 20 to 45 percent Feature films produced in Britain: 65 Circuits Management Assn. formed, composed of Odeon and G-B cinema circuits Gabriel Pascal leaves for Hollywood Korda acquires Shepperton Studios as new hdqrs. for London Films Del Giudice loses control of Two Cities to Rank; founds Pilgrim Pictures (–1950) Croydon leaves Ealing, joins Rank's Highbury Studios as dir. of prod. *Sequence* (Lindsay Anderson, ed.), film journal, founded by Anderson, Karel Reisz, and Tony Richardson Death of G. B. Samuelson, Marcel Varnel	*Black Narcissus* (d: Powell and Pressburger, p: Archers/IP) *Brighton Rock* (D: J. Boulting, p: ABPC) *Captain Boycott* (d: Launder, p: Individual Pictures/IP) *The Courtneys of Curzon Street* (d: Wilcox, p: Imperadio) *Dear Murderer* (d: Crabtree, p: Gainsborough) *Fame Is the Spur* (d: R. Boulting, p: Two Cities) *Hue and Cry* (d: Crichton, p: Ealing) *An Ideal Husband* (d: A. Korda, p: London Films) *It Always Rains on Sunday* (d: Hamer, p: Ealing) *Mine Own Executioner* (d: Kimmins, p: Harefield/London Films) *Nicholas Nickleby* (d: Cavalcanti, p: Ealing) *The October Man* (d: Baker, p: Two Cities) *Odd Man Out* (d: Reed, p: Two Cities) *They Made Me a Fugitive* (d: Cavalcanti, p: Gloria-Alliance) *The Upturned Glass* (d: Huntington, p: Triton)
1948	Birth of Prince Charles Mahatma Gandhi assassinated Berlin Airlift (–1949); Marshall Plan inaugurated (–1951) British mandate in Palestine expires; State of Israel proclaimed Ceylon and Burma gain independence British Citizenship Act grants passports to all Commonwealth citizens Railroads, canals, and road transport nationalized T. S. Eliot wins Nobel Prize for Literature Aldeburgh Festival founded by Benjamin Britten Th: *The Browning Version* (Rattigan) Lit: *The Gathering Storm* (Churchill), *The*	Dalton Duty rescinded; compromise Anglo-American film agreement stipulates that only $17 million to leave country annually: remaining foreign profits to be reinvested in Britain; stimulates U.S. prod. in Britain Cinematograph Film Act raises quota ceiling for domestic prods. to 45 percent Radcliffe Report sets guidelines for reorganization of BFI; proposes increasing membership, education and publication programs; lectures; film theater; regional theaters; Natl. Film School; revision and expansion of *Sight and Sound*; London Film Festival; and foundation of Experimental Film	*Anna Karenina* (d: Duvivier, p: London Films) *The Fallen Idol* (d: Reed, p: London Films) *Hamlet* (d: Olivier, p: Two Cities) *London Belongs to Me* (d: Gilliat, p: Individual Pictures/IP) *Oliver Twist* (d: Lean, p: Cineguild/IP) *Quartet* (d: Annakin, Crabtree, French, and Smart, p: Gainsborough) *The Red Shoes* (d: Powell and Pressburger, p: Archers/IP) *The Winslow Boy* (d: Asquith, p: London Films/BLPA)

	Selected Historical and Cultural Events, including Radio and Television	Balcon and the British Film Industry	Selected British Films
1948, continued	*Heart of the Matter* (Greene)	Fund/Production Board W. P. Lipscomb succeeds MacPhail as story sup., Ealing (–1951) Danischewsky becomes assoc. producer, Ealing; S. John Woods succeeds him as publicity dir. First Ealing color prods., *Saraband for Dead Lovers* (d: Dearden) and *Scott of the Antarctic* (d: Frend) Balcon knighted for services to film industry Hammer Films formed; studios at Bray Feature films produced in Britain: 102 Death of Edward Black	
1949	North Atlantic Treaty Organization (NATO) formed Eire becomes independent Republic of Ireland, with capital at Dublin Gas industry nationalized Lit: *Landscape into Art* (Clark), *Love in a Cold Climate* (N. Mitford), *1984* (Orwell)	Natl. Film Finance Corp. (NFFC) created by Cinematograph Film Production (Special Loans) Act; Balcon honorary advisor (–1953); loans to independent producers include £2 million to Korda's British Lion Rank sells Shepherd's Bush studios to television Islington studios closed Weekly cinema attendance drops to 27 million (from 31 million in 1946) Feature films produced in Britain: 120 Walter Forde retires from films Saville returns to Britain Gavin Lambert becomes ed. of *Sight and Sound* (–1956) Death of Will Hay, Tom Walls	*Kind Hearts and Coronets* (d: Hamer, p: Ealing) *The Passionate Friends* (d: Lean, p: Cineguild/Pinewood) *Passport to Pimlico* (d: Cornelius, p: Ealing) *The Queen of Spades* (d: Dickinson, p: ABPC/World Screenplays) *The Rocking Horse Winner* (d: Pelissier, p: Two Cities) *The Small Back Room* (d: Powell and Pressburger, p: Archers/London Films/BLPA) *The Third Man* (d: Reed, p: London Films/BLPA) *Whisky Galore!* (d: Mackendrick, p: Ealing)
1950	Birth of Princess Anne People's Republic of China recognized Iron and steel industries nationalized Stone of Scone stolen from Westminster Abbey by Scottish nationalists; returned four months later Bertrand Russell wins Nobel Prize for Literature Death of George Orwell, G. B. Shaw	Eady Plan est.: levy imposed on box-office receipts to finance foundation of British Film Production Fund; will support domestic prod. through NFFC and, in future, Natl. Film School, Children's Film Foundation, and BFI Experimental Film Fund/Prod. Board; voluntary, Fund becomes statutory in 1957 Board of Film Censors introduces X rating Feature films produced in Britain: 131 Jules Dassin, Carl Foreman, and Joseph Losey emigrate to Britain Death of Humphrey Jennings	*The Blue Lamp* (d: Dearden, p: Ealing) *Chance of a Lifetime* (d: Miles, p: Pilgrim Pictures) *The Clouded Yellow* (d: R. Thomas, p: Carillon) *Gone to Earth* (d: Powell and Pressburger, p: London Films/Vanguard Prods.) *The Happiest Days of Your Life* (d: Launder, p: Individual Pictures/BLPA) *Madeleine* (d: Lean, p: Cineguild/Pinewood) *Night and the City* (d: Dassin, p: 20th Cent. Prods.) *Odette* (d: Wilcox, p: Imperadio) *Seven Days to Noon* (d: J. Boulting, p: London Films/BLPA) *So Long at the Fair* (d: Fisher and Darnborough, p: Gainsborough) *Stage Fright* (d: Hitchcock, p: WB-FN) *State Secret* (d: Gilliat, p: Individual Pictures/BLPA) *Waterfront* (d: M. Anderson, p: Conqueror)
1951	Sir Winston Churchill (Conservative) becomes Prime Minister Burgess/Maclean spy scandal; defect to U.S.S.R. Royal Festival Hall, London, built Festival of Britain, May–Sept., marks centenary of Great Exhibition of	Balcon becomes chairman (–1954) of Group 3 (managing dir., John Baxter; hdqrs., Beaconsfield Studios), set up by British Film Prod. Fund to provide low-budget features by new directing talents; first film, *Judgment Deferred* (d: Baxter), released 1952	*The Browning Version* (d: Asquith, p: Two Cities/Javelin) *High Treason* (d: R. Boulting, p: Conqueror) *The Lady with a Lamp* (d: Wilcox, p: Imperadio) *Laughter in Paradise* (d: Zampi,

	Selected Historical and Cultural Events, including Radio and Television	Balcon and the British Film Industry	Selected British Films
1951, continued	Industry of All Nations Cornerstone laid for British National Theatre, South Bank, London New Coventry Cathedral design competition won by Basil Spence; construction will begin 1956 (–1962) Abbey Theatre destroyed by fire, Dublin; later rebuilt Music: *Billy Budd,* opera (Britten); *The Pilgrim's Progress* (Vaughan Williams) Lit: *The Cruel Sea* (Monsarrat), *The End of the Affair* (Greene)	Balcon becomes chairman of BFI Experimental Film Fund (–1966), offering grants to young independent filmmakers Balcon acknowledges contributions of Ealing assoc. producers with full producer credit Telekinema opens at Festival of Britain; demonstrates 3-D, widescreen, and stereo systems Children's Film Foundation begun, funded by Eady Plan, to make short features for children's matinees; to be distributed by Rank Denham studios closed Feature films produced in Britain: 125 Balcon's only daughter, Jill, weds Cecil Day-Lewis, future Poet Laureate Death of Will Barker, Robert Flaherty, Ivor Novello	p: Transocean) *The Lavender Hill Mob* (d: Crichton, p: Ealing) *The Magic Box* (d: J. Boulting, p: Festival) *The Man in the White Suit* (d: Mackendrick, p: Ealing) *Outcast of the Islands* (d: Reed, p: London Films/BLPA) *Pool of London* (d: Dearden, p: Ealing) *The Tales of Hoffmann* (d: Powell and Pressburger, p: Archers/London Films/BLPA) *Tom Brown's Schooldays* (d: Parry, p: Talisman) *Where No Vultures Fly* (d: Watt, p: Ealing)
1952	Death of King George VI; Elizabeth II succeeds to throne Mau Mau Rebellion, Kenya Four-day smog in London kills ca. 4,700 First British atomic tests, Monte Bello Islands, W. Australia Laurel and Hardy tour British music halls (–1953) Th: Christie's *The Mousetrap* begins record-breaking run, London Lit: *Collected Poems* (Dylan Thomas), *Men at Arms* (E. Waugh)	Courtauld, financier, leaves Britain for health reasons, ending support of Ealing (since 1931); Balcon negotiates loan from NFFC Feature films produced in Britain: 114 Success of *The African Queen* encourages U.S. investment in Brit. prod. Crown Film Unit closes Telekinema becomes home of BFI's Natl. Film Theatre	*The African Queen* (d: Huston, p: Romulus/Horizon) *Angels One Five* (d: More O'Ferrall, p: Templar) *Brandy for the Parson* (d: Eldridge, p: Group 3) *The Card* (d: Neame, p: BFM) *The Cruel Sea* (d: Frend, p: Ealing) *Cry, the Beloved Country* (d: Z. Korda, p: London Films/BLPA) *The Holly and the Ivy* (d: More O'Ferrall, p: London Films/BLPA) *The Importance of Being Earnest* (d: Asquith, p: BFM) *The Pickwick Papers* (d: Langley, p: Renown) *Secret People* (d: Dickinson, p: Ealing) *The Sound Barrier* (d: Lean, p: London Films/BLPA) *The Titfield Thunderbolt* (d: Crichton, p: Ealing)
1953	Coronation of Queen Elizabeth II Death of Queen Mary Iron and steel industries and road transport denationalized Hillary and Norgay conquer Mount Everest Joan Littlewood becomes dir. of Theatre Workshop (–1961) Churchill wins Nobel Prize for Literature Music: *Gloriana,* opera (Britten), *Sinfonia Antartica,* no. 7 (Vaughan Williams) Th: *Witness for the Prosecution* (Christie) Lit: *Casino Royale,* first James Bond novel (Fleming), *The Go-Between* (Hartley) Death of Dylan Thomas	Television's threat to cinemas accelerates with successful BBC coverage of coronation CinemaScope premieres with *The Robe,* Odeon Theatre, Leicester Square, London Feature films produced in Britain: 117 Death of Cecil Hepworth, Richard Massingham	*The Beggar's Opera* (d: Brook, p: Imperadio) *Genevieve* (d: Cornelius, p: Sirius) *The Heart of the Matter* (d: More O'Ferrall, p: London Films/BLPA) *Innocents in Paris* (d: Parry, p: Romulus) *The Kidnappers* (d: Leacock, p: Group 3) *The Man Between* (d: Reed, p: London Films/BLPA) *O Dreamland* (d: L. Anderson, p: BFI Exp. Film Fund) *The Story of Gilbert and Sullivan* (d: Gilliat, p: London Films/BLPA)
1954	South-East Asia Treaty Organization (SEATO) formed Last wartime rationing ended Roger Bannister runs mile in 3 min., 59.4 sec., setting new world's record	*Animal Farm* (Halas & Batchelor) first completed Brit. animated feature Cinerama opens at London Casino Korda's British Lion announces huge losses	*The Beachcomber* (d: M. Box, p: London Independent) *The Belles of St. Trinian's* (d: Launder, p: BL/London Films) *Carrington, V.C.* (d: Asquith, p: Remus)

	Selected Historical and Cultural Events, including Radio and Television	Balcon and the British Film Industry	Selected British Films
1954, continued	Construction of GPO Tower, London, begun (–1965) Independent Television Authority (ITA) created; assigns and administers commercial television station licenses Th: *The Boy Friend* (Wilson), *The Chalk Garden* (Bagnold), *Salad Days* (Slade), *Separate Tables* (Rattigan), *Under Milkwood* (Dylan Thomas, posth.) Lit: *Lord of the Flies* (Golding) Death of James Hilton	Feature films produced in Britain: 138 Death of Gabriel Pascal	*The Divided Heart* (d: Crichton, p: Ealing) *Doctor in the House* (d: R. Thomas, p: Group 3) *Father Brown* (d: Hamer, p: Facet) *Hobson's Choice* (d: Lean, p: London Films/BLPA) *The Purple Plain* (d: Parrish, p: Two Cities) *Thursday's Children* (d/p: L. Anderson and Brenton)
1955	Anthony Eden (Conservative) becomes Prime Minister Britain and U.S. agree to cooperate on atomic energy research Commercial television broadcasting begins in Britain (ITV); first television commercial transmitted: Gibbs S. R. Toothpaste Mary Quant opens boutique, King's Rd., Chelsea Music: *The Midsummer Marriage*, opera (Tippett) Lit: *The Quiet American* (Greene)	Mackendrick to U.S. Ealing Studios sold to BBC TV for £300,000, to pay off NFFC loan *Dixon of Dock Green*, based on Ealing film *The Blue Lamp* (1950), becomes popular BBC TV series (–1976) New British Lion Co. formed, acquires net assets of orig. co. Feature films produced in Britain: 150	*The Bespoke Overcoat* (d: Clayton, p: Remus) *Cast a Dark Shadow* (d: Gilbert, p: Frobisher) *The Colditz Story* (d: Hamilton, p: Ivan Foxwell) *The Dam Busters* (d: M. Anderson, p: ABPC) *Geordie* (d: Launder, p: Argonaut) *I Am a Camera* (d: Cornelius, p: Remus) *The Ladykillers* (d: Mackendrick, p: Ealing) *The Prisoner* (d: Glenville, p: Facet/London Independent) *The Quartermass Experiment* (d: Guest, p: Hammer) *Richard III* (d: Olivier, p: London Films/Big Ben) *Summer Madness/Summertime* (d: Lean, p: London Films/Lopert Prods.)
1956	Suez Crisis; gasoline and oil rationing result First atomic power station in Britain begins operations, Calder Hall Clean Air Act bans burning of smoky fuels Granada Television begins transmissions, Manchester ITA licenses Independent Television Network, alliance of 15 independent stations English Stage Co. leases Royal Court Theatre, London; George Devine, Dir.; Tony Richardson, Asst. Dir. Th: *Look Back in Anger* (Osborne), *The Quare Fellow* (Behan) Lit: *Diamonds Are Forever* (Fleming), *History of the English-Speaking Peoples* (Churchill) Death of Max Beerbohm, A. A. Milne	Ealing Studios becomes Ealing Films, relocates at M-G-M's Boreham Wood First *Free Cinema* program at Natl. Film Theatre (six series of nonfiction films by Free Cinema filmmakers shown in next three years) BFI and the London *Observer* sponsor exhibition *60 Years of Cinema*, London Penelope Houston becomes ed. of *Sight and Sound* Feature films produced in Britain: 110 Death of Alexander Korda	*The Battle of the River Plate* (d: Powell and Pressburger, p: Archers/Rank) *The Green Man* (d: Day, p: Grenadier) *The Intimate Stranger* (d: Losey, p: Anglo-Guild-Merton Park) *Invitation to the Dance* (d: Kelly, p: M-G-M Brit.) *Momma Don't Allow* (d: Reisz and Richardson, p: BFI Exp. Film Fund) *1984* (d: M. Anderson, p: Holiday) *Private's Progress* (d: J. Boulting, p: Charter)
1957	Queen Elizabeth visits Canada and U.S., addresses UN General Assembly Harold Macmillan (Conservative) becomes Prime Minister European Common Market est.; becomes effective Jan. 1, 1958 Wolfenden Reports on homosexuality and prostitution Britain explodes hydrogen bomb near Christmas Island Suez Canal reopened First Carnaby St. boutique opened	Cinematograph Act passed: quota extended two yrs.; Eady levy becomes statutory, funds to be administered by Brit. Film Fund Agency; NFFC reorganized and extended 10 yrs. Maurice Elvey retires from films, ending 44-yr. directorial career Natl. Film Theatre moves to permanent home under Waterloo Bridge, South Bank; holds first London Film Festival; films include *The Seventh Seal, Throne of Blood, Nights of Cabiria,*	*The Bridge on the River Kwai* (d: Lean, p: Horizon) *Every Day Except Christmas* (d: L. Anderson, p: Graphic Films/Ford Motor Co.) *A King in New York* (d: Chaplin, p: Attica Film Co.) *Nice Time* (d: Goretta and Tanner, p: BFI Exp. Film Fund) *Night of the Demon* (d: J. Tourneur, p: Sabre) *The Prince and the Showgirl* (d: Olivier,

	Selected Historical and Cultural Events, including Radio and Television	Balcon and the British Film Industry	Selected British Films
1957, continued	Queen's Christmas broadcast televised for first time The Royal Ballet, Sadler's Wells, founded Th: *Endgame* (Beckett), *The Entertainer* (Osborne) Lit: *On the Beach* (Shute), *Room at the Top* (Braine) Death of Malcolm Lowry	and *A Face in the Crowd* First film of Hammer horror cycle, *The Curse of Frankenstein* (d: Fisher) Feature films produced in Britain: 108 Death of Jack Buchanan	p: Olivier/Monroe) *Saint Joan* (d: Preminger, p: Wheel Prods.) *The Smallest Show on Earth* (d: Dearden, p: Hallmark) *Time without Pity* (d: Losey, p: Harlequin)
1958	Life Peerages Act passed Campaign for Nuclear Disarmament (CND) founded; first 50-mile march for Nuclear Disarmament, London-Aldermaston West Indies Federation formed (–1962) Riots between teddy boys and blacks at Notting Hill, London, and Nottingham Debutantes presented at Court for last time London Planetarium opened; first in Britain State opening of Parliament and Queen's Speech televised Restoration plans for Stonehenge announced Th: *The Birthday Party* (Pinter), *Five Finger Exercise* (Shaffer), *A Taste of Honey* (Delaney) Lit: *The Greengage Summer* (Godden), *Saturday Night and Sunday Morning* (Sillitoe) Death of Marie Stopes, Ralph Vaughan Williams	John Osborne and Tony Richardson form Woodfall Films; first prod., *Look Back in Anger* (d: Richardson), released 1959 *Carry On, Sergeant* (d: Gerald Thomas, p: Insignia), first in "Carry On" series Filippo Del Giudice retires to monastery in Rome Odeon and Gaumont cinema circuits combine Feature films produced in Britain: 138 Death of Adrian Brunel, Henry Cornelius, Graham Cutts, W. P. Lipscomb	*Amelia and the Angel* (d: Russell, p: BFI Exp. Film Fund) *Carve Her Name with Pride* (d: Gilbert, p: Keyboard) *Dracula* (d: Fisher, p: Hammer/Cadogan) *Dunkirk* (d: Norman, p: Ealing) *Gideon's Day* (d: Ford, p: Col. Brit.) *Indiscreet* (d: Donen, p: Grandon) *The Inn of the Sixth Happiness* (d: Robson, p: 20th Cent.-Fox) *A Night to Remember* (d: Baker, p: Rank) *Nowhere to Go* (d: Holt, p: Ealing) *Orders to Kill* (d: Asquith, p: Lynx) *Revenge of Frankenstein* (d: Fisher, p: Hammer/Cadogan)
1959	European Free Trade Association formed; Britain becomes member 1960 (–1972) First section of London-Birmingham Motorway (M1) opened Christopher Cockerell invents hovercraft Television coverage of General Election Mermaid Theatre opened, first in City of London since Shakespeare's time; founder/dir., Bernard Miles; first prod.: *Lock Up Your Daughters* (Miles) Th: *Billy Liar* (Waterhouse), *The Long and the Short and the Tall* (Hall) Lit: *Goldfinger* (Fleming), *Memento Mori* (Spark)	ABPC, Elstree, buys up Ealing assets; completes film in progress, *The Siege of Pinchgut* (d: Watt) Bryanston Films Ltd. est.; Balcon, Chairman (–1965); guarantees bank financing, with distribution through British Lion; first release, *The Battle of the Sexes* (d: Crichton; p: Prometheus) Allied Film Makers, prod. co., formed by Attenborough, Jack Hawkins, Dearden and Relph, and Bryan Forbes and Guy Green; financed by Rank and Natl. Provincial Bank; Rank, distrib./exhibitor (–1964) British Film Academy merges with Society of Film & Television Arts Feature films produced in Britain: 121 Death of Lupino Lane, G. A. Smith	*The Devil's Disciple* (d: Hamilton, p: Hecht-Hill-Lancaster) *The Hound of the Baskervilles* (d: Fisher, p: Hammer) *The Horse's Mouth* (d: Neame, p: Knightsbridge) *I'm All Right, Jack* (d: J. Boulting, p: Charter Films) *The Mouse That Roared* (d: Arnold, p: Open Road) *The Mummy* (d: Fisher, p: Hammer) *Room at the Top* (d: Clayton, p: Remus) *Sapphire* (d: Dearden, p: Artna) *Shake Hands with the Devil* (d: M. Anderson, p: Troy Pennebaker) *Tiger Bay* (d: Lee Thompson, p: IA) *We Are the Lambeth Boys* (d: Reisz, p: Ford Motor Co.)
1960	Birth of Prince Andrew Princess Margaret weds Antony Armstrong-Jones, Lord Snowdon Macmillan makes "winds of change" speech in Africa; Cyprus and Nigeria become independent Television sets number 10.5 million Picasso retrospective, Tate Gallery, London Peter Hall appointed managing dir. of Royal Shakespeare Co. Music: *A Midsummer Night's Dream*,	Weekly cinema attendance drops to 10 million (from over 22 million in 1955) Films Act passed; extends quota to 1967 Cinematograph Act passed; concerned with foreign co-prods. Entertainments Duty abolished Feature films produced in Britain: 122 University lectureship in film est. at Slade School of Art, London; first lecturer, Thorold Dickinson *Peeping Tom* (d/p: Powell) and *Psycho* (d: Hitchcock, p: Paramount)	*Cone of Silence* (d: Frend, p: Aubrey Baring Prods.) *The Entertainer* (d: Richardson, p: Woodfall) *The League of Gentlemen* (d: Dearden, p: AFM) *Our Man in Havana* (d: Reed, p: Kingsmead) *The Running, Jumping, and Standing Still Film* (d: Lester, p: Sellers Prods.) *Saturday Night and Sunday Morning* (d: Reisz, p: Woodfall)

	Selected Historical and Cultural Events, including Radio and Television	Balcon and the British Film Industry	Selected British Films
1960, continued	opera (Britten) TV: *Coronation Street* (Granada TV) begins broadcasting Th: *The Caretaker* (Pinter), *A Man for All Seasons* (Bolt), *Oliver!*, musical (Bart) Lit: *The Loneliness of the Long Distance Runner* (Sillitoe)	condemned by press	*School for Scoundrels* (d: Hamer, p: Guardsman) *Sink the Bismarck!* (d: Gilbert, p: 20th Cent.-Fox) *Sons and Lovers* (d: Cardiff, p: 20th Cent.-Fox) *The Trials of Oscar Wilde* (d: Hughes, p: Viceroy/Warwick) *Tunes of Glory* (d: Neame, p: Colin Lesslie/Knightsbridge)
1961	Negotiations begin for British entry into Common Market South Africa leaves Commonwealth; Sierra Leone and Tanganyika independent Farthings no longer legal tender Spy trials in London: Gordon Lonsdale, George Blake, the Krogers Royal Ballet visits U.S.S.R. Th: *Beyond the Fringe,* revue (Moore and Cook); *The Collection* (Pinter); *The Knack* (Jellicoe); *Luther* (Osborne) Lit: *The Prime of Miss Jean Brodie* (Spark) Birth of Lady Diana Spencer	Economic uncertainties of industry bring increase in independent prods. Feature films produced in Britain: 122 Kubrick emigrates to Britain Death of Filippo Del Giudice, George Formby	*The Day the Earth Caught Fire* (d: Guest, p: Melina) *The Greengage Summer* (d: Gilbert, p: Saville Prods./PKL Pictures) *The Guns of Navarone* (d: Lee Thompson, p: Open Road) *The Innocents* (d: Clayton, p: Achilles) *Night of the Eagle/Burn, Witch, Burn!* (d: Hayers, p: IA) *The Queen's Guards* (d: Powell, p: Imperial) *A Taste of Honey* (d: Richardson, p: Woodfall) *Victim* (d: Dearden, p: Parkway) *Whistle Down the Wind* (d: Forbes, p: AFM/Beaver)
1962	Commonwealth Immigrants Act controls immigration into Britain Uganda independent Transport Act creates British Railways Board The London *Sunday Times* issues first color supplement Music: *King Priam,* opera (Tippett) TV: Pilkington Report rejects pay-TV, proposes more airtime and more channels; *That Was the Week That Was* (BBC) (–1963) Lit: *A Clockwork Orange* (Burgess), *The Golden Notebook* (Lessing)	Saville retires from films Feature films produced in Britain: 117 First James Bond film, *Dr. No* (d: Terence Young, p: Eon Prods.) Death of Angus MacPhail	*Billy Budd* (d: Ustinov, p: Anglo-Allied) *The Damned* (d: Losey, p: Hammer/Swallow) *A Kind of Loving* (d: Schlesinger, p: Vic Films) *Lawrence of Arabia* (d: Lean, p: Horizon) *Lolita* (d: Kubrick, p: Anglo-Amalgamated/Seven Arts/Anya/Transworld) *The Loneliness of the Long-Distance Runner* (d: Richardson, p: Woodfall) *The L-Shaped Room* (d: Forbes, p: Romulus)
1963	Sir Alec Douglas-Home (Conservative) becomes Prime Minister Harold Wilson elected leader of Labour Party DeGaulle vetoes Britain's entry into Common Market Profumo affair Nuclear test-ban treaty signed by Britain, U.S., and U.S.S.R. Glasgow-London mail train robbery (£2.5 million) Beatlemania hits Britain National Theatre's first season at Old Vic opens with production of *Hamlet;* Olivier, dir. Th: *Alfie* (Naughton), *The Bed Sitting Room* (Antrobus and Milligan), *Oh What a Lovely War* (Theatre Workshop) Death of Aldous Huxley, Sir David Low	Balcon's last personal prod. released, *Sammy Going South* (d: Mackendrick, p: Balcon Prods./Bryanston/Seven Arts) *Tom Jones* (d: Richardson, p: Woodfall/UA) international hit; financed by U.S. co.; prod. had been refused by Bryanston as being beyond its resources Feature films produced in Britain: 114 Death of Robert Hamer	*Billy Liar!* (d: Schlesinger, p: Vic Films/Waterhall) *The Caretaker* (d: Donner, p: Caretaker) *The Chalk Garden* (d: Neame, p: Quota Rentals) *Doctor Strangelove...* (d: Kubrick, p: Hawk) *From Russia with Love* (d: Young, p: Eon Prods.) *The Haunting* (d: Wise, p: Argyle Enterprises) *Lord of the Flies* (d: Brooks, p: Two Arts) *The Servant* (d: Losey, p: Springbok) *Sparrows Can't Sing* (d: Littlewood, p: Carthage) *This Sporting Life* (d: L. Anderson, p: IA)
1964	Birth of Prince Edward Harold Wilson (Labour) becomes Prime	Last Bryanston release, *The System* (d: Michael Winner, p: Kenneth	*Becket* (d: Glenville, p: Keep/Par.) *Culloden* (d: Watkins, p: BBC)

	Selected Historical and Cultural Events, including Radio and Television	Balcon and the British Film Industry	Selected British Films
1964, continued	Minister Govt. grants licenses to drill for oil and gas in North Sea Easter riots of Mods vs. Rockers in Brighton, other sea resorts "Brain Drain": British scientists migrate in great numbers to U.S. Court of Session, Edinburgh, rules that Harris Tweed must be made entirely in Outer Hebrides TV: BBC-2 inaugurated, introducing 625-line image, Continental standard Beatles make first trip to U.S.; Rolling Stones become popular in Britain and U.S.; The Who formed, London Th: *Entertaining Mr. Sloane* (Orton), *Inadmissible Evidence* (Osborne), *Marat-Sade...* (Weiss), *The Royal Hunt of the Sun* (Shaffer) Lit: *In His Own Write* (Lennon) Death of Lady Nancy Astor, Lord Beaverbrook, Brendan Behan, Ian Fleming, Sean O'Casey, Dame Edith Sitwell	Shipman Prods.) Balcon becomes chairman of British Lion (–1966) Feature films produced in Britain: 113 Herbert Wilcox declares bankruptcy Death of Alfred Junge	*Goldfinger* (d: Hamilton, p: Eon Prods./Danjac) *A Hard Day's Night* (d: Lester, p: Proscenium) *It Happened Here* (d/p: Brownlow and Mollo) *King and Country* (d: Losey, p: BHE) *The Masque of the Red Death* (d: Corman, p: Anglo-Amalgamated/Alta Vista) *The Pumpkin Eater* (d: Clayton, p: Romulus) *Seance on a Wet Afternoon* (d: Forbes, p: AFM/Beaver)
1965	Rhodesia makes unilateral declaration of independence; Britain introduces oil embargo, economic sanctions Natural gas discovered in North Sea 750th anniversary of Magna Carta, 700th anniversary of Parliament, 900th anniversary of Westminster Abbey Consortium of television independents' pay-TV experiment (–1967) Private commercial radio stations established off British coast GPO Tower opens, London Dead Sea Scrolls exhibited at British Museum Dave Clark Five popular Th: *The Homecoming* (Pinter), *The Killing of Sister George* (Marcus) Lit: *The Looking Glass War* (Le Carré), *Thunderball* (Fleming, posth.) Death of Sir Winston Churchill, T. S. Eliot, W. Somerset Maugham	Bryanston sold to Associated Rediffusion, television co. Feature films produced in Britain: 95 Death of H. Bruce Woolfe	*Darling...* (d: Schlesinger, p: Vic Films/Appia) *Help!* (d: Lester, p: Subafilms) *The Hill* (d: Lumet, p: Seven Arts) *The Ipcress File* (d: Furie, p: Lowndes-Steven) *The Knack...and How to Get It* (d: Lester, p: Woodfall) *The Nanny* (d: Holt, p: Hammer/Seven Arts) *Othello* (d: Burge, p: BHE) *Repulsion* (d: Polanski, p: Tekli) *The Spy Who Came in from the Cold* (d: Ritt, p: Salem) *Young Cassidy* (d: Cardiff and Ford, p: Sextant)
1966	Prime Minister Wilson announces "standstill" in wages and prices Aviation executive Freddie Laker founds charter airline London *Times* changes format, placing news instead of ads on front page Th: *Staircase* (Dyer) Lit: *The Birds Fall Down* (R. West), *The Comedians* (Greene) Death of C. S. Forester, Evelyn Waugh	BFI Experimental Film Fund reconstituted as BFI Production Board; Balcon, Chairman (–1972); Bruce Beresford, Head of Production (–1971) London Film-makers' Co-op formed by avant-garde and independent filmmakers 75 percent of Brit. first features exhibited are U.S.-financed Feature films produced in Britain: 93 Death of Erich Pommer	*Alfie* (d: Gilbert, p: Sheldrake) *Cul-de-Sac* (d: Polanski, p: Tekli/Compton) *Fahrenheit 451* (d: Truffaut, p: Vineyard/Anglo-Enterprises/Universal) *The Family Way* (d: R. Boulting, p: Janbox) *Georgy Girl* (d: Narizzano, p: Everglades) *A Man for All Seasons* (d: Zinnemann, p: Highroad) *Marat-Sade...* (d: Brook, p: Marat-Sade Prods.) *Morgan...A Suitable Case for Treatment* (d: Reisz, p: Quintra/BL) *The Quiller Memorandum* (d: M. Anderson, p: Carthay) *The War Game* (d: Watkins, p: BBC)

	Selected Historical and Cultural Events, including Radio and Television	Balcon and the British Film Industry	Selected British Films
1966, continued			*The Whisperers* (d: Forbes, p: Seven Pines)
			The Wrong Box (d: Forbes, p: Salamander)
1967	Queen Elizabeth and Prince Philip visit Canada for Centennial celebrations	BFI launches regional film theaters; first, Bristol Arts Centre	*Accident* (d: Losey, p: Royal Avenue Chelsea)
	Jeremy Thorpe elected leader of Liberal Party	Feature films produced in Britain: 82	*Blow-Up* (d: Antonioni, p: Bridge)
	Pound devalued	Death of Anatole de Grunwald, Maurice Elvey	*The Burning* (d: Frears, p: BFI Prod. Bd.)
	"Hot line" est. between Kremlin and 10 Downing St.		*Dance of the Vampires* (d: Polanski, p: Cadre/Filmways/M-G-M)
	Abortion legalized; contraceptives supplied free under Family Planning Act		*Far from the Madding Crowd* (d: Schlesinger, p: Vic Films/Appia)
	Yachtsman Francis Chichester completes 226-day solo voyage around world; knighted by Queen at Greenwich		*How I Won the War* (d: Lester, p: Petersham)
	Twiggy takes fashion world by storm		*Privilege* (d: Watkins, p: World Film Services/Memorial Enterprises)
	Queen Elizabeth II (Cunard Line) launched; *Queen Mary* sold to Long Beach, Calif.		*Quartermass and the Pit* (d: Baker, p: Hammer)
	Cecil Day-Lewis becomes Poet Laureate (–1972)		*Two for the Road* (d: Donen, p: Donen Enterprises)
	TV: *The Forsyte Saga* series (BBC); BBC begins first regular color transmissions in Europe		*Ulysses* (d: Strick, p: Ulysses Prods.)
	Th: *A Day in the Death of Joe Egg* (Nichols), *Hadrian VII* (Luke), *The Man in the Glass Booth* (R. Shaw), *Rosencrantz and Guildenstern Are Dead* (Stoppard)		
	Death of Sir Victor Gollancz, Margaret Kennedy, John Masefield, Joe Orton		
1968	Britain rejects renewed claim by Argentina to Falkland Islands	90 percent of Brit. first features U.S.-financed	*Blind White Duration* (d/p: LeGrice)
	Mass demonstrations in London against Vietnam War	Feature films produced in Britain: 83	*If . . .* (d: L. Anderson, p: Memorial Enterprises)
	Commonwealth Immigration and Race Relations Acts passed; govt. restricts immigration from India, Pakistan, West Indies, and Rhodesia	Queen's Award for Industry presented to Hammer Films	*Inadmissible Evidence* (d: Page, p: Woodfall)
	Arizona developers buy London Bridge	Pinewood Studios receives Oscar for Technical Achievement	*The Lion in Winter* (d: Harvey, p: Haworth)
	Midi fails to replace miniskirt	Natl. Film Theatre inaugurates John Player Lectures; Godard scheduled for first lecture; first to appear, Richard Lester	*Oliver!* (d: Reed, p: Romulus)
	Theatres Act abolishes Lord Chamberlain's powers of theater censorship, in effect since 1737	Death of Anthony Asquith	*Romeo and Juliet* (d: Zeffirelli, p: BHE/Verona)
	Music: *The Prodigal Son,* a church parable (Britten)		*Secret Ceremony* (d: Losey, p: Universal/World/Paul Heller)
			Twisted Nerve (d: R. Boulting, p: Charter)
			2001: A Space Odyssey (d: Kubrick, p: Hawk/M-G-M)
			Witchfinder General (d: Reeves, p: AIP/Tigon)
			Yellow Submarine (d: Dunning, p: Apple)
1969	Prince Charles invested as Prince of Wales, Caernarvon	Balcon publishes autobiography, *A Lifetime of Films*	*The Assassination Bureau* (d: Dearden, p: Heathfield)
	Oil discovered in North Sea	Rank retires as chairman of Rank Org.; succeeded by John Davis	*The Battle of Britain* (d: Hamilton, p: Spitfire)
	Worldwide inflation	Hammer Films closes Bray Studios	*The Dance of Death* (d: Giles, p: BHE/Natl. Th.)
	General Post Office made public corp.	Feature films produced in Britain: 88	*Hamlet* (d: Richardson, p: Woodfall)
	Ulster troubles begin; British troops sent to Belfast to quell rioting	Death of Iris Barry	*Isadora* (d: Reisz, p: Universal)
	Student riots at London School of Economics and Political Science force several-week closing		*Kes* (d: Loach, p: Kestrel/Woodfall)
	MP Enoch Powell (Conservative)		*Mare's Tail* (d/p: Larcher)
			Oh! What a Lovely War

	Selected Historical and Cultural Events, including Radio and Television	Balcon and the British Film Industry	Selected British Films
1969, continued	proposes govt.-financed repatriation of black and Asian residents Voting age lowered from 21 to 18 Royal Academy of Arts, London, celebrates 200th anniversary Pantsuits become acceptable daily wear for women TV: *Civilisation* series (BBC); U.S. PBS inaugurates *Masterpiece Theatre,* anthology of British TV dramas; *Monty Python's Flying Circus,* comedy series (BBC-1; –1974); Open University founded Th: *In Celebration* (Storey), *The National Health* (Nichols), *What the Butler Saw* (Orton, posth.)		(d: Attenborough, p: Accord) *The Prime of Miss Jean Brodie* (d: Neame, p: 20th Cent.-Fox) *The Royal Hunt of the Sun* (d: Lerner, p: Royal/Benmar/Security) *Women in Love* (d: Russell, p: Brandywine)
1970	Edward Heath (Conservative) becomes Prime Minister Gambia becomes independent republic within Commonwealth School-leaving age raised to 16 BBC Radio London goes on the air "Skinheads" harass Pakistani immigrants First jumbo jets (Boeing 747s) go into BOAC service Beatles break up TV: *The Six Wives of Henry VIII* series (BBC) Th: *Home* (Storey), *A Midsummer Night's Dream* (Shakespeare; Peter Brook prod.) *Oh! Calcutta* (Tynan), *A Voyage Round My Father* (Mortimer) Death of E. M. Forster, Lord Bertrand Russell	Natl. Film Theatre Two (NFT2) opens; first screening, *Loving Memory* (d: Tony Scott, p: BFI Prod. Bd./ Woodfall) Board of Film Censors draws up new ratings: U (general exhibition), A (general exhibition, but parental guidance for under-14), AA (restricted: 14 and over), X (restricted: 18 and over) Films Act extends NFFC, broadens Brit. Film Fund Agency (created 1957) financing to include BFI Prod. Bd. and Natl. Film School; extends 30 percent quota through 1980 *Cinema City* exhibition sponsored by Natl. Film Archive and the London *Sunday Times* celebrates 75 yrs. of cinema EMI and M-G-M become partners in running Elstree Studios; former M-G-M lot at Boreham Wood closed ABPC becomes EMI Film & Theatre Corp.; cinemas still known as ABC Feature films produced in Britain: 92	*Bronco Bullfrog* (d: Platts-Mills, p: Maya) *Entertaining Mr. Sloane* (d: Hickox, p: Canterbury) *The Go-Between* (d: Losey, p: World Film Services) *King Lear* (d: Brook, p: Filmways/ Lanterna/Athena) *Leo the Last* (d: Boorman, p: Char-Wink-Boor/Calisbury) *Let It Be* (d: Lindsay-Hogg, p: Apple) *Performance* (d: Roeg and Cammell, p: Goodtimes Enterprises) *Ryan's Daughter* (d: Lean, p: Faraway) *10 Rillington Place* (d: Fleischer, p: Genesis/Filmways/Col.) *Times For* (d: Dwoskin, p: Alan Power/ Q Films)
1971	Decimal currency adopted Northern Ireland violence worsens; govt. institutes policies of preventive detention and internment without trial; 172 killed Post Office Tower bombed, London Postal strike continues 47 days Rolls-Royce Ltd., declaring bankruptcy, nationalized *Concorde* makes first transatlantic flight TV: *Elizabeth R* series (BBC); *Upstairs, Downstairs* series (London Weekend Television) begins (–1975) Th: *Butley* (Gray), *The Changing Room* (Storey), *Old Times* (Pinter) Death of Tyrone Guthrie	Natl. Film School est., Beaconsfield; first dir., Colin Young Death of Basil Dearden, Seth Holt	*And Now for Something Completely Different* (d: McNaughton, p: Kettledrum/Python) *Bleak Moments* (d: Leigh, p: Autumn Prods./Memorial Enterprises/BFI Prod. Bd.) *The Boy Friend* (d: Russell, p: M-G-M/ EMI/Russflix) *A Clockwork Orange* (d: Kubrick, p: WB) *The Devils* (d: Russell, p: WB) *Focus* (d/p: Gidal) *Sunday, Bloody Sunday* (d: Schlesinger, p: Schlesinger/Joseph Janni)
1972	Prime Minister Heath signs treaty admitting Britain to Common Market, effective Jan. 1, 1973 Direct rule imposed on Northern Ireland; violence continues: 467 killed during yr.; 13 killed on "Bloody	Cinematograph Films Act repeals Sunday Entertainments Act (1932), abolishes Cinematograph Fund, and creates separate quota category for films of Common Market countries Michael Relph succeeds Balcon as	*Diamonds Are Forever* (d: Hamilton, p: Eon Prods.) *Family Life* (d: Loach, p: Kestrel/Anglo/ EMI) *Frenzy* (d: Hitchcock, p: Pinewood) *The Ruling Class* (d: Medak, p: Jules

	Selected Historical and Cultural Events, including Radio and Television	Balcon and the British Film Industry	Selected British Films
1972, continued	Sunday," Londonderry; Dublin mob destroys British Embassy Coal strike continues 47 days Tutankhamen exhibition at British Museum Sir John Betjeman becomes Poet Laureate (–1984) BBC celebrates 50th anniversary Independent Television Authority (est. 1956) becomes Independent Broadcasting Authority (IBA); jurisdiction broadened to include independent radio stations TV: *America* series (BBC), *War and Peace* series (BBC) Th: *Jesus Christ Superstar* (Rice and Webber), *Jumpers* (Stoppard), *Time and Time Again* (Ayckbourn) Lit: *The Day of the Jackal* (Forsyth) Death of Duke of Windsor, Cecil Day-Lewis, Dame Margaret Rutherford	chairman of BFI Prod. Bd. Feature films produced in Britain: 96 Death of John Grierson, Sir Compton Mackenzie, J. Arthur Rank	Buck/Jack Hawkins) *Sleuth* (d: Mankiewicz, p: Palomar Pictures International) *Young Winston* (d: Attenborough, p: Col.)
1973	Princess Anne weds Captain Mark Phillips Northern Ireland violence continues; 250 killed; bombings in London, Midlands Energy crisis precipitates electricity cutbacks, three-day work wk., fuel conservation The Bahamas become independent after 300 yrs. of Brit. rule First commercial radio stations, London Broadcasting Co. (24-hr. news) and Capital Radio (pop music), begin transmission TV: *The World at War* series (Thames Television) Music: *Death in Venice,* opera (Britten) Th: *Equus* (Shaffer), *The Party* (Griffiths), *The Rocky Horror Show* (O'Brien) Lit: *The Honorary Consul* (Greene), *Watership Down* (Adams) Death of W. H. Auden, Sir Noël Coward, Nancy Mitford, J. R. R. Tolkien	Brit.-financed films made in Britain and abroad: 86 VAT (Value Added Tax) imposed on cinema seat prices Death of Ernest Lindgren, George Pearson, Dennis Price	*Butley* (d: Pinter, p: Am. Film Th.) *The Day of the Jackal* (d: Zinnemann, p: Warwick/Universal) *A Doll's House* (d: Losey, p: World Film Services/Films la Boétie) *Don't Look Now* (d: Roeg, p: BL) *England Made Me* (d: Duffell, p: Atlantic) *O Lucky Man!* (d: L. Anderson, p: Memorial Enterprises/Sam)
1974	Harold Wilson (Labour) becomes Prime Minister IRA terrorists bomb Tower of London and Houses of Parliament; retaliatory bombing during Dublin rush hr. Kidnapping attempt on Princess Anne, London Covent Garden market moved across Thames to Nine Elms Video cassette recorders become available for home use TV: *Shoulder to Shoulder* series (BBC) Th: *The Norman Conquests* (Ayckbourn), *Travesties* (Stoppard) Lit: *Tinker, Tailor, Soldier, Spy* (Le Carré) Death of Jacob Bronowski, Cyril Connolly	Brit.-financed films made in Britain and abroad: 66 Shepperton Studios suffers substantial financial losses Assn. of Cinematograph and Television Technicians proposes nationalization or worker-ownership of film industry Death of Compton Bennett, Clive Brook, Michael Truman	*The Abdication* (d: Harvey, p: WB) *Ireland: Behind the Wire* (d/p: Berwick Street Collective) *Mahler* (d: Russell, p: David Puttnam, Goodtimes Enterprises/Ken Russell Films) *Murder on the Orient Express* (d: Lumet, p: EMI/GW Films) *The Odessa File* (d: Neame, p: Domino/Oceanic Prods.) *The Optimist of Nine Elms* (d: Simmons, p: Cheetah/Sagittarius)

	Selected Historical and Cultural Events, including Radio and Television	Balcon and the British Film Industry	Selected British Films
1975	British vote to stay in Common Market Margaret Thatcher becomes leader of Conservative Party Inflation rate jumps 25 percent First Brit. commercial North Sea oil rig produces "Cod War" between Iceland and Britain (–1976) Peter Hall becomes dir. of National Theatre TV: *Edward the Seventh* series (ATV), *Fawlty Towers,* 1st series (2nd series, 1979) (BBC) Th: *The Bed Before Yesterday* (Travers), *Comedians* (Griffiths), *No Man's Land* (Pinter) Lit: *The Raj Quartet* (completed; begun 1968; Paul Scott) Death of Eamon De Valéra, Julian Huxley, Arnold Toynbee, Sir P. G. Wodehouse	British Lion merges with EMI Brit.-financed films made in Britain and abroad: 46 Death of Muir Mathieson	*The Autobiography of a Princess* (d: Ivory, p: Merchant-Ivory) *The Homecoming* (d: Hall, p: Seven Keys) *Lisztomania* (d: Russell, p: David Puttnam, Goodtimes Enterprises/Visual Programme Systems) *The Man Who Fell to Earth* (d: Roeg, p: BL) *The Man Who Would Be King* (d: Huston, p: Col.) *Monty Python and the Holy Grail* (d: Gilliam and Jones, p: EMI/Python) *Moon over the Alley* (d: Despins, p: BFI Prod. Bd.) *Night Cleaners* (d/p: Berwick Street Collective) *The Rocky Horror Picture Show* (d: Sharman, p: Fox) *The Romantic Englishwoman* (d: Losey, p: Dial Films/Meric-Matalan) *Winstanley* (d: Brownlow and Mollo, p: BFI Prod. Bd.)
1976	Queen Elizabeth and Prince Philip attend U.S. Bicentennial celebrations; open XXI Olympic Games, Montreal James Callaghan (Labour) becomes Prime Minister Peace People's Movement marches against Ulster violence British Ambassador to Republic of Ireland killed by landmine, Dublin Race riots, Notting Hill, London Jeremy Thorpe, amidst scandal, resigns as head of Liberal Party; succeeded by David Steel Britain and France begin transatlantic *Concorde* service to Washington, D.C.; to New York in 1977 John Curry skating gold medalist, Innsbruck Winter Olympics National Theatre moves from Old Vic to South Bank, London Unexpurgated edition of *The Diary of Samuel Pepys* (final volume) published TV: *I, Claudius* series (BBC) Death of Baron Benjamin Britten, Dame Agatha Christie, Dame Edith Evans, Field Marshal Viscount Montgomery, Dame Sybil Thorndike	British Academy of Film & Television Arts (organized 1975, pres.: Princess Anne) opens new hdqrs., London Govt. report, "The Future of the British Film Industry," recommends appt. of Minister of the Arts and central British Film Authority, which would oversee BFI, Natl. Film School, and NFFC Tax of 75 percent on worldwide earnings of foreign producers resident in Britain discourages foreign investment Assn. of Independent Producers formed Goldcrest Films est.	*Barry Lyndon* (d: Kubrick, p: Hawk/Peregrine/WB) *Bill Douglas Trilogy* (completed): *My Childhood* ('72), *My Ain Folk* ('73), *My Way Home* ('76) (d: Douglas, p: BFI Prod. Bd.) *Bugsy Malone* (d: Parker, p: David Puttnam, Goodtimes Enterprises/Bugsy Malone Prods.) *Robin and Marian* (d: Lester, p: Rastar/Col.) *The Slipper and the Rose* (d: Forbes, p: Paradine) *Tommy* (d: Russell, p: Robert Stigwood Org.)
1977	Queen Elizabeth II's Silver Jubilee; Queen visits all parts of kingdom, including Northern Ireland North Sea oil spill Freddie Laker's discount Skytrain begins operations (goes into receivership, 1982) Notting Hill Carnival riots Punk fashions in London Christie's *The Mousetrap* celebrates 25th anniversary, Ambassador's Theatre, London Th: *Bedroom Farce* (Ayckbourn), *The Elephant Man* (Pomerance), *Privates on*	Feature films produced in Britain: 80 Death of Sir Michael Balcon, Basil Dean, Charles Frend, Herbert Wilcox	*A Bridge Too Far* (d: Attenborough, p: Joseph E. Levine) *Death on the Nile* (d: Guillermin, p: EMI) *The Duellists* (d: Scott, p: David Puttnam, Enigma Prods./Scott Free Enterprises) *Joseph Andrews* (d: Richardson, p: Woodfall) *A Portrait of the Artist as a Young Man* (d: Strick, p: Ulysses Film Prods.) *Riddles of the Sphinx* (d: Mulvey and Wollen, p: BFI Prod. Bd.) *The Spy Who Loved Me* (d: Gilbert, p: Eon Prods.)

	Selected Historical and Cultural Events, including Radio and Television	Balcon and the British Film Industry	Selected British Films
1977, continued	*Parade* (Nichols) Death of Richard Addinsell, Sir Anthony Eden, Sir Terence Rattigan, Cyril Ritchard		
1978	Oil discovered off west coast of Scotland World's first test-tube baby born in England Princess Margaret and Lord Snowdon divorced Publication of the London *Times* and *Sunday Times* suspended after labor-management dispute over new technology TV: *Edward and Mrs. Simpson* series (Thames Television), *Pennies from Heaven* series (BBC) Th: *Betrayal* (Pinter), *Evita* (Webber and Rice), *Plenty* (Hare), *Whose Life Is It Anyway?* (Clark) Lit: *The Far Pavilions* (Kaye), *The Human Factor* (Greene), *Life in the English Country House* (Girouard)	Feature films produced in Britain: 50 Death of Jack Hulbert	*Before Hindsight* (d: Lewis, p: Metropolis Pictures/BFI Prod. Bd.) *Midnight Express* (d: Parker, p: David Puttnam, Casablanca FilmWorks/Col.) *Nighthawks* (d: Peck and Hallam, p: Four Corners/Nashburgh) *Stevie* (d: Enders, p: First Artists/Grand Metropolitan) *Vertical Features Remake* (d/p: Greenaway) *A Walk Through H* (d: Greenaway, p: BFI Prod. Bd.)
1979	Margaret Thatcher (Conservative) becomes first woman Prime Minister Lord Mountbatten of Burma murdered by IRA terrorists Pope John Paul II visits Republic of Ireland Industrial unrest BBC celebrates 25 yrs. of Television News TV: *To the Manor Born* comedy series (BBC)	London International Film School est., Covent Garden Thorn Electrical Industries and EMI Films Inc. merge to form Thorn-EMI, Elstree Studios Feature films produced in Britain: 54 Death of Dame Gracie Fields, Vincent Korda, Victor Saville	*Alien* (d: Scott, p: Brandywine/Ronald Shusett Prods./Fox) *Black Jack* (d: Loach, p: Kestrel/NFFC) *Correction, Please or How We Got Into Pictures* (d: Burch, p: Arts Council of Gr. Brit.) *The First Great Train Robbery* (d: Crichton, p: Starling Prods.) *Moonraker* (d: Gilbert, p: Eon Prods/Les Productions Artistes Associés) *Quadrophenia* (d: Roddam, p: The Who/Polytel) *Radio On* (d: Petit, p: BFI/Road Movies/NFFC) *Rude Boy* (d: Hazan and Mingay, p: Buzzy Enterprises) *Scum* (d: Clarke, p: Berwick St. Films/Boyd's) *The Secret Policeman's Ball* (d: Graef, p: Films of Record/Amnesty Intl.) *That Sinking Feeling* (d: Forsyth, p: Forsyth/Minor Miracle Film Coop/The Sinking Feeling Film Coop.) *Yanks* (d: Schlesinger, p: CIP/UA/Joseph Janni-Lester Persky Prods.)
1980	Callaghan resigns as leader of Labour Party Worldwide recession. Record interest rates; inflation escalates; manufacturing declines Unemployment exceeds 2 million; 335,000 workers laid off, Jan.–Sept.; steel workers' strike (3 months) Govt. announces plan to reduce state control of electricity, Post Office, and British Transport Docks IRA prisoners' hunger strike, Belfast (1 month); Ulster death toll for decade over 2,000 Easter weekend violence, Scarborough	BFI Publishing founded Rank Org. withdraws from film prod.; holdings have shifted to hotels, real estate, and copying machines Feature films produced in Britain: 61 Death of Dame Cicely Courtneidge, Terence Fisher, Sir Alfred Hitchcock, Peter Sellers	*Bad Timing* (d: Roeg, p: Rank/The Recorded Picture Co.) *The Elephant Man* (d: Lynch, p: Brooksfilms) *The Falls* (d: Greenaway, p: BFI Prod. Bd.) *The Gamekeeper* (d: Loach, p: ATV) *McVicar* (d: Clegg, p: Who Films) *The Shining* (d: Kubrick, p: Hawk/Producer Circle) *The Tempest* (d: Jarman, p: Boyd's)

	Selected Historical and Cultural Events, including Radio and Television	Balcon and the British Film Industry	Selected British Films
1980, continued	and other seaside resorts Sixpence ceases to be legal tender Stone Age art discovered in Wye Valley *Times* crossword celebrates 50th anniversary TV: *Hollywood* series (Thames Television) Th: *Amadeus* (Shaffer), *The Dresser* (Harwood), *Educating Rita* (Russell) Death of Sir Cecil Beaton, John Lennon, Sir Oswald Mosley, Ben Travers, Kenneth Tynan		
1981	Prince Charles weds Lady Diana Spencer Unemployment reaches ca. 3 million; unemployed black youths riot in Brixton, Toxteth, Wood Green, and Salford British Telecom takes over telephone services froam Post Office Belize, Antigua, and Barbados independent Citizens' Band radio becomes legal Last reunion of Boer War veterans, London First London marathon; ca. 7,000 entrants TV: *Brideshead Revisited* series (Granada) Th: *Another Country* (Mitchell), *Cats* (Webber)	National Film Finance Corp. Act reorganizes NFFC; Film Levy Finance Act reorganizes Brit. Film Fund Agency Feature films produced in Britain: 52 Death of Len Lye, Jessie Matthews	*Chariots of Fire* (d: Hudson, p: Allied Stars/David Puttnam, Enigma Prods./Fox/Goldcrest) *Clash of the Titans* (d: Davis, p: Peerford Films, for M-G-M/Titan Prods.) *The French Lieutenant's Woman* (d: Reisz, p: Juniper Films) *Gregory's Girl* (d: Forsyth, p: Lake Film Prods.) *Outland* (d: Hyams, p: Ladd Co. [Gr. Brit.] Ltd.) *Priest of Love* (d: Miles, p: Milesian Film Prods.) *Raise the Titanic!* (d: Jameson, p: Marble Arch/ITC) *Time Bandits* (d: Gilliam, p: HandMade) *Voice Over* (d: Monger, p: Monger/Welsh Arts Council)
1982	Birth of Prince William to Prince Charles and Princess Diana Falkland Islands campaign Labor and race riots mark summer British Nationality Act est. three classes of citizenship: British, British Dependent Territories, and British Overseas Wildlife and Countryside Act passed, providing for voluntary local management agreements Royal Shakespeare Co. moves to Barbican Theatre; first prods., *Henry IV, Parts I and II* Last performance of D'Oyly Carte Opera Co. Th: *Noises Off* (Frayn)	Channel 4 begins operations; commissions programs/films for broadcast. First film shown: *Walter* (d: Frears, p: Central Prods., for Channel 4). In its first yr., commissions 20 films, four of which *(Angel, The Draughtsman's Contract, Moonlighting, and Remembrance)* receive theatrical exposure First London Multi-Media Market held; video dominates Several independent London cinemas become clubs to avoid Eady payments Feature films produced in Britain: 38 Cinema attendance 60.2 million, down 65 percent from 1971 (176 million) Death of Alberto Cavalcanti, Stanley Holloway, Dame Celia Johnson	*Brimstone and Treacle* (d: Loncraine, p: Namara Films/Pennies from Heaven) *Britannia Hospital* (d: L. Anderson, p: Film & General Prods.) *The Draughtsman's Contract* (d: Greenaway, p: BFI Prod. Bd./Channel 4) *Experience Preferred–But Not Essential* (d: Duffell, p: David Puttnam, Enigma Prods./Goldcrest/Channel 4) *Gandhi* (d: Attenborough, p: Indo-British Films, for Goldcrest) *Moonlighting* (d: Skolimowski, p: Michael White, for Channel 4) *Privates on Parade* (d: Blakemore, p: HandMade) *P'Tang Yang Kipperbang* (d: Apted, p: David Puttnam, Enigma Prods./Goldcrest/Channel 4) *Remembrance* (d: Gregg, p: Colin Gregg Film Prods., for Channel 4) *Scrubbers* (d: Zetterling, p: HandMade) *An Unsuitable Job for a Woman* (d: Petit, p: Boyd's, for Goldcrest) *Victor/Victoria* (d: Edwards, p: Peerford)
1983	IRA terrorism continues; Christmas bombing, Harrods, London Welsh miners' strike BBC and ITV Companies begin "breakfast TV" programming Death of Sir Adrian Boult, Sir Kenneth Clark, Richard Llewellyn, Sir William	Quota abolished by Parliament *Gandhi* wins eight Oscars Producers and dirs. propose reduction of Eady levy on cinema admissions; also propose tax on television, cable, and satellite film sales to support production fund	*Ascendancy* (d: Bennett, p: BFI Prod. Bd./Channel 4) *The Dresser* (d: Yates, p: World Film Services, for Col./Goldcrest) *Educating Rita* (d: Gilbert, p: Acorn) *The Gold Diggers* (d: Potter, p: BFI Prod. Bd.)

	Selected Historical and Cultural Events, including Radio and Television	**Balcon and the British Film Industry**	**Selected British Films**
1983, continued	Walton	Feature films produced in Britain: 42 Twelve times as many people watch films on television as in cinemas Television-funded films proliferate. Channel 4 becomes major source of financing; of 15 British films shown at London Film Festival, 11 involve financing from TV, nine by Channel 4 Death of Georges Auric, David Macdonald, David Niven, Sir Ralph Richardson	*Local Hero* (d: Forsyth, p: David Puttnam, Enigma Prods./Goldcrest) *Merry Christmas Mr. Lawrence* (d: Oshima, p: The Recorded Picture Co.) *Monty Python's The Meaning of Life* (d: Jones, p: Celandine Films/Monty Python Partnership, for Universal) *The Ploughman's Lunch* (d: Eyre, p: Greenpoint/A.C. and D./ Goldcrest/Channel 4) *Red Monarch* (d: Gold, p: David Puttnam, Enigma Prods./Goldcrest/Channel 4) *Terence Davies Trilogy* (completed): *Children* ('76), *Madonna and Child* ('80), *Death and Transfiguration* ('83) (d: Davies, p: BFI Prod. Bd./ Natl. Film School/Greater London Arts Assn.)
1984	Common Market deliberates status of Great Britain Miners' strike York Minster fire Th: *Benefactors* (Frayn), *The Common Pursuit* (Gray), *Starlight Express*, musical (Webber) Death of Sir John Betjeman, J. B. Priestley	Chancellor of Exchequer's proposed budget (effective 1986) decreases financial incentives for foreign investment in domestic prod. (e.g., capital allowances to be restructured; Britain's 60 percent income tax to be applicable to visiting actors and dirs.) United British Artists, film, theater, and cable co., organized; founding members: Richard Johnson, Glenda Jackson, Diana Rigg, John Hurt, Albert Finney, Harold Pinter Fire destroys 007 stage, Pinewood Studios Death of Richard Burton, Thorold Dickinson, Walter Forde, Joseph Losey, James Mason, Paul Rotha	*Another Country* (d: Kanievska, p: Castlezone, for Goldcrest/NFFC) *The Bounty* (d: Donaldson, p: Bounty Pictures/De Laurentiis) *Cal* (d: O'Connor, p: David Puttnam, Enigma Prods./Goldcrest) *The Far Pavilions* (d: Duffell, p: Geoffrey Reeve, for Goldcrest/Home Box Office) *Give My Regards to Broad Street* (d: Webb, p: MPL Communications) *Greystoke...* (d: Hudson, p: WEA Records, for WB) *The Killing Fields* (d: Joffe, p: David Puttnam, Enigma Prods./Goldcrest) *Nineteen Eighty-Four* (d: Radford, p: Virgin Films) *Passage to India* (d: Lean, p: Brabourne and Goodwin, for Goldcrest/Thorn EMI)
1985		British Film Year 50th anniversary of founding of Natl. Film Archive	

Filmography

Geoff Brown and Rachael Low

THIS FILMOGRAPHY was originally compiled for the German monograph *Der Produzent: Michael Balcon und der englische Film,* published in 1981 on the occasion of a Balcon retrospective at the Berlin Film Festival. Grateful acknowledgment is made to Catherine A. Surowiec and Howard Feinstein of The Museum of Modern Art's Department of Film for their additions to and emendations of the material for this publication.

NOTES

The films are listed by date of production. If the release date—that of the first public showing—differs from the year of production, it appears at the end of the entry (in a few instances, the date of the first trade showing is used instead). Titles throughout are those assigned at the film's original British release; alternate titles are listed as well, including those for U.S. release. All films are features, unless otherwise noted. Exceptions are featurettes (40–60 min) and shorts (less than 40 min). Full credits for films shown in the exhibition *British Film* at The Museum of Modern Art are available in the program notes accompanying the series.

KEY TO ABBREVIATIONS

Assoc Pr: Associate Producer
Pr: Producer
Prod Staff: Production Staff
Co-Pr: Co-Producer
Prod Sup: Production Supervisor
Sup: Supervisor
Dir: Director
Co-Dir: Co-Director
Asst. Dir: Assistant Director
Sc: Screenwriter/screenplay
Co-Sc: Co-Screenwriter
Dial: Dialogue writer
Add Dial: Additional dialogue written by
Add Scenes: Additional scenes written by
Adapt: Adaptation by/Adapter
Intertitles: Intertitles written by
Comm: Commentary
Narr: Narration
Ph: Cinematographer
Ed: Editor
Sup Ed: Supervising Editor
A.D.: Art Director/Art direction by
Prod Des: Production Designer/Production Design by
collab: Collaborator
Mus: Music composed by
Mus Arr: Music arranged by
Mus Dir: Music Director
Lyr: Lyrics by
Add Songs: Additional songs by
Rel: Released

1921

The Story of Oil. Victory Motion Pictures, for the Anglo-American Oil Company. *Pr:* Michael Balcon, Sidney Bernstein. *Dir:* Victor Saville (compiled and adapted from **The Conquest of Oil,** U.S., 1919, made by the U.S. Bureau of Mines and The Standard Oil Company)

Liquid Sunshine. Victory Motion Pictures, for the Anglo-American Oil Company. *Pr:* Michael Balcon, Sidney Bernstein. *Dir:* Victor Saville (compiled and adpated from **The Conquest of Oil,** U.S., 1919, made by the U.S. Bureau of Mines and The Standard Oil Company)

1923

Woman to Woman. Balcon-Saville-Freedman. *Dir:* Graham Cutts. *Sc:* Cutts, Alfred Hitchcock, based on the play by Michael Morton. *Ph:* Claude McDonnell. *Ed:* Alma Reville. *A.D.:* Hitchcock. *With:* Betty Compson, Clive Brook, Josephine Earle. *Rel:* 1924

1924

The White Shadow/U.S.: **White Shadows.** Balcon-Saville-Freedman. *Dir:* Graham Cutts. *Sc:* Cutts, Alfred Hitchcock, based on a novel by Michael Morton. *Ph:* Claude McDonnell. *Ed/A.D.:* Hitchcock. *With:* Betty Compson, Clive Brook

The Prude's Fall. Balcon-Saville-Freedman. *Dir:* Graham Cutts. *Sc/A.D.:* Alfred Hitchcock. *Ph:* Hal Young. *With:* Jane Novak, Julanne Johnston, Warwick Ward

The Passionate Adventure. Gainsborough. *Dir:* Graham Cutts. *Sc:* Alfred Hitchcock, Michael Morton. *Ph:* Claude McDonnell. *A.D.:* Hitchcock. *With:* Alice Joyce, Clive Brook, Lillian Hall-Davies, Victor McLaglen

1925

The Blackguard. Gainsborough/UFA. *Co-Pr:* Erich Pommer. *Dir:* Graham Cutts. *Sc/A.D.:* Alfred Hitchcock. *Ph:* Theodor Sparkuhl. *With:* Walter Rilla, Jane Novak, Bernhard Goetzke. Filmed in Berlin

The Rat. Gainsborough. *Dir:* Graham Cutts. *Sc:* Cutts, from the play by David L'Estrange [Ivor Novello and Constance Collier]. *Ph:* Hal Young. *A.D.:* C. W. Arnold. *With:* Ivor Novello, Mae Marsh, Isabel Jeans. *Rel:* 1926

Gainsborough Burlesque Films (series). Gainsborough. *Dir:* Adrian Brunel. *Sc:* Brunel, J. O. C. Orton, Edwin Greenwood. *Ph:* Henry Harris. *With:* Adrian Brunel, Mrs. Miles Mander, Jack Buchanan. **The Typical Budget. Cut It Out: A Day in the Life of a Censor. Battling Bruisers. The Blunderland of Big Game. So This Is Jollygood.** Shorts

1926

The Steve Donoghue Series. Gainsborough/C & M Productions. *Dir:* Walter West. *Ph:* Hal Young. **Riding for a King.** *With:* Steve Donoghue, Carlyle Blackwell, June, Miles Mander. **Beating the Book.** *With:* Donoghue, Blackwell, Violet Hopson. **The Golden Spurs.** *With:* Donoghue, Irene Russell. **The Stolen Favourite.** *With:* Donoghue, Lillian Pitchford. Shorts

The Sea Urchin. Gainsborough. *Dir/Sc:* Graham Cutts, based on the play by John Hastings Turner. *Ph:* Hal Young. *A.D.:* C. W. Arnold. *With:* Betty Balfour, George Hackathorne.

The Pleasure Garden. Gainsborough/Emelka (Münchener Lichtspielkunst AG). *Co-Pr:* Erich Pommer. *Dir:* Alfred Hitchcock. *Sc:* Eliot Stannard, based on the novel by Oliver Sandys. *Ph:* Gaetano di Ventimiglia. *A.D.:* Ludwig Reiber, C. W. Arnold. *With:* Virginia Valli, Carmelita Geraghty, Miles Mander, John Stuart, Nita Naldi. *Rel:* 1927. Filmed in Munich

The Triumph of the Rat. Gainsborough/Piccadilly. *Assoc Pr:* Carlyle Blackwell. *Dir:* Graham Cutts. *Sc:* Cutts, Reginald Fogwell. *Titles:* Roland Pertwee. *Ph:* Hal Young. *A.D.:* Bertram Evans. *With:* Ivor Novello, Isabel Jeans. *Rel:* 1927

The Lodger: A Story of the London Fog/U.S.: ***The Case of Jonathan Drew.*** Gainsborough. *Dir:* Alfred Hitchcock. *Sc:* Hitchcock, Eliot Stannard, based on the novel by Mrs. Marie Belloc Lowndes. *Titles:* Ivor Montagu. *Intertitle design:* E. McKnight Kauffer. *Ph:* Hal Young, Gaetano di Ventimiglia. *Ed:* Montagu. *A.D.:* C.W. Arnold, Bertram Evans. *With:* Ivor Novello, June, Malcolm Keen.

The Mountain Eagle/U.S.: ***Fear O'God.*** Gainsborough/Emelka (Münchener Lichtspielkunst AG). *Dir:* Alfred Hitchcock. *Sc:* Eliot Stannard. *Story:* Charles Lapworth. *Ph:* Gaetano di Ventimiglia. *A.D.:* Willy and Ludwig Reiber. *With:* Bernhard Goetzke, Nita Naldi, Malcolm Keen. *Rel:* 1927. Filmed in Munich

---------------------- 1927 ----------------------

Blighty. Gainsborough/Piccadilly. *Assoc. Pr:* Carlyle Blackwell. *Dir:* Adrian Brunel. *Sc:* Eliot Stannard. *Story:* Ivor Montagu, Charles McEvoy. *Ph:* J. J. Cox. *Sup Ed:* Montagu. *A.D.:* Bertram Evans. *With:* Ellaline Terriss, Lillian Hall-Davies, Jameson Thomas, Nadia Sibirskaïa, Godfrey Winn. *Rel:* 1928

The Queen Was in the Parlour/U.S.: ***Forbidden Love.*** Gainsborough/Piccadilly/UFA (FPG Film Produktion GmbH). *Pr:* Herman Fellner. *Dir:* Graham Cutts. *Sc:* Cutts, based on the play by Noël Coward. *Ph:* Otto Kanturek. *A.D.:* O.F. Werndorff. *With:* Lili Damita, Paul Richter, Harry Liedtke, Rudolf Klein-Rogge. *Rel:* 1928. Filmed in Berlin

Downhill/U.S.: ***When Boys Leave Home.*** Gainsborough. *Dir:* Alfred Hitchcock. *Sc:* Eliot Stannard, based on the play by David L'Estrange [Ivor Novello and Constance Collier]. *Ph:* Claude McDonnell. *Ed:* Lionel Rich, Ivor Montagu. *A.D.:* Bertram Evans. *With:* Ivor Novello, Isabel Jeans, Ian Hunter, Lillian Braithwaite, Annette Benson, Robin Irvine.

The Rolling Road. Gainsborough/Piccadilly. *Assoc Pr:* Carlyle Blackwell. *Dir:* Graham Cutts. *Sc:* Violet E. Powell. *Ph:* Hal Young. *Ed:* Ivor Montagu. *A.D.:* Bertram Evans. *With:* Carlyle Blackwell, Flora le Breton

Easy Virtue. Gainsborough. *Dir:* Alfred Hitchcock. *Sc:* Eliot Stannard, based on the play by Noël Coward. *Ph:* Claude McDonnell. *Ed:* Ivor Montagu. *A.D.:* Clifford Pember. *With:* Isabel Jeans, Franklin Dyall, Robin Irvine, Ian Hunter, Benita Hume

The Ghost Train. Gainsborough/UFA (FPG Film der Phoebus-Film AG). *Pr:* Herman Fellner. *Dir:* Geza von Bolvary. *Sc:* Benno Vigny, Adolf Lantz, based on the play by Arnold Ridley. *Ph:* Otto Kanturek. *A.D.:* O. F. Werndorff. *With:* Guy Newall, Ilse Bois. *Rel:* 1928. Filmed in Berlin

One of the Best. Gainsborough/Piccadilly. *Assoc Pr:* Carlyle Blackwell. *Dir:* T. Hayes Hunter. *Sc:* Patrick L. Mannock, based on the play by Seymour Hicks and George Edwardes. *Ph:* James Wilson. *A.D.:* Clifford Pember. *With:* Carlyle Blackwell, Walter Butler, Eve Gray, Elsa Lanchester, Harold Huth. *Rel:* 1928

---------------------- 1928 ----------------------

The Constant Nymph. Gainsborough. *Assoc Pr:* Basil Dean. *Dir:* Adrian Brunel. *Sc:* Dean, Margaret Kennedy, Alma Reville, based on the play by Kennedy and Dean, and Kennedy's novel. *Ph:* James Wilson, Dave Gobett. *A.D.:* George Harris. *With:* Ivor Novello, Mabel Poulton, Benita Hume, Frances Doble, Mary Clare, Elsa Lanchester

The Vortex. Gainsborough. *Assoc Pr:* S. C. Balcon. *Dir:* Adrian Brunel. *Sc:* Eliot Stannard, based on the play by Noël Coward. *Intertitles:* Roland Pertwee. *Ph:* James Wilson. *A.D.:* Clifford Pember. *With:* Ivor Novello, Willette Kershaw, Frances Doble

A South Sea Bubble. Gainsborough. *Dir:* T. Hayes Hunter. *Sc:* Angus MacPhail, Alma Reville, based on the novel by Roland Pertwee. *Ph:* Walter Blakeley. *Ed:* Arthur Tavares. *With:* Ivor Novello, Benita Hume, Annette Benson. *Rel:* 1929

The Gallant Hussar. Gainsborough/Felsom-Film, for Deutsche Vereins Film AG (Defa, German Fox). *Pr:* Herman Fellner, Josef Somlo. *Dir:* Geza von Bolvary. *Sc:* Dr. A. Bardos, Margarete Maria Langen. *Ph:* Eduard Hoesch. *A.D.:* O. F. Werndorff, Emil Hasler. *With:* Ivor Novello, Evelyn Holt. Filmed in Berlin

A Light Woman/Dolores. Gainsborough. *Dir:* Adrian Brunel. *Sc:* Brunel, Angus MacPhail, Dale Laurence [Mrs. Adey Brunel]. *Ph:* Claude McDonnell. *With:* Benita Hume, Gerald Ames

The First Born. Mander Production Syndicate/Gainsborough. *Assoc Pr/Dir:* Miles Mander. *Sc:* Mander, Alma Reville, based on Mander's play *Those Common People*. *Titles:* Ian Dalrymple. *Ph:* Walter Blakeley. *Ed:* Arthur Tavares. *A.D.:* C. W. Arnold. *With:* Miles Mander, Madeleine Carroll, John Loder. *Rel:* 1929

---------------------- 1929 ----------------------

Number Seventeen. Gainsborough/Felsom-Film, for Deutsche Vereins Film AG (Defa, German Fox). *Pr:* Herman Fellner, Josef Somlo. *Dir:* Geza von Bolvary. *Sc:* Benno Vigny, Adolf Lantz, based on the play by J. Jefferson Farjeon. *Ph:* Eduard Hoesch. *A.D.:* O. F. Werndorff. *With:* Guy Newall, Lien Dyers. Filmed in Berlin. Silent and sound versions

The Return of the Rat. Gainsborough. *Dir:* Graham Cutts. *Sc:* Angus MacPhail, Edgar C. Middleton, A. Neil Lyons. *Ph:* Roy Overbaugh. *A.D.:* Alan McNab. *With:* Ivor Novello, Isabel Jeans, Mabel Poulton, Marie Ault, Gordon Harker. Silent version *rel.* 1929; sound version *rel.* 1930

The Wrecker. Gainsborough. *Assoc Pr:* S. C. Balcon. *Dir:* Geza von Bolvary. *Sc:* Angus MacPhail, based on the play by Arnold Ridley and Bernard Merivale. *Intertitles:* Reginald Berkeley. *Ph:* Otto Kanturek, James Wilson. *Ed:* Arthur Tavares. *A.D.:* Oscar Werndorff. *With:* Carlyle Blackwell, Benita Hume, Gordon Harker. Silent version completed 1928; *rel.* with sound, 1929

Armistice. Gainsborough. *Assoc Pr/Dir:* Victor Saville. *Sc:* Poem "In Flanders Field," by John McCrae. *With:* Henry Ainley, Bands of H.M. Coldstream Guards, H.M. Welsh Guards and Men's Choir. Short.

In a Monastery Garden. Gainsborough. *Dir:* Adrian Brunel. *Mus:* "In a Monastery Garden," by Albert W. Ketèlbey. *With:* Geoffrey Gwyther, Men's Choir and Orchestra. Short

City of Play. Gainsborough. *Dir:* Denison Clift. *Sc:* Angus MacPhail, Clift. *Story:* Clift. *Ph:* Claude McDonnell. *With:* Chili Bouchier, Pat Aherne, Andrews Engelmann. Silent version completed July 1929; *rel.* with sound later in year

Taxi for Two. Gainsborough. *Dir/Sc:* Alexander Esway. *Dial Dir:* Denison Clift. *Dial:* Ian Dalrymple, Angus MacPhail.

Ph: James Wilson. *Ed:* Dalrymple. *With:* John Stuart, Mabel Poulton, Gordon Harker. Silent and sound versions

Woman to Woman. Gainsborough/Burlington/Tiffany-Stahl. *Dir:* Victor Saville. *Sc:* Saville, Nicholas Fodor, based on the play by Michael Morton. *Ph:* Benjamin Kline. *With:* Betty Compson, Juliette Compton, George Barraud. *Rel:* 1930. Filmed in Hollywood

──────────────── **1930** ────────────────

Sugar and Spice (series). Gainsborough. *Dir:* Alexander Oumansky. **Alfresco.** *With:* Hal Swain's Kit Kat Band, Elsie Carlisle. **Toyland.** *With:* The Benedetti Brothers, Freddie Bartholomew. **Black and White.** *With:* Elsie Carlisle, Johnny Nit. **Classic v. Jazz.** *With:* Hal Swain's Kit Kat Band, the Adajio Trio. **Gypsy Land.** *With:* Balam, Sedelli, Valli, the Adajio Trio. **Dusky Melodies.** *With:* Johnny Nit, Lew Hardcastle's Band, the Gainsborough Girls. Made as a revue feature, **The Gainsborough Picture Show,** but *rel.* as shorts only

Gainsborough Gems (series). Gainsborough. **Martini and His Band No. 1. Martini and His Band No. 2. Billie Barnes. George Mozart in Domestic Troubles. Hal Swain's Sax-o-Five. Elsie Percival and Ray Raymond. Pete Mandell and His Rhythm Masters No. 1. Pete Mandell and His Rhythm Masters No. 2. Dick Henderson. The Blue Boys No. 1. The Blue Boys No. 2. Lewis Hardcastle's Dusky Syncopaters. The Walsh Brothers. The Volga Singers. Ena Reiss.** Shorts

Just for a Song. Gainsborough. *Dir/Sc:* V. Gareth Gundrey. *Story:* Desmond Carter. *Ph:* James Wilson. *With:* Lillian Davis, Constance Carpenter, Cyril Ritchard, Dick Henderson. Contained color sequence

The Crooked Billet. Gainsborough. *Dir:* Adrian Brunel. *Sc:* Angus MacPhail, based on the play by Dion Titheradge. *Ph:* Claude McDonnell. *Ed:* Ian Dalrymple. *Mus Dir:* Louis Levy. *With:* Carlyle Blackwell, Madeleine Carroll, Miles Mander, Gordon Harker. Silent version completed 1929; sound version *rel.* 1930

Journey's End. Gainsborough/Welsh-Pearson/Tiffany-Stahl. *Assoc Pr:* George Pearson. *Dir:* James Whale. *Sc:* Joseph Moncure March, based on the play by R. C. Sherriff. *Ph:* Benjamin Kline. *Ed:* Claude Berkeley. *A.D.:* Hervey Libbert. *With:* Colin Clive, Anthony Bushell, David Manners, Billy Bevan. Filmed in Hollywood

Balaclava/U.S.: **Jaws of Hell.** Gainsborough. *Dir:* Maurice Elvey. *Dial Dir:* Milton Rosmer. *Sc:* Angus MacPhail, W. P. Lipscomb, V. Gareth Gundrey, Rosmer, Robert Stevenson. *Story:* Boyd Cable [Ernest Ewart], based on the poem *The Charge of the Light Brigade* by Alfred Lord Tennyson. *Ph:* James Wilson. *Ed:* Arthur Tavares, Ian Dalrymple. *Mus Dir:* Louis Levy. *With:* Benita Hume, Cyril McLaglen, Miles Mander. Silent version completed 1928, never released; sound version *rel.* 1930

Symphony in Two Flats. Gainsborough. *Dir:* V. Gareth Gundrey. *Sc:* Angus MacPhail, Gundrey, based on the play by Ivor Novello. *Ph:* James Wilson. *With:* Ivor Novello, Benita Hume, Cyril Ritchard. *Rel:* 1931

Ashes. Gainsborough. *Dir:* Frank Birch. *Sc:* Angus MacPhail. *With:* Ernest Thesiger, Herbert Mundin, Elsa Lanchester. Short

A Warm Corner. Gainsborough. *Dir:* Victor Saville. *Sc:* Angus MacPhail, Saville. *Ph:* Fred A. Young. *A.D.:* Walter Murton. *With:* Leslie Henson, Heather Thatcher, Belle Chrystall. *Rel:* 1931

──────────────── **1931** ────────────────

P. C. Josser. Gainsborough. *Dir:* Milton Rosmer. *Sc:* Con West, Herbert Sargent, based on West's music hall sketch "The Police Force." *Ph:* William Shenton, Horace Wheddon. *With:* Ernie Lotinga

Hot Heir. Gainsborough. *Assoc Pr:* S. C. Balcon. *Dir:* W. P. Kellino. *Sc:* Angus MacPhail. *Songs:* J. J. Gilbert, Noel Gay. *With:* Charles Austin, Bobbie Comber. Short

Harry Lauder Songs (series). Gainsborough/Welsh-Pearson. *Dir:* George Pearson. *With:* Harry Lauder. **I Love a Lassie. Somebody's Waiting for Me. I Love to Be a Sailor. Roamin' in the Gloamin'. Tobermory. Nanny. The Saftest of the Family. She's My Daisy.** Shorts

Who Killed Doc Robin? Gainsborough. *Assoc Pr:* S. C. Balcon. *Dir:* W. P. Kellino. *Sc:* Angus MacPhail. *With:* Clifford Heatherley, Dennis Wyndham. Short

Bull Rushes. Gainsborough. *Assoc Pr:* S. C. Balcon. *Dir:* W. P. Kellino. *Sc:* Angus MacPhail. *With:* Wallace Lupino, Reginald Gardiner. Short. *Rel:* 1932

Third Time Lucky. Gainsborough. *Dir:* Walter Forde. *Sc:* Angus MacPhail, based on the play by Arnold Ridley. *Ph:* William Shenton. *Ed:* Ian Dalrymple. *A.D.:* Walter Murton. *With:* Bobby Howes, Gordon Harker, Garry Marsh

The Sport of Kings. Gainsborough. *Dir:* Victor Saville. *Sc:* Angus MacPhail, based on the play by Ian Hay. *Ph:* Fred A. Young. *With:* Leslie Henson, Hugh Wakefield, Gordon Harker

The Stronger Sex. Gainsborough. *Dir:* V. Gareth Gundrey. *Sc:* Angus MacPhail, Gundrey, based on the play by John Valentine. *Ph:* James Wilson. *With:* Colin Clive, Adrianne Allen, Gordon Harker, Elsa Lanchester

Aroma of the South Seas. Gainsborough. *Dir:* W. P. Kellino. *Sc:* Angus MacPhail. *With:* Reginald Gardiner, Wallace Lupino, Moore Marriott. Short

The Ringer. Gainsborough/British Lion. *Dir:* Walter Forde. *Sc:* Angus MacPhail, Robert Stevenson, based on the play *The Ringer* and the novel *The Gaunt Stranger* by Edgar Wallace. *Ph:* Alex Bryce, Leslie Rowson. *Ed:* Ian Dalrymple. *A.D.:* Norman Arnold. *With:* Franklin Dyall, Gordon Harker, Carol Goodner

The Lady of the Lake. Gainsborough. *Dir:* James A. Fitzpatrick. *Sc:* Fitzpatrick, Angus MacPhail, based on the poem by Sir Walter Scott. *With:* Percy Marmont, Benita Hume. Silent version completed 1928, never released; sound version *rel.* 1931

A Night in Montmartre. Gainsborough. *Dir:* Leslie Hiscott. *Sc:* Angus MacPhail, based on the play by Miles Malleson and Walter Peacock. *Ph:* Sydney Blythe. *With:* Franklin Dyall, Hugh Williams, Heather Angel, Kay Hammond. *Rel:* 1932

The Man They Couldn't Arrest. Gainsborough. *Dir:* T. Hayes Hunter. *Sc:* Angus MacPhail, Hunter, Arthur Wimperis. *Ph:* Leslie Rowson. *With:* Hugh Wakefield, Gordon Harker. *Rel:* 1932

My Old China. Gainsborough. *Assoc Pr:* S. C. Balcon. *Dir:* W. P. Kellino. *Sc:* Angus MacPhail. *With:* Clifford Heatherley, Reginald Gardiner, Constance Carpenter. Short

The Ghost Train. Gainsborough. *Assoc Pr:* Philip Samuel. *Dir:* Walter Forde. *Sc:* Angus MacPhail, Lajos Biro, based on the play by Arnold Ridley. *Ph:* Leslie Rowson. *Ed:* Ian Dalrymple. *A.D.:* Walter Murton. *With:* Jack Hulbert, Cicely Courtneidge, Donald Calthrop, Ann Todd, Cyril Raymond, Angela Baddeley. *Rel:* 1932

Hindle Wakes. Gainsborough. *Dir:* Victor Saville. *Sc:* Angus MacPhail, Saville, based on the play by Stanley Houghton. *Ph:* Mutz Greenbaum. *Ed:* R. E. Dearing. *A.D.:* Andrew Mazzei. *Mus Dir:* W. L. Trytel. *With:* Sybil Thorndike, Edmund Gwenn, Belle Chrystall, John Stuart, Norman McKinnell. *Rel:* 1932

The Calendar/U.S.: **Bachelor's Folly.** Gainsborough/British

Lion. *Assoc Pr:* Herbert Smith. *Dir:* T. Hayes Hunter. *Sc:* Angus MacPhail, Robert Stevenson, Bryan Wallace, based on the play by Edgar Wallace. *Ph:* Bernard Knowles, Alex Bryce. *Ed:* Ian Dalrymple. *With:* Herbert Marshall, Edna Best, Gordon Harker, Nigel Bruce. *Rel:* 1932

Michael and Mary. Gainsborough. *Dir:* Victor Saville. *Sc:* Angus MacPhail, Robert Stevenson. *Dial:* Monckton Hoffe. *Adapt:* Saville, based on the play by A. A. Milne. *Ph:* Leslie Rowson. *Ed:* Ian Dalrymple, John Goldman. *A.D.:* Vetchinsky. *Mus Dir:* Louis Levy. *With:* Herbert Marshall, Edna Best, Elizabeth Allan, Frank Lawton

Sunshine Susie/U.S.: **The Office Girl.** Gainsborough. *Dir:* Victor Saville. *Sc:* Robert Stevenson, Angus MacPhail, Saville, Noel Wood-Smith. *Adapt:* Saville, from the German sc. *Die Privatsekretärin* by Franz Schulz. *Ph:* Mutz Greenbaum. *Ed:* Ian Dalrymple. *A.D.:* Vetchinsky. *Mus:* Paul Abraham. *Lyr:* Desmond Carter. *Mus Dir:* Louis Levy. *With:* Renate Müller, Jack Hulbert, Owen Nares, Morris Harvey. *Rel:* 1932

———————————— 1932 ————————————

Lord Babs. Gainsborough. *Dir:* Walter Forde. *Sc:* Angus MacPhail, Clifford Grey, based on the play by Keble Howard. *Ph:* Leslie Rowson. *Ed:* Ian Dalrymple. *A.D.:* Vetchinsky. *Songs:* Vivian Ellis, Grey. *With:* Bobby Howes, Jean Colin, Alfred Drayton

The Frightened Lady/U.S.: **Criminal at Large.** Gainsborough/British Lion. *Assoc Pr:* Herbert Smith. *Dir:* T. Hayes Hunter. *Sc:* Angus MacPhail, Bryan Wallace, based on the play by Edgar Wallace. *Ph:* Bernard Knowles, Alex Bryce. *Ed:* Ralph Kemplen, Ian Dalrymple. *A.D.:* Norman Arnold. *With:* Norman McKinnell, Cathleen Nesbitt, Emlyn Williams, Gordon Harker

The Faithful Heart/U.S.: **Faithful Hearts.** Gainsborough. *Dir:* Victor Saville. *Sc:* Robert Stevenson, Angus MacPhail, Lajos Biro, Saville. *Add Dial:* W. P. Lipscomb. *Adapt:* Saville, based on the play by Monckton Hoffe. *Ph:* Mutz Greenbaum. *Ed:* Ian Dalrymple. *A.D.:* Vetchinsky. *Mus Dir:* Louis Levy. *With:* Herbert Marshall, Edna Best, Anne Grey, Athole Stewart

White Face. Gainsborough/British Lion. *Dir:* T. Hayes Hunter. *Sc:* Angus MacPhail, Bryan Wallace, based on the play *Persons Unknown* by Edgar Wallace. *Ph:* Bernard Knowles, Alex Bryce. *A.D.:* Norman Arnold. *With:* Hugh Williams, Gordon Harker, Nora Swinburne

Jack's the Boy/U.S.: **Night and Day.** Gainsborough. *Dir:* Walter Forde. *Sc:* W. P. Lipscomb. *Story:* Jack Hulbert, Douglas Furber. *Ph:* Leslie Rowson. *Ed:* Ian Dalrymple, John Goldman. *A.D.:* Vetchinsky. *Songs:* Vivian Ellis, Douglas Furber. *Mus Dir:* Louis Levy. *With:* Jack Hulbert, Cicely Courtneidge, Winifred Shotter

Love on Wheels. Gainsborough. *Dir:* Victor Saville. *Sc:* Robert Stevenson. *Dial:* Douglas Furber. *Adapt:* Saville, Angus MacPhail, based on a German screenplay. *Ph:* Mutz Greenbaum. *Ed:* Ian Dalrymple, Derek Twist. *A.D.:* Vetchinsky. *Songs:* Jean Gilbert, Douglas Furber. *Mus Dir:* Louis Levy. *With:* Jack Hulbert, Gordon Harker, Leonora Corbett, Edmund Gwenn

Baroud/U.S.: **Love in Morocco.** Rex Ingram Productions. *Pr/Dir:* Rex Ingram. *Co-Dir:* Alice Terry. *Sc:* Ingram, Peter Spencer. *Story:* Ingram, Benno Vigny. *Ph:* Léonce-Henri Burel, P. Portier, A. Allegier, Marcel Lucien, T. Tomatis. *Ed:* Lothar Wolff. *A.D.:* Jean Lafitte, Henri Menessier. *Mus Dir:* Louis Levy. *With:* Rex Ingram, Rosita Garcia, Laura Salerni, Dennis Hoey, Pierre Batcheff. *Rel:* 1933. Filmed in Morocco and Nice

Marry Me. Gainsborough. *Dir:* William Thiele. *Sc:* Angus MacPhail, Anthony Asquith, from the German sc. *Mädchen zum Heiraten.* *Ph:* Bernard Knowles. *Mus:* Michael Krausz. *Lyr:*

Desmond Carter, Frank Eyton. *With:* Renate Müller, Harry Green, George Robey, Ian Hunter, Maurice Evans. *Rel:* 1933

There Goes the Bride. Gainsborough/British Lion. *Dir:* Albert de Courville. *Sc:* W. P. Lipscomb, Fred Raymond, based on the German sc. *Ich Bleib' bei Dir.* *Ph:* Mutz Greenbaum, Alex Bryce. *A.D.:* Norman Arnold. *Songs:* Noel Gay, Fred Raymond. *With:* Jessie Matthews, Owen Nares, Carol Goodner. *Rel:* 1933

Tell Me To-Night/U.S.: **Be Mine Tonight.** Cine-Allianz Tonfilm. *Pr:* Herman Fellner, Josef Somlo. *Dir:* Anatole Litvak. *Sc:* J. O. C. Orton, based on the German sc. *Das Lied einer Nacht.* *Ph:* Fritz Arno Wagner. *A.D.:* Werner Schlichting. *Mus:* Puccini, Flotow, Rossini, di Capua, Mischa Spoliansky. *Eng Lyr:* Frank Eyton. *With:* Jan Kiepura, Magda Schneider, Sonnie Hale, Edmund Gwenn, Athene Seyler. *Rel:* 1933. Filmed in Germany

Happy Ever After. UFA. *Pr:* Erich Pommer. *Dir:* Paul Martin, Robert Stevenson. *Sc:* Jack Hulbert, Douglas Furber, based on the German sc. *Ein Blonder Traum* by Walter Reisch and Billy Wilder. *With:* Jack Hulbert, Lilian Harvey, Cicely Courtneidge, Sonnie Hale, Edward Chapman. *Rel:* 1933. Filmed in Germany

Rome Express. Gaumont-British. *Assoc Pr:* Philip Samuel. *Dir:* Walter Forde. *Sc:* Sidney Gilliat. *Story:* Clifford Grey. *Ph:* Gunther Krampf. *Ed:* Frederick Y. Smith, Ian Dalrymple. *A.D.:* Andrew Mazzei. *With:* Conrad Veidt, Esther Ralston, Cedric Hardwicke, Gordon Harker, Joan Barry, Donald Calthrop. *Rel:* 1933

After the Ball. Gaumont-British. *Dir:* Milton Rosmer. *Sc:* J. O. C. Orton. *Adapt:* H. M. Harwood, based on the German sc. *Opernredoute.* *Ph:* Percy Strong. *Ed:* Derek Twist. *A.D.:* Alfred Junge. *Mus:* Otto Stransky. *Lyr:* Clifford Grey. *With:* Esther Ralston, Basil Rathbone. *Rel:* 1933

The Midshipmaid. Gaumont-British. *Dir:* Albert de Courville. *Sc:* Stafford Dickens, based on the play by Ian Hay and Commander Stephen King-Hall. *A.D.:* Alfred Junge. *Mus:* Noel Gay. *With:* Jessie Matthews, John Mills, Nigel Bruce, Anthony Bushell, Basil Sydney. *Rel:* 1933

———————————— 1933 ————————————

The Man from Toronto. Gainsborough. *Dir:* Sinclair Hill. *Sc:* W. P. Lipscomb, based on the play by Douglas Murray. *Ph:* Leslie Rowson. *A.D.:* Vetchinsky. *With:* Jessie Matthews, Ian Hunter, Frederick Kerr

They're Off! Gaumont-British. *Pr:* Clayton Hutton. *Dir:* John Rawlins. *With:* Bud Flanagan and Chesney Allen. Short

Sign Please. Gaumont-British. *Pr:* Clayton Hutton. *Dir:* John Rawlins. *Sc:* Sidney Gilliat, based on the sketch "The Salesmen" by Fred Karno. *With:* Charlie Naughton and Jimmie Gold. Short

The Good Companions. Gaumont-British/Welsh-Pearson. *Assoc Pr:* George Pearson. *Prod Staff:* Angus MacPhail, Louis Levy, Ian Dalrymple, George Gunn. *Dir:* Victor Saville. *Sc:* W. P. Lipscomb, based on the novel by J. B. Priestley and the play by Priestley and Edward Knoblock. *Ph:* Bernard Knowles. *Ed:* Frederick Y. Smith. *A.D.:* Alfred Junge. *Mus:* George Posford. *Lyr:* Douglas Furber. *With:* Jessie Matthews, Edmund Gwenn, Mary Glynne, John Gielgud, Max Miller, Finlay Currie

Soldiers of the King/U.S.: **The Woman in Command.** Gainsborough. *Dir:* Maurice Elvey. *Sc:* J. O. C. Orton, W. P. Lipscomb, Jack Hulbert. *Story:* Douglas Furber. *Ph:* Leslie Rowson, Percy Strong. *Ed:* Ian Dalrymple. *A.D.:* Vetchinsky. *Song:* Noel Gay. *Mus Dir:* Louis Levy. *With:* Cicely Courtneidge, Edward Everett Horton, Anthony Bushell, Dorothy Hyson

King of the Ritz. Gainsborough/British Lion. *Assoc Pr:* Herbert Smith. *Dir:* Carmine Gallone. *Sc:* Ivor Montagu, based on the play *Le Roi de Palace. Ph:* Leslie Rowson, Alex Bryce. *Ed:* Arthur Tavares. *A.D.:* Norman Arnold. *Mus:* Raoul Moretti. *Lyr:* Clifford Grey. *With:* Stanley Lupino, Betty Stockfield

Tooth Will Out. Gaumont-British. *Pr:* Clayton Hutton. *Dir:* Frank Cadman. *Sc:* John Dighton, Hugh Stewart, based on a sketch by Fred Karno. *With:* Jack Williams, Joey Porter. Short

F.P. 1. UFA. *Pr:* Erich Pommer. *Dir:* Karl Hartl. *Sc:* Robert Stevenson, based on the German sc. *F.P. 1 Antwortet Nicht* by Walter Reisch and Kurt Siodmak. *With:* Conrad Veidt, Leslie Fenton, Jill Esmond. Filmed in Berlin

The Lucky Number. Gainsborough. *Prod Staff:* Angus MacPhail, Louis Levy, Ian Dalrymple, George Gunn. *Dir/Sc:* Anthony Asquith. *Story:* Franz Schulz. *Ph:* Gunther Krampf, Derick Williams. *Ed:* Dan Birt. *A.D.:* Vetchinsky. *Mus:* Mischa Spoliansky. *Lyr:* Douglas Furber. *With:* Clifford Mollison, Gordon Harker, Joan Wyndham

Sleeping Car. Gaumont-British. *Assoc Pr:* R. B. Wainwright. *Dir:* Anatole Litvak. *Sc:* Franz Schulz. *With:* Madeleine Carroll, Ivor Novello, Laddie Cliff, Kay Hammond, Claude Allister

Post Haste. Gaumont-British. *Pr:* Clayton Hutton. *Dir:* Frank Cadman. *Sc:* Sidney Gilliat, based on the sketch "G.P.O." by Fred Karno. *With:* Jack Williams, Joey Porter. Short

Waltz Time. Gaumont-British. *Pr:* Herman Fellner. *Dir:* William Thiele. *Sc:* A. P. Herbert, based on the operetta *Die Fledermaus. Ed:* Derek Twist. *A.D.:* Alfred Junge. *Mus:* Johann Strauss, Jr. *Mus Dir:* Louis Levy. *With:* Evelyn Laye, Fritz Schultz, Gina Malo

It's a Boy. Gainsborough. *Prod Staff:* Angus MacPhail, Ian Dalrymple, Louis Levy, George Gunn. *Dir:* Tim Whelan. *Sc:* Leslie Howard Gordon, John Paddy Carstairs, based on the play by Austin Melford. *Ph:* Mutz Greenbaum. *Ed:* Harold Young. *A.D.:* Vetchinsky. *With:* Leslie Henson, Edward Everett Horton, Heather Thatcher

The Dreamers. Gaumont-British. *Pr:* Clayton Hutton. *Dir:* Frank Cadman. *Ph:* Stanley Rodwell. *With:* Bud Flanagan and Chesney Allen. Short

Falling for You. Gainsborough. *Prod Staff:* Angus MacPhail, Louis Levy, Ian Dalrymple, George Gunn. *Dir:* Jack Hulbert, Robert Stevenson. *Sc:* Hulbert, Douglas Furber, Stevenson. *Story:* Sidney Gilliat. *Ph:* Bernard Knowles. *Ed:* R. E. Dearing. *A.D.:* Vetchinsky. *Mus:* Vivian Ellis. *Lyr:* Furber. *With:* Jack Hulbert, Cicely Courtneidge, Tamara Desni, Garry Marsh

The Only Girl/U.S.: ***Heart Song.*** UFA. *Pr:* Erich Pommer. *Dir:* Friedrich Hollaender. *Sup:* Robert Stevenson, John Heygate. *Sc:* Stevenson, Heygate, based on the German sc. *Ich und die Kaiserin. Lyr:* Frank Eyton. *With:* Lilian Harvey, Charles Boyer, Mady Christians, Ernest Thesiger, Maurice Evans. Filmed in Berlin

Britannia of Billingsgate. Gaumont-British. *Dir:* Sinclair Hill. *Sc:* Ralph Stock. *Ph:* Mutz Greenbaum. *A.D.:* Alfred Junge. *Mus:* George Posford. *Lyr:* Holt Marvel. *With:* Violet Loraine, Gordon Harker, Kay Hammond, John Mills

The Prince of Wales. Gaumont-British. *Ph:* H.R.H. The Prince of Wales et al. *Ed:* Ian Dalrymple

Orders Is Orders. Gaumont-British. *Dir:* Walter Forde. *Sc:* Sidney Gilliat, Leslie Arliss, based on the play by Ian Hay. *Ph:* Glen MacWilliams. *Ed:* Derek Twist. *A.D.:* Alfred Junge. *With:* Charlotte Greenwood, James Gleason, Ian Hunter, Cedric Hardwicke, Ray Milland. *Rel:* 1934

The Ghoul. Gaumont-British. *Dir:* T. Hayes Hunter. *Sc:* Leonard Hines, Roland Pertwee, John Hastings Turner. *Adapt:* Rupert Downing, based on the novel by Frank King.

Ph: Gunther Krampf. *Ed:* Ian Dalrymple, Dan Birt. *A.D.:* Alfred Junge. *Mus Dir:* Louis Levy. *With:* Boris Karloff, Cedric Hardwicke, Ernest Thesiger, Dorothy Hyson, Anthony Bushell

I Was a Spy. Gaumont-British. *Prod Staff:* Angus MacPhail, Ian Dalrymple, Louis Levy, George Gunn. *Dir:* Victor Saville. *Sc:* W. P. Lipscomb. *Ph:* Charles Van Enger. *Ed:* Frederick Y. Smith. *A.D.:* Alfred Junge. *With:* Madeleine Carroll, Herbert Marshall, Conrad Veidt, Gerald du Maurier, Edmund Gwenn

Early to Bed. UFA. *Pr:* Erich Pommer. *Dir:* Ludwig Berger. *Sc:* Robert Stevenson, based on the German sc. *Ich bei Tag und Du bei Nacht. Mus:* Werner R. Heymann. *Lyr:* Rowland Leigh. *With:* Sonnie Hale, Edmund Gwenn, Fernand Gravey, Heather Angel. Filmed in Berlin

The Fire Raisers. Gaumont-British. *Assoc Pr:* Jerome Jackson. *Dir:* Michael Powell. *Sc:* Powell, Jackson. *Ph:* Leslie Rowson. *Ed:* Derek Twist. *A.D.:* Alfred Junge. *With:* Leslie Banks, Anne Grey, Carol Goodner. *Rel:* 1934

Just Smith. Gaumont-British. *Dir:* Tom Walls. *Sc:* J. O. C. Orton, based on the play *Never Come Back* by Frederick Lonsdale. *A.D.:* Alfred Junge. *With:* Tom Walls, Carol Goodner, Anne Grey

Channel Crossing. Gaumont-British. *Dir:* Milton Rosmer. *Sc:* W. P. Lipscomb, Cyril Campion. *Story:* Lipscomb, Angus MacPhail. *Ph:* Phil Tannura. *Ed:* Dan Birt. *A.D.:* Alfred Junge. *With:* Matheson Lang, Constance Cummings, Edmund Gwenn, Anthony Bushell, Max Miller, Dorothy Dickson, Nigel Bruce

A Cuckoo in the Nest. Gaumont-British. *Prod Staff:* Angus MacPhail, Ian Dalrymple, Louis Levy, George Gunn. *Dir:* Tom Walls. *Sc:* A.R. Rawlinson, based on the play by Ben Travers. *Adapt/Dial:* Travers. *Ph:* Glen MacWilliams. *Ed:* Helen Lewis. *A.D.:* Alfred Junge. *With:* Tom Walls, Ralph Lynn, Robertson Hare, Yvonne Arnaud, Mary Brough

Friday the Thirteenth. Gainsborough. *Prod Staff:* Angus MacPhail, Ian Dalrymple, George Gunn, Louis Levy. *Dir:* Victor Saville. *Sc:* G. H. Moresby-White. *Dial:* Emlyn Williams. *Story:* Sidney Gilliat, Moresby-White. *Ph:* Charles Van Enger. *Ed:* R. E. Dearing. *A.D.:* Alfred Junge, Vetchinsky. *With:* Jessie Matthews, Ralph Richardson, Robertson Hare, Edmund Gwenn, Gordon Harker, Max Miller, Emlyn Williams, Frank Lawton, Belle Chrystall, Ursula Jeans, Sonnie Hale

Aunt Sally/U.S.: ***Along Came Sally.*** Gainsborough. *Dir:* Tim Whelan. *Sc:* Guy Bolton. *Story:* Whelan. *Ph:* Charles Van Enger. *Ed:* Derek Twist. *A.D.:* Vetchinsky. *Mus:* Harry Woods. *With:* Cicely Courtneidge, Sam Hardy, Billy Milton. *Rel:* 1934

The Constant Nymph. Gaumont-British. *Dir:* Basil Dean. *Sc:* Dean, Margaret Kennedy, Dorothy Farnum, based on the play by Kennedy and Dean and the novel by Kennedy. *Ph:* Mutz Greenbaum. *A.D.:* Alfred Junge. *Mus:* Eugene Goossens. *With:* Brian Aherne, Victoria Hopper, Leonora Corbett. *Rel:* 1934

Turkey Time. Gaumont-British. *Dir:* Tom Walls. *Sc:* Ben Travers, based on his play. *Ph:* Charles Van Enger. *A.D.:* Alfred Junge. *With:* Tom Walls, Ralph Lynn, Robertson Hare, Dorothy Hyson. *Rel:* 1934

───────────────── **1934** ─────────────────

Jack Ahoy! Gaumont-British. *Dir:* Walter Forde. *Sc:* Sidney Gilliat, J. O. C. Orton. *Dial:* Jack Hulbert, Leslie Arliss, Gerard Fairlie, Austin Melford. *Ph:* Bernard Knowles. *Ed:* Ralph Kemplen. *A.D.:* Alfred Junge. *Mus:* Bretton Byrd. *With:* Jack Hulbert

The Night of the Party/U.S.: ***The Murder Party.*** Gaumont-

British. *Assoc Pr:* Jerome Jackson. *Dir:* Michael Powell. *Sc:* Ralph Smart, based on the play by Roland Pertwee and John Hastings Turner. *Ph:* Glen MacWilliams. *A.D.:* Alfred Junge. *With:* Leslie Banks, Ian Hunter, Ernest Thesiger

Red Ensign/U.S.: **Strike!** Gaumont-British. *Assoc Pr:* Jerome Jackson. *Dir:* Michael Powell. *Sc:* Powell, Jackson. *Ph:* Leslie Rowson. *Ed:* Geoffrey Barkas. *A.D.:* Alfred Junge. *With:* Leslie Banks, Carol Goodner, Frank Vosper

Waltzes from Vienna/U.S.: **Strauss' Great Waltz.** Tom Arnold Productions. *Pr:* Tom Arnold. *Dir:* Alfred Hitchcock. *Sc:* Guy Bolton, Alma Reville, based on the musical play by Bolton adapted from the German play *Walzerkrieg.* *Ph:* Glen MacWilliams. *Ed:* Charles Frend. *A.D.:* Oscar Werndorff. *Mus:* Johann Strauss (Sr. and Jr.). *Mus Dir:* Louis Levy. *With:* Jessie Matthews, Edmund Gwenn, Fay Compton, Esmond Knight, Frank Vosper. Filmed at Gaumont-British studios, Shepherd's Bush

The Battle/U.S.: **Thunder in the East.** Lianofilm Production. *Pr:* Léon Garganoff. *Dir:* Nicolas Farkas. *Sc:* Robert Stevenson, based on the French sc. *La Bataille.* *With:* Charles Boyer, John Loder, Merle Oberon, Betty Stockfield, Miles Mander. Filmed in France

Evergreen. Gaumont-British. *Dir:* Victor Saville. *Sc:* Marjorie Gaffney, based on the musical play by Benn W. Levy. *Adapt/Dial:* Emlyn Williams. *Ph:* Glen MacWilliams. *Ed:* Ian Dalrymple, Paul Capon. *A.D.:* Alfred Junge, Peter Proud. *Songs:* Richard Rodgers, Lorenz Hart. *Add Songs:* Harry Woods. *Mus Dir:* Louis Levy. *With:* Jessie Matthews, Sonnie Hale, Betty Balfour, Barry Mackay

A Cup of Kindness. Gaumont-British. *Dir:* Tom Walls. *Sc:* Ben Travers, based on his play. *Ph:* Phil Tannura. *Ed:* Alfred Roome. *A.D.:* Alfred Junge. *Mus Dir:* Louis Levy. *With:* Tom Walls, Ralph Lynn, Robertson Hare, Claude Hulbert, Dorothy Hyson

Princess Charming. Gaumont. *Dir:* Maurice Elvey. *Sc/Dial:* L. du Garde Peach. *Ph:* Mutz Greenbaum. *A.D.:* Ernö Metzner. *Mus:* Ray Noble. *Lyr:* Max Kester. *Mus Dir:* Louis Levy. *With:* Evelyn Laye, George Grossmith, Max Miller, Yvonne Arnaud

Man of Aran. Gainsborough. *Dir:* Robert Flaherty. *Asst Dir:* Pat Mullen. *Sc:* Robert and Frances Flaherty. *Collab:* John Goldman. *Ph:* R. Flaherty. *Field laboratory:* John Taylor. *Ed:* Goldman. *Mus:* John Greenwood, based on folk music of Aran. *Mus Dir:* Louis Levy. *With:* Colman "Tiger" King, Maggie Dirrane, Michael Dillane, Pat Mullen

Wild Boy. Gainsborough. *Dir:* Albert de Courville. *Sc:* Stafford Dickens. *With:* Sonnie Hale, Bud Flanagan, Chesney Allen, Lyn Harding, Leonora Corbett

Chu-Chin-Chow. Gainsborough. *Assoc Pr:* Philip Samuel. *Dir:* Walter Forde. *Sc/Dial:* Edward Knoblock, Sidney Gilliat, L. du Garde Peach, based on the musical play by Oscar Asche. *Ph:* Mutz Greenbaum. *Ed:* Derek Twist. *A.D.:* Ernö Metzner. *Songs:* Frederic Norton. *Mus Dir:* Louis Levy. *With:* George Robey, Fritz Kortner, Anna May Wong, John Garrick

Wings over Everest. Gaumont-British. *Assoc Pr:* Ivor Montagu. *Dir:* Geoffrey Barkas, Montagu. *Ph:* S. R. Bonnett, A. L. Fisher, J. Rosenthal. *Ed:* Montagu. Featurette

Little Friend. Gaumont-British. *Assoc Pr:* Robert Stevenson. *Dir:* Berthold Viertel. *Sc:* Margaret Kennedy, Christopher Isherwood. *Adapt:* Viertel, based on the novel *Kleine Freundin* by Ernst Lothar. *Ph:* Gunther Krampf. *Ed:* Ian Dalrymple. *A.D.:* Alfred Junge. *Mus:* Ernst Toch. *With:* Matheson Lang, Lydia Sherwood, Nova Pilbeam, Jean Cadell, Jimmy Hanley

My Song for You. Gaumont-British/Cine-Allianz Tonfilm. *Assoc Pr:* Jerome Jackson. *Dir:* Maurice Elvey. *Sc:* Richard Benson, based on the German sc. *Ein Lied für Dich.* *Ph:*

Charles Van Enger. *Ed:* Charles Frend. *A.D.:* Alfred Junge. *Mus:* Willy Schmidt-Gentner, Bronislau Kaper, Walter Jurmann. *Add Mus:* Mischa Spoliansky. *Lyr:* Frank Eyton. *Mus Dir:* Louis Levy. *With:* Jan Kiepura, Sonnie Hale, Emlyn Williams

The Unfinished Symphony/U.S.: **Lover Divine.** Cine-Allianz Tonfilm/Willi Forst Produktion. *Pr:* Arnold Pressburger. *Dir:* Willi Forst. *Sup:* Anthony Asquith. *Sc:* Benn Levy, based on the German sc. *Leise flehen meine Lieder* by Forst. *With:* Hans Jaray, Marta Eggerth, Helen Chandler. Filmed in Vienna

My Old Dutch. Gainsborough. *Assoc Pr:* Ivor Montagu. *Dir:* Sinclair Hill. *Sc:* Marjorie Gaffney, Bryan Wallace, Michael Hogan. *Adapt:* Wallace, Leslie Arliss, based on the play by Albert Chevalier and Arthur Shirley. *Ph:* Leslie Rowson. *With:* Betty Balfour, Gordon Harker, Florrie Forde

Evensong. Gaumont-British. *Dir:* Victor Saville. *Sc/Dial/Lyr:* Edward Knoblock. *Adapt:* Dorothy Farnum, based on the play by Knoblock and Beverley Nichols and the novel by Nichols. *Ph:* Mutz Greenbaum. *Ed:* Otto Ludwig. *A.D.:* Alfred Junge. *Mus:* Mischa Spoliansky. *Mus Dir:* Louis Levy. *With:* Evelyn Laye, Fritz Kortner, Emlyn Williams

Jew Süss/U.S.: **Power.** Gaumont-British. *Dir:* Lothar Mendes. *Sc/Dial:* A. R. Rawlinson. *Adapt:* Dorothy Farnum, based on the novel *Jud Süss* by Lion Feuchtwanger. *Ph:* Bernard Knowles, Roy Kellino. *Ed:* Otto Ludwig. *A.D.:* Alfred Junge. *Mus Dir:* Louis Levy. *With:* Conrad Veidt, Benita Hume, Cedric Hardwicke, Gerald du Maurier. *Rel:* 1935

The Camels Are Coming. Gainsborough. *Assoc Pr:* Robert Stevenson. *Dir:* Tim Whelan. *Sc:* Guy Bolton. *Dial:* Jack Hulbert. *Story:* Whelan, Russell Medcraft. *Ph:* Glen MacWilliams, Bernard Knowles. *Ed:* Frederick Y. Smith. *A.D.:* Oscar Werndorff. *Musical Numbers:* Ray Noble, Max Kester, Noel Gay. *Mus Dir:* Louis Levy. *With:* Jack Hulbert, Anna Lee

Lady in Danger. Gaumont-British. *Dir:* Tom Walls. *Sc:* Marjorie Gaffney, based on the play *O Mistress Mine* by Ben Travers. *Adapt/Dial:* Travers. *Ph:* Phil Tannura. *Ed:* Helen Lewis. *A.D.:* Alfred Junge. *Mus Dir:* Louis Levy. *With:* Tom Walls, Yvonne Arnaud. *Rel:* 1935

Road House. Gaumont-British. *Dir:* Maurice Elvey. *Sc:* Leslie Arliss, Austin Melford, based on the play by Walter Hackett. *Ph:* Leslie Rowson. *A.D.:* Alfred Junge. *With:* Violet Loraine, Gordon Harker, Emlyn Williams. *Rel:* 1935

The Iron Duke. Gaumont-British. *Dir:* Victor Saville. *Sc:* H. M. Harwood, Bess Meredyth. *Ph:* Curt Courant, Leslie Rowson. *Ed:* Ian Dalrymple. *A.D.:* Alfred Junge. *Mus Dir:* Louis Levy. *With:* George Arliss, Gladys Cooper, Ellaline Terriss. *Rel:* 1935

The Man Who Knew Too Much. Gaumont-British. *Assoc Pr:* Ivor Montagu. *Dir:* Alfred Hitchcock. *Sc:* Edwin Greenwood, A. R. Rawlinson. *Add Dial:* Emlyn Williams. *Ph:* Curt Courant. *Ed:* H. St. C. Stewart. *A.D.:* Alfred Junge, Peter Proud. *Mus:* Arthur Benjamin. *Mus Dir:* Louis Levy. *With:* Leslie Banks, Edna Best, Peter Lorre, Nova Pilbeam, Frank Vosper, Pierre Fresnay. *Rel:* 1935

Dirty Work. Gaumont-British. *Dir:* Tom Walls. *Sc:* Ben Travers, based on his play. *Ph:* Phil Tannura. *Ed:* Alfred Roome. *A.D.:* Alfred Junge. *Mus Dir:* Louis Levy. *With:* Ralph Lynn, Gordon Harker, Robertson Hare, Lilian Bond. *Rel:* 1935

———————————— **1935** ————————————

My Heart Is Calling. Gaumont-British/Cine-Allianz Tonfilm. *Pr:* Arnold Pressburger. *Assoc Pr:* Ivor Montagu. *Dir:* Carmine Gallone. *Sc:* Richard Benson, based on the German sc. *Mein Herz Ruft nach Dir.* *Adapt/Dial:* Sidney Gilliat. *Ph:* Glen MacWilliams. *Ed:* Ralph Kemplen. *A.D.:* John Harman. *Mus:* Robert Stolz. *Lyr:* T. Connor, Harry S. Pepper. *Mus Dir:*

Louis Levy. *With:* Jan Kiepura, Marta Eggerth, Sonnie Hale

The Phantom Light. Gainsborough. *Assoc Pr:* Jerome Jackson. *Dir:* Michael Powell. *Sc:* Ralph Smart, based on the play *The Haunted Light* by Evadne Price and Joan Roy Byford. *Ph:* Roy Kellino. *Ed:* Derek Twist. *A.D.:* Vetchinsky. *Mus Dir:* Louis Levy. *With:* Gordon Harker, Binnie Hale, Ian Hunter

Things Are Looking Up. Gaumont-British. *Dir:* Albert de Courville. *Sc:* Stafford Dickens, Con West. *Ph:* Charles Van Enger. *With:* Cicely Courtneidge, Max Miller, William Gargan, Dick Henderson, Suzanne Lenglen

Temptation. Milo-Film. *Dir:* Max Neufeld. *With:* Frances Day, Stewart Rome. Filmed in France; Eng-lang version of **Antonia, Romance Hongroise**

Oh, Daddy. Gainsborough. *Dir:* Graham Cutts, Austin Melford. *Sc:* Melford, based on his play. *Ph:* Mutz Greenbaum. *Ed:* Charles Frend. *With:* Frances Day, Leslie Henson, Robertson Hare, Barry Mackay, Marie Lohr

Fighting Stock. Gainsborough. *Dir:* Tom Walls. *Sc:* Ben Travers. *Ph:* Phil Tannura. *Ed:* Charles Frend. *A.D.:* Oscar Werndorff. *Mus Dir:* Louis Levy. *With:* Tom Walls, Ralph Lynn, Robertson Hare, Marie Lohr

Bulldog Jack/U.S.: **Alias Bulldog Drummond.** Gaumont-British. *Dir:* Walter Forde. *Sc:* J. O. C. Orton, Sidney Gilliat, Gerard Fairlie. *Story/Add Dial:* Jack Hulbert. Based on the stories and characters of "Sapper" [H.C. McNeile]. *Ph:* Mutz Greenbaum. *Ed:* Otto Ludwig. *A.D.:* Alfred Junge. *Mus Dir:* Louis Levy. *With:* Jack Hulbert, Fay Wray, Claude Hulbert, Ralph Richardson

Heat Wave. Gainsborough. *Assoc Pr:* Jerome Jackson. *Dir:* Maurice Elvey. *Sc:* Austin Melford, Leslie Arliss, Jerome Jackson. *Ph:* Glen MacWilliams. *Songs:* Maurice Sigler, Al Goodhart, Al Hoffman. *With:* Albert Burdon, Anna Lee

Forever England/U.S.: **Born for Glory/Torpedo Raider.** Gaumont-British. *Dir:* Walter Forde. *2nd Unit Dir:* Anthony Asquith. *Sc/Adapt:* J. O. C. Orton, based on the novel *Brown on Resolution* by C. S. Forester. *Ph:* Bernard Knowles. *Ed:* Otto Ludwig. *A.D.:* Alfred Junge. *With:* John Mills, Betty Balfour, Barry Mackay, Jimmy Hanley

The 39 Steps. Gaumont-British. *Assoc Pr:* Ivor Montagu. *Dir:* Alfred Hitchcock. *Sc/Adapt:* Alma Reville, Charles Bennett, based on the novel by John Buchan. *Ph:* Bernard Knowles. *Ed:* Derek Twist. *A.D.:* Oscar Werndorff, Albert Jullion. *Mus Dir:* Louis Levy. *With:* Robert Donat, Madeleine Carroll

The Clairvoyant/U.S.: **The Evil Mind.** Gainsborough. *Dir:* Maurice Elvey. *Sc:* Charles Bennett, Bryan Wallace, based on the novel *Der Hellseher* by Ernst Lothar. *Ph:* Glen MacWilliams. *Ed:* Paul Capon. *A.D.:* Alfred Junge. *Mus:* Arthur Benjamin. *Mus Dir:* Louis Levy. *With:* Claude Rains, Fay Wray

The Divine Spark. Alleanza Cinematografica Italiana. *Pr:* Arnold Pressburger. *Dir:* Carmine Gallone. *Sc:* Emlyn Williams, Richard Benson. *Story:* Walter Reisch. *Ph:* Franz Planer. *Ed:* Fritz Pressburger. *A.D.:* Werner Schlichting. *Mus:* Bellini, Rossini. *With:* Marta Eggerth, Phillips Holmes, Benita Hume. *Rel:* 1936. Filmed in Rome; Eng-lang version of **Casta Diva**

Me and Marlborough. Gaumont-British. *Dir:* Victor Saville. *Sc:* Marjorie Gaffney, W. P. Lipscomb. *Dial:* Ian Hay. *Ph:* Curt Courant. *Ed:* Michael Gordon. *A.D.:* Alfred Junge. *Song:* Noel Gay. *Mus. Dir:* Louis Levy. *With:* Cicely Courtneidge, Tom Walls, Barry Mackay

Boys Will Be Boys. Gainsborough. *Dir:* William Beaudine. *Sc:* Will Hay, Robert Edmunds, based on the "Narkover" characters of "Beachcomber" (J.B. Morton) in the London *Daily Express*. *Ph:* Charles Van Enger. *Ed:* Alfred Roome. *A.D.:* Vetchinsky. *Title Song:* The Two Leslies [Leslie Sarony, Leslie

Holmes]. *Mus Dir:* Louis Levy. *With:* Will Hay, Gordon Harker, Jimmy Hanley

Stormy Weather. Gainsborough. *Dir:* Tom Walls. *Sc:* Ben Travers. *Ph:* Phil Tannura. *Ed:* Alfred Roome. *A.D.:* Vetchinsky. *Mus Dir:* Louis Levy. *With:* Tom Walls, Ralph Lynn, Yvonne Arnaud, Robertson Hare. *Rel:* 1936

Car of Dreams. Gaumont-British. *Dir:* Graham Cutts, Austin Melford. *Sc:* Melford. *Adapt:* Stafford Dickens, Richard Benson, based on the Hungarian sc. *Meseauto*. *Ph:* Mutz Greenbaum. *A.D.:* Alfred Junge. *Mus:* Mischa Spoliansky. *Lyr:* Frank Eyton. *With:* John Mills, Grete Mosheim, Robertson Hare

The Passing of the Third Floor Back. Gaumont-British. *Assoc Pr:* Ivor Montagu. *Dir:* Berthold Viertel. *Sc:* Michael Hogan, Alma Reville, based on the play by Jerome K. Jerome. *Ph:* Curt Courant. *Ed:* Derek Twist. *Mus Dir:* Louis Levy. *With:* Conrad Veidt, Anna Lee, René Ray. *Rel:* 1936

The Guv'nor/U.S.: **Mister Hobo.** Gaumont-British. *Assoc Pr:* S. C. Balcon. *Dir:* Milton Rosmer. *Sc:* Guy Bolton, Maude Howell, based on the French sc. *Rothschild*. *Ph:* Mutz Greenbaum. *A.D.:* Alfred Junge. *With:* George Arliss, Gene Gerrard, Patric Knowles. *Rel:* 1936

First a Girl. Gaumont-British. *Assoc Pr:* S. C. Balcon. *Dir:* Victor Saville. *Sc:* Marjorie Gaffney, based on the German sc. *Viktor und Viktoria* by Reinhold Schünzel. *Ph:* Glen MacWilliams. *Ed:* A. Barnes. *A.D.:* Oscar Werndorff. *Songs:* Maurice Sigler, Al Goodhart, Al Hoffman. *Mus Dir:* Louis Levy. *With:* Jessie Matthews, Sonnie Hale, Griffith Jones, Anna Lee. *Rel:* 1936

The Tunnel/U.S.: **Transatlantic Tunnel.** Gaumont-British. *Assoc Pr:* S. C. Balcon. *Dir:* Maurice Elvey. *Sc/Dial:* L. du Garde Peach. *Add Dial:* Clemence Dane. *Adapt:* Kurt Siodmak, based on the German sc. *Der Tunnel*. *Ph:* Gunther Krampf. *Ed:* Charles Frend. *A.D.:* Ernö Metzner. *Mus Dir:* Louis Levy. *With:* Richard Dix, Leslie Banks, Madge Evans, Helen Vinson, C. Aubrey Smith. *Rel:* 1936

Foreign Affairs. Gainsborough. *Dir:* Tom Walls. *Sc:* Ben Travers. *Ph:* Roy Kellino. *Ed:* Alfred Roome. *A.D.:* Vetchinsky. *Mus Dir:* Louis Levy. *With:* Tom Walls, Ralph Lynn, Robertson Hare, Marie Lohr, Norma Varden. *Rel:* 1936

King of the Damned. Gaumont-British. *Dir:* Walter Forde. *Sc:* Charles Bennett, Sidney Gilliat. *Ph:* Bernard Knowles. *Ed:* C. Randell. *A.D.:* Oscar Werndorff. *Mus Dir:* Louis Levy. *With:* Conrad Veidt, Helen Vinson, Noah Beery. *Rel:* 1936

——————————— **1936** ———————————

Jack of All Trades/U.S.: **The Two of Us.** Gainsborough. *Dir:* Robert Stevenson, Jack Hulbert. *Sc:* J. O. C. Orton, based on the play *Youth at the Helm* by Hubert Griffith, based on a German play. *Dial:* Hulbert, Austin Melford. *Ph:* Charles Van Enger. *Ed:* Terence Fisher. *A.D.:* Vetchinsky. *Songs:* Maurice Sigler, Al Goodhart, Al Hoffman. *Mus Dir:* Louis Levy. *With:* Jack Hulbert, Gina Malo, Robertson Hare

First Offence. Gainsborough. *Dir:* Herbert Mason. *Sc:* Stafford Dickens, Austin Melford, based on the French sc. *Mauvaise Graine,* by Billy Wilder. *Ph:* Arthur Crabtree. *Ed:* Michael Gordon. *A.D.:* Walter Murton. *Mus Dir:* Louis Levy. *With:* John Mills, Lilli Palmer

Rhodes of Africa/U.S.: **Rhodes/Rhodes, the Empire Builder.** Gaumont-British. *Dir:* Berthold Viertel. *Assoc Pr/2nd Unit Dir:* Geoffrey Barkas. *Sc:* Leslie Arliss, Michael Barringer. *Dial:* Miles Malleson. *Ph:* Bernard Knowles, S. R. Bonnett. *Ed:* Derek Twist. *A.D.:* Oscar Werndorff. *Mus Dir:* Louis Levy. *With:* Walter Huston, Oscar Homolka, Basil Sydney, Peggy Ashcroft

Pot Luck. Gainsborough. *Dir:* Tom Walls. *Sc:* Ben Travers. *Ph:*

Roy Kellino, Arthur Crabtree. *Ed:* Alfred Roome. *A.D.* Walter Murton. *Mus Dir:* Louis Levy. *With:* Tom Walls, Ralph Lynn, Robertson Hare

Tudor Rose/U.S.: *Nine Days a Queen.* Gainsborough. *Assoc Pr:* Edward Black, Sidney Gilliat. *Dir/Sc:* Robert Stevenson. *Dial:* Miles Malleson. *Ph:* Mutz Greenbaum. *Ed:* Terence Fisher. *A.D.:* Vetchinsky. *Mus Dir:* Louis Levy. *With:* Nova Pilbeam, Cedric Hardwicke, John Mills, Sybil Thorndike, Desmond Tester, Felix Aylmer

Secret Agent. Gaumont-British. *Assoc Pr:* Ivor Montagu. *Dir:* Alfred Hitchcock. *Sc:* Charles Bennett, based on the play by Campbell Dixon, adapted from Somerset Maugham's novel *Ashenden. Dial:* Ian Hay. *Ph:* Bernard Knowles. *Ed:* Charles Frend. *A.D.:* Oscar Werndorff, Albert Jullion. *Mus Dir:* Louis Levy. *With:* Madeleine Carroll, John Gielgud, Peter Lorre, Robert Young

It's Love Again. Gaumont-British. *Dir:* Victor Saville. *Sc:* Marion Dix. *Ph:* Glen MacWilliams. *Ed:* A. L. Barnes. *A.D.:* Alfred Junge. *Songs:* Sam Coslow, Harry Woods. *Mus Dir:* Louis Levy. *With:* Jessie Matthews, Robert Young, Sonnie Hale

Where There's a Will. Gainsborough. *Assoc Pr:* Edward Black, Sidney Gilliat. *Dir:* William Beaudine. *Sc:* Will Hay, Robert Edmunds, Beaudine. *Story:* Leslie Arliss, Gilliat. *Ph:* Charles Van Enger. *Ed:* Terence Fisher. *A.D.:* Vetchinsky. *Mus Dir:* Louis Levy. *With:* Will Hay, Graham Moffatt, Gina Malo, Hartley Power

Seven Sinners/U.S.: *Doomed Cargo.* Gaumont-British. *Dir:* Albert de Courville. *Sc:* Sidney Gilliat, Frank Launder. *Adapt:* L. du Garde Peach, based on the play *The Wrecker* by Arnold Ridley and Bernard Merivale. *Ph:* Mutz Greenbaum. *Ed:* Michael Gordon. *A.D.:* Ernö Metzner. *Mus:* Bretton Byrd. *Mus Dir:* Louis Levy. *With:* Edmund Lowe, Constance Cummings, Thomy Bourdelle, Felix Aylmer

Everything Is Thunder. Gaumont-British. *Assoc Pr:* S. C. Balcon. *Dir:* Milton Rosmer. *Sc:* J. O. C. Orton, Marion Dix. *Ph:* Gunther Krampf. *A.D.:* Alfred Junge. *With:* Constance Bennett, Oscar Homolka, Douglass Montgomery

The Flying Doctor. National Productions (Australia)/Gaumont-British. *Dir:* Miles Mander. *Sc:* J. O. C. Orton, Mander, based on the novel by Robert Waldron. *Ph:* Derick Williams. *Ed:* Orton, R. Maslyn Williams, Edna Turner. *A.D.:* Richard Ridgway. *Mus:* Willy Redstone, Alf J. Lawrence. *With:* Charles Farrell, Mary Maguire, James Raglan, Joe Valli. *Rel:* 1936 in Australia, 1937 in Britain. Filmed in Sydney, Australia

East Meets West. Gaumont-British. *Assoc Pr:* Haworth Bromly. *Dir:* Herbert Mason. *Co-Dir:* Maude Howell. *Sc/Story:* Edwin Greenwood. *Adapt:* Howell. *Ph:* Bernard Knowles. *Ed:* Charles Frend. *A.D.:* Oscar Werndorff. *Mus Dir:* Louis Levy. *With:* George Arliss, Lucie Mannheim, Romney Brent, Godfrey Tearle

The Man Who Changed His Mind/U.S.: *The Man Who Lived Again/Doctor Maniac/Brain Snatcher.* Gainsborough. *Assoc Pr:* Edward Black, Sidney Gilliat. *Dir:* Robert Stevenson. *Sc:* Gilliat, L. du Garde Peach, John L. Balderston, based on the story "The Devil Goes Calling" by du Garde Peach. *Ph:* Jack Cox. *Ed:* R. E. Dearing, Alfred Roome. *A.D.:* Vetchinsky. *Mus Dir:* Louis Levy. *With:* Boris Karloff, Anna Lee, John Loder

Everybody Dance. Gainsborough. *Assoc Pr:* Edward Black, Sidney Gilliat. *Dir:* Charles Reisner. *Sc:* Leslie Arliss. *Ph:* Jack Cox. *Ed:* R. E. Dearing, Terence Fisher. *A.D.:* Vetchinsky. *Songs:* Mack Gordon, Harry Revel. *Mus Dir:* Louis Levy. *With:* Cicely Courtneidge, Ernest Truex

All In. Gainsborough. *Dir:* Marcel Varnel. *Sc:* Leslie Arliss, Val

Guest. *Ph:* Arthur Crabtree. *With:* Ralph Lynn, Gina Malo

His Lordship/U.S.: *Man of Affairs.* Gaumont-British. *Assoc Pr:* S. C. Balcon. *Dir:* Herbert Mason. *Sc:* L. du Garde Peach, Edwin Greenwood, Maude Howell. *Ph:* Gunther Krampf. *A.D.:* Alfred Junge. *With:* George Arliss, René Ray. *Rel:* 1937

Strangers on Honeymoon. Gaumont-British. *Assoc Pr:* Haworth Bromly. *Dir:* Albert de Courville. *Sc:* Laird Doyle, Ralph Spence, Sidney Gilliat, Bryan Wallace, based on the novel *The Northing Tramp* by Edgar Wallace. *Ph:* Mutz Greenbaum. *Ed:* C. Randell. *A.D.:* Ernö Metzner. *With:* Constance Cummings, Noah Beery. *Rel:* 1937

Sabotage/U.S.: *A Woman Alone.* Gaumont-British. *Assoc Pr:* Ivor Montagu. *Dir:* Alfred Hitchcock. *Sc:* Charles Bennett, Alma Reville, based on the novel *The Secret Agent* by Joseph Conrad. *Ph:* Bernard Knowles. *Ed:* Charles Frend. *A.D.:* Oscar Werndorff. *Mus Dir:* Louis Levy. *With:* Sylvia Sidney, Oscar Homolka, John Loder, Desmond Tester. Working title: *The Hidden Power. Rel:* 1937

Windbag the Sailor. Gainsborough. *Dir:* William Beaudine. *Sc:* Marriott Edgar, Stafford Dickens, Will Hay. *Story:* Robert Stevenson, Leslie Arliss. *Ph:* Jack Cox. *Ed:* R. E. Dearing, Terence Fisher. *A.D.:* Vetchinsky, A. Cox. *Mus Dir:* Louis Levy. *With:* Will Hay, Moore Marriott, Graham Moffatt. *Rel:* 1937

──────── 1937 ────────

O.H.M.S./U.S.: *You're in the Army Now.* Gaumont-British. *Assoc Pr:* Geoffrey Barkas. *Dir:* Raoul Walsh. *Sc:* Austin Melford, A. R. Rawlinson, Bryan Wallace. *Ph:* Roy Kellino. *Ed:* Charles Saunders. *A.D.:* Edward Carrick. *Mus Dir:* Louis Levy. *With:* Anna Lee, John Mills, Wallace Ford, Grace Bradley

Head over Heels. Gaumont-British. *Assoc Pr:* S. C. Balcon. *Dir:* Sonnie Hale. *Sc:* Marjorie Gaffney, Fred Thompson, Dwight Taylor. *Ph:* Glen MacWilliams. *A.D.:* Alfred Junge. *Songs:* Mack Gordon, Harry Revel. *With:* Jessie Matthews, Robert Flemyng

The Great Barrier/U.S.: *Silent Barriers.* Gaumont-British. *Assoc Pr:* Gunther Stapenhorst. *Dir:* Milton Rosmer. *2nd Unit Dir:* Geoffrey Barkas. *Sc:* Michael Barrington, Rosmer. *Ph:* Glen MacWilliams, Robert Martin, S. R. Bonnett. *Ed:* Charles Frend. *A.D.:* Walter Murton. *Mus:* Hubert Bath. *Mus Dir:* Louis Levy. *With:* Richard Arlen, Lilli Palmer, Barry Mackay, J. Farrell MacDonald

King Solomon's Mines. Gaumont-British. *Dir:* Robert Stevenson. *Assoc Pr/2nd Unit Dir:* Geoffrey Barkas. *Sc:* Michael Hogan, Roland Pertwee, based on the novel by H. Rider Haggard. *Dial:* Pertwee. *Ph:* Glen MacWilliams. *Ed:* Michael Gordon. *A.D.:* Alfred Junge. *Mus:* Mischa Spoliansky. *Lyr:* Eric Maschwitz. *With:* Roland Young, Cedric Hardwicke, Paul Robeson, Anna Lee, John Loder

──────── 1938 ────────

A Yank at Oxford. M-G-M British. *Dir:* Jack Conway. *Sc:* Leon Gordon, Roland Pertwee. *Story:* Sidney Gilliat, Michael Hogan. *Ph:* Harold Rosson, Cyril Knowles. *Sup Ed:* Margaret Booth. *Ed:* Charles Frend. *A.D.:* L. P. Williams. *Mus:* Hubert Bath, Edward Ward. *Mus Dir:* Bath. *With:* Robert Taylor, Lionel Barrymore, Vivien Leigh, Maureen O'Sullivan, Griffith Jones, Edmund Gwenn

The Gaunt Stranger/U.S.: *The Phantom Strikes.* Northwood Enterprises/CAPAD. *Assoc Pr:* S. C. Balcon. *Dir:* Walter Forde. *Sc:* Sidney Gilliat, based on the play *The Ringer* and the novel *The Gaunt Stranger* by Edgar Wallace. *Ph:* Ronald Neame. *Ed:* Charles Saunders. *A.D.:* Oscar Werndorff. *Mus:* Ernest Irving. *With:* Sonnie Hale, Wilfrid Lawson, Alexander

Knox, Patricia Roc. *Rel:* 1939. Filmed at ATP studios, Ealing

The Ware Case. CAPAD/Associated Star. *Assoc Pr:* S. C. Balcon. *Dir:* Robert Stevenson. *Sc:* Roland Pertwee, Stevenson, based on the play by George Pleydell Bancroft. *Ph:* Ronald Neame. *Ed:* Charles Saunders. *A.D.:* Oscar Werndorff. *Mus:* Ernest Irving. *With:* Clive Brook, Jane Baxter, Barry K. Barnes, Edward Rigby, Peter Bull. *Rel:* 1939. Filmed at ATP studios, Ealing

---------------------- **1939** ----------------------

Let's Be Famous. Associated Talking Pictures. *Assoc Pr:* S. C. Balcon. *Dir:* Walter Forde. *Sc:* Roger MacDougall, Allan MacKinnon. *Ph:* Ronald Neame, Gordon Dines. *Ed:* Ray Pitt. *A.D.:* Oscar Werndorff. *Mus:* Noel Gay. *Lyr:* Gay, Frank Eyton, Ralph Butler. *With:* Jimmy O'Dea, Betty Driver, Sonnie Hale, Milton Rosmer. Filmed at Ealing

Trouble Brewing. Associated Talking Pictures. *Pr:* Jack Kitchin. *Dir:* Anthony Kimmins. Sc: Kimmins, Angus MacPhail, Michael Hogan. *Ph:* Ronald Neame. *Ed:* Ernest Aldridge. *A.D.:* Wilfrid Shingleton. *Songs:* George Formby, Harry Gifford, Fred E. Cliffe. *With:* George Formby, Googie Withers, Garry Marsh. Filmed at Ealing

There Ain't No Justice. Ealing Studios/CAPAD. *Assoc Pr:* Sergei Nolbandov. *Dir:* Pen Tennyson. *Sc:* Tennyson, Nolbandov, James Curtis, based on Curtis's novel. *Ph:* Mutz Greenbaum. *Ed:* Ray Pitt. *A.D.:* Wilfrid Shingleton. *Mus:* Ernest Irving. *With:* Jimmy Hanley, Phyllis Stanley, Edward Rigby, Edward Chapman

The Four Just Men/U.S.: **The Secret Four.** Ealing Studios/CAPAD. *Assoc Pr:* S. C. Balcon. *Dir:* Walter Forde. *Sc:* Angus MacPhail, Sergei Nolbandov, based on the novel by Edgar Wallace. *Ph:* Ronald Neame. *Ed:* Charles Saunders. *A.D.:* Wilfrid Shingleton. *Mus:* Ernest Irving. *With:* Hugh Sinclair, Griffith Jones, Francis L. Sullivan, Frank Lawton, Anna Lee

Cheer Boys Cheer. Associated Talking Pictures. *Assoc Pr:* S. C. Balcon. *Dir:* Walter Forde. *Sc:* Roger MacDougall, Allan MacKinnon. *Story:* Ian Dalrymple, Donald Bull. *Ph:* Ronald Neame. *Ed:* Ray Pitt. *A.D.:* Wilfrid Shingleton. *Mus:* Ernest Irving. *With:* Nova Pilbeam, Edmund Gwenn, Jimmy O'Dea, Peter Coke. Filmed at Ealing

Young Man's Fancy. Ealing Studios/CAPAD. *Assoc Pr:* S. C. Balcon. *Dir:* Robert Stevenson. *Sc:* Roland Pertwee. *Story:* Stevenson. *Ph:* Ronald Neame. *Ed:* Charles Saunders, Ralph Kemplen. *A.D.:* Wilfrid Shingleton. *Mus Dir:* Ernest Irving. *With:* Griffith Jones, Anna Lee, Seymour Hicks, Martita Hunt, Felix Aylmer. *Rel:* 1940

Happy Families. Ealing Studios, for National Service Department of the Ministry of Labour. *Prod Sup:* Bryan Wallace. *Dir:* Walter Forde. *With:* Edmund Gwenn, John Mills, Frank Lawton. Short

Come On George. Associated Talking Pictures. *Pr:* Jack Kitchin. *Dir:* Anthony Kimmins. *Sc:* Kimmins, Leslie Arliss, Val Valentine. *Ph:* Ronald Neame. *Ed:* Ray Pitt. *A.D.:* Wilfrid Shingleton. *Songs:* George Formby, Fred E. Cliffe, Harry Gifford, Alan Nicholson. *With:* George Formby, Pat Kirkwood. *Rel:* 1940. Filmed at Ealing

---------------------- **1940** ----------------------

Return to Yesterday. Ealing Studios/CAPAD. *Assoc Pr:* S. C. Balcon. *Dir:* Robert Stevenson. *Sc:* Stevenson, Roland Pertwee, Angus MacPhail, based on the play *Goodness, How Sad* by Robert Morley. *Ph:* Ronald Neame. *Ed:* Charles Saunders. *A.D.:* Wilfrid Shingleton. *Mus:* Ernest Irving. *With:* Clive Brook, Anna Lee, Dame May Whitty

The Proud Valley. Ealing Studios/CAPAD. *Assoc Pr:* Sergei Nolbandov. *Dir:* Pen Tennyson. *Sc:* Tennyson, Jack Jones, Louis Golding. *Ph:* Glen MacWilliams, Roy Kellino. *Ed:* Ray Pitt. *A.D.:* Wilfrid Shingleton. *Mus Dir:* Ernest Irving. *With:* Paul Robeson, Edward Chapman, Simon Lack, Rachel Thomas

Let George Do It!/U.S.: **Murder in Bergen.** Associated Talking Pictures. *Assoc Pr:* Basil Dearden. *Dir:* Marcel Varnel. *Sc:* John Dighton, Austin Melford, Angus MacPhail, Dearden. *Ph:* Ronald Neame. *Ed:* Ray Pitt. *A.D.:* Wilfrid Shingleton. *Songs:* George Formby, Harry Gifford, Fred E. Cliffe, Eddie Latto. *Mus Dir:* Ernest Irving. *With:* George Formby, Phyllis Calvert, Garry Marsh, Romney Brent, Coral Browne. Filmed at Ealing

All Hands. Ealing Studios, for Ministry of Information. *Dir/Sc:* John Paddy Carstairs. *With:* John Mills, Leueen McGrath. Short

Dangerous Comment. Ealing Studios, for Ministry of Information. *Dir:* John Paddy Carstairs. *Sc:* Roland Pertwee, Roger MacDougall. *Story:* Carstairs. *With:* Frank Lawton, Edward Lexy, Penelope Dudley Ward, Roland Culver. Short

Now You're Talking. Ealing Studios, for Ministry of Information. *Dir:* John Paddy Carstairs. *Sc:* Basil Dearden, Roger MacDougall, Jeffrey Dell. *With:* Sebastian Shaw, Edward Chapman, Dorothy Hyson. Short

Saloon Bar. Ealing Studios. *Assoc Pr:* Culley Forde. *Dir:* Walter Forde. *Sc:* Angus MacPhail, John Dighton. *Ph:* Ronald Neame. *Ed:* Ray Pitt. *A.D.:* Wilfrid Shingleton. *Mus Dir:* Ernest Irving. *With:* Gordon Harker, Elizabeth Allan, Mervyn Johns

Convoy. Ealing Studios. *Assoc Pr:* Sergei Nolbandov. *Dir:* Pen Tennyson. *Sc:* Patrick Kirwan, Tennyson. *Ph:* Gunther Krampf, Roy Kellino. *Ed:* Ray Pitt. *A.D.:* Wilfrid Shingleton. *Mus:* Ernest Irving. *With:* Clive Brook, John Clements, Edward Chapman

Food for Thought. Ealing Studios, for Ministry of Information. *Pr:* John Croydon. *Dir:* Adrian Brunel. *With:* Mabel Constanduros, Muriel George. Short

Sea Fort. Ealing Studios, for Ministry of Information. *Pr:* Cavalcanti. *Dir/Sc:* Ian Dalrymple. *Ph:* Ernest Palmer. *Ed:* Ernest Aldridge. *Narr:* Patric Curwen. Short

Salvage with a Smile. Ealing Studios, for Ministry of Information and Ministry of Supply. *Pr:* John Croydon. *Dir:* Adrian Brunel. *Sc:* Brunel. *Ph:* Leslie Rowson. *Ed:* Ernest Aldridge. *With:* Aubrey Mallalieu, Ronald Shiner, Kathleen Harrison. Short

Mastery of the Sea. Ealing Studios, in collaboration with the Royal Navy and Merchant Marine. *Assoc Pr:* Cavalcanti. *Ph:* Roy Kellino. *Ed:* Robert Hamer, Frances Cockburn. *Mus Dir:* Ernest Irving. *Narr:* Edward Chapman

Kitten on the Quay. Ealing Studios, for Ministry of Information. *Dir:* St. John Cooper. Animation short

Sailors Three/U.S.: **Three Cockeyed Sailors.** Ealing Studios. *Assoc Pr:* Culley Forde. *Dir:* Walter Forde. *Sc:* Angus MacPhail, Gordon Wellesley. *Story:* MacPhail, Austin Melford, John Dighton. *Ph:* Gunther Krampf, Basil Emmott. *Ed:* Ray Pitt. *A.D.:* Wilfrid Shingleton. *Mus:* Noel Gay, Harry Parr-Davies. *Lyr:* Frank Eyton, Phil Park. *With:* Tommy Trinder, Claude Hulbert, Michael Wilding

Spare a Copper. Associated Talking Pictures. *Assoc Pr:* Basil Dearden. *Dir:* John Paddy Carstairs. *Sc:* Roger MacDougall, Dearden, Austin Melford. *Ph:* Bryan Langley. *Ed:* Ray Pitt. *A.D.:* Wilfrid Shingleton. *Songs:* Roger MacDougall, George Formby, Fred E. Cliffe, Harry Gifford. *With:* George Formby, Dorothy Hyson, Bernard Lee. *Rel:* 1941. Filmed at Ealing

Young Veteran. Ealing Studios. *Pr:* Cavalcanti. *Asst:* Basil Dearden, Monja Danischewsky. *Comm/Narr:* Michael Frank

[Frank Owen]. *Sup Ed:* Ray Pitt. *Ed:* Charles Crichton. *With:* Men of His Majesty's Forces, Arthur Christiansen, St. John Cooper. Short

Cable Laying. Ealing Studios. *Dir:* John Paddy Carstairs. Short

Signals Office (Divisional). Ealing Studios, for the British Army. *Dir:* John Paddy Carstairs. Short

Signals Office (Corps). Ealing Studios, for the British Army. *Dir:* John Paddy Carstairs. Short

--------------------------- 1941 ---------------------------

The Ghost of St. Michael's. Ealing Studios. *Assoc Pr:* Basil Dearden. *Dir:* Marcel Varnel. *Sc:* Angus MacPhail, John Dighton. *Ph:* Derick Williams. *Ed:* B. J. Jarvis. *A.D.:* Wilfrid Shingleton, *collab.* Cavalcanti. *With:* Will Hay, Claude Hulbert, Charles Hawtrey, Raymond Huntley, Felix Aylmer

Yellow Caesar. Ealing Studios. *Pr/Dir:* Cavalcanti. *Comm/Narr:* Michael Frank [Frank Owen], with Michael Foot. *Add scenes/ Dial:* Adrian Brunel. *Ed:* Charles Crichton. *With:* Benito Mussolini. Short

Turned Out Nice Again. Associated Talking Pictures. *Assoc Pr:* Basil Dearden. *Dir:* Marcel Varnel. *Sc:* Austin Melford, John Dighton, Dearden, based on the play *As You Are* by Hugh Mills, Wells Root. *Ph:* Gordon Dines. *Ed:* Robert Hamer. *A.D.:* Wilfrid Shingleton, *collab.* Cavalcanti. *Songs:* Roger MacDougall, Eddie Latto. *With:* George Formby, Peggy Bryan, Elliot Mason, Edward Chapman, O. B. Clarence. Filmed at Ealing

Guests of Honor. Ealing Studios. *Pr:* Cavalcanti. *Asst:* Monja Danischewsky. *Dir:* Ray Pitt. *Comm:* Frank Owen, Michael Foot. *Ph:* Douglas Slocombe. *Ed:* Charles Crichton. *Mus Dir:* Ernest Irving. Short

Freedom Must Have Wings. Ealing Studios, for the French Army. *Dir:* Compton Bennett. Short

Ships with Wings. Ealing Studios. *Assoc Pr:* S. C. Balcon. *Dir:* Sergei Nolbandov. *Sc:* Patrick Kirwan, Austin Melford, Diana Morgan, Nolbandov. *Ph:* Mutz Greenbaum, Wilkie Cooper, Roy Kellino, Eric Cross. *Ed:* Robert Hamer. *A.D.:* Wilfrid Shingleton. *Mus:* Geoffrey Wright. *Lyr:* Diana Morgan. *Mus Dir:* Ernest Irving. *With:* John Clements, Leslie Banks, Jane Baxter, Basil Sydney, Edward Chapman. *Rel:* 1942

Black Sheep of Whitehall. Ealing Studios. *Assoc Pr:* S. C. Balcon. *Dir:* Basil Dearden, Will Hay. *Sc:* Angus MacPhail, John Dighton. *Ph:* Gunther Krampf, Eric Cross. *Ed:* Ray Pitt. *A.D.:* Tom Morahan. *Mus Dir:* Ernest Irving. *With:* Will Hay, John Mills, Basil Sydney, Felix Aylmer. *Rel:* 1942

--------------------------- 1942 ---------------------------

The Big Blockade. Ealing Studios. *Assoc Pr:* Cavalcanti. *Dir:* Charles Frend. *Sc:* Angus MacPhail. *Comm:* Frank Owen. *Ph:* Wilkie Cooper, Douglas Slocombe. *Ed:* Charles Crichton, Compton Bennett. *A.D.:* Tom Morahan. *Mus:* Richard Addinsell. *With:* Leslie Banks, Michael Redgrave, John Mills, Michael Rennie, Will Hay, Robert Morley

The Foreman Went to France/U.S.: **Somewhere in France.** Ealing Studios. *Assoc Pr:* Cavalcanti. *Dir:* Charles Frend. *Sc:* Angus MacPhail, John Dighton, Leslie Arliss. *Story:* J. B. Priestley, based on the experiences of Melbourne Johns. *Ph:* Wilkie Cooper. *Ed:* Robert Hamer. *A.D.:* Tom Morahan. *Mus:* William Walton. *With:* Tommy Trinder, Constance Cummings, Clifford Evans, Robert Morley, Gordon Jackson

Go to Blazes! Ealing Studios, for Ministry of Information. *Dir:* Walter Forde. *Sc:* Angus MacPhail, Diana Morgan. *Ph:* Ernest Palmer. *With:* Will Hay. Short

The Next of Kin. Ealing Studios, for Directorate of Army Kinematography. *Assoc Pr:* S. C. Balcon. *Dir:* Thorold Dickinson. *Sc:* Dickinson, Sir Basil Bartlett, Angus MacPhail, John Dighton. *Ph:* Ernest Palmer. *Ed:* Ray Pitt. *A.D.:* Tom Morahan. *Mus:* William Walton. *With:* Mervyn Johns, Nova Pilbeam, Geoffrey Hibbert

The Goose Steps Out. Ealing Studios. *Assoc Pr:* S. C. Balcon. *Dir:* Basil Dearden, Will Hay. *Sc:* Angus MacPhail, John Dighton. *Ph:* Ernest Palmer. *Ed:* Ray Pitt. *A.D.:* Tom Morahan. *Mus Dir:* Bretton Byrd. *With:* Will Hay, Charles Hawtrey, Frank Pettingell, Julien Mitchell

Find, Fix and Strike. Ealing Studios. *Pr:* Cavalcanti. *Assoc Pr:* Charles Crichton. *Dir:* Compton Bennett. *Comm:* Lord Elton. *Ph:* Roy Kellino, Douglas Slocombe. *Mus Dir:* Ernest Irving. *Rel:* 1943. Short

Went the Day Well?/U.S.: **48 Hours.** Ealing Studios. *Assoc Pr:* S. C. Balcon. *Dir:* Cavalcanti. *Sc:* John Dighton, Diana Morgan, Angus MacPhail. *Story:* Graham Greene. *Ph:* Wilkie Cooper, Douglas Slocombe. *Ed:* Sidney Cole. *A.D.:* Tom Morahan. *Mus:* William Walton. *With:* Leslie Banks, Basil Sydney, Frank Lawton, Elizabeth Allan, Valerie Taylor

Mighty Penny. Ealing Studios, for Red Cross Association. *Dir:* John Paddy Carstairs. Short

Raid on France. Ealing Studios. *Dir:* Compton Bennett. With footage from the last 2 reels of **The Next of Kin.** Short

Meet Mr. Joad. Empire Film Productions. *Dir:* Eric Williams. *With:* C. E. M. Joad. Filmed at Ealing. Short

--------------------------- 1943 ---------------------------

Nine Men. Ealing Studios. *Assoc Pr:* Charles Crichton. *Dir/Sc:* Harry Watt. Based on the story "Umpity Poo" by Gerald Kersh. *Ph:* Roy Kellino. *Sup Ed:* Sidney Cole. *Ed:* Crichton. *A.D.:* Duncan Sutherland. *Mus:* John Greenwood, Eric Coates. *With:* Jack Lambert, Gordon Jackson, Frederick Piper, Grant Sutherland, Bill Blewitt

Greek Testament. Ealing Studios. *Pr:* Cavalcanti. *Asst:* Charles Crichton. *Dir:* Charles Hasse. *Comm:* Frank Owen, Angus MacPhail. *Story:* Monja Danischewsky. *Ph:* Douglas Slocombe, Ernest Palmer, Charles Masset. *Sup Ed:* Sidney Cole. *Ed:* Lito Carruthers. *A.D.:* Michael Relph. *Mus:* Ernest Irving. *With:* Vrassidas Capernaros, officers and men of the Greek Navy. Featurette

The Bells Go Down. Ealing Studios. *Assoc Pr:* S. C. Balcon. *Dir:* Basil Dearden. *Sc:* Roger MacDougall, *collab.* Stephen Black, based on Black's book *The Bells Go Down: The Diary of a London A.F.S. Man.* *Ph:* Ernest Palmer. *Sup Ed:* Sidney Cole. *Ed:* Mary Habberfield. *A.D.:* Michael Relph. *Mus:* Roy Douglas. *With:* Tommy Trinder, James Mason, Mervyn Johns, Finlay Currie

Undercover/U.S.: **Underground Guerrillas.** Ealing Studios. *Assoc Pr:* S. C. Balcon. *Dir:* Sergei Nolbandov. *Sc:* John Dighton, Monja Danischewsky. *Story:* George Slocombe. *Ph:* Wilkie Cooper. *Sup Ed:* Sidney Cole. *Ed:* Eily Boland. *A.D.:* Duncan Sutherland. *Mus:* Frederic Austin. *With:* John Clements, Godfrey Tearle, Tom Walls, Michael Wilding

My Learned Friend. Ealing Studios. *Assoc Pr:* S. C. Balcon. *Dir:* Basil Dearden, Will Hay. *Sc:* John Dighton, Angus MacPhail. *Ph:* Wilkie Cooper. *Ed:* Charles Hasse. *A.D.:* Michael Relph. *Song:* Peter Noble. *Mus:* Ernest Irving. *With:* Will Hay, Claude Hulbert, Mervyn Johns, Ernest Thesiger

Did You Ever See a Dream Walking? Ealing Studios, for National Savings Committee. *Dir:* Basil Dearden. *With:* Claude Hulbert, Enid Trevor. Short

Save Your Shillings and Smile. Ealing Studios, for National Savings Committee. *Dir:* Harry Watt. *With:* Tommy Trinder, Carol Lynne. Short

The Saving Grace. Ealing Studios, for National Savings Committee. *Dir:* Charles Frend. *With:* Tom Walls, Mervyn Johns. Short

The Sky's the Limit. Ealing Studios, for National Savings Committee. *Pr:* Cavalcanti. With footage from **Ships with Wings** (1941). Short

Fleet Air Arm. Ealing Studios, for Ministry of Information. *Dir:* Compton Bennett. With footage from **Find, Fix and Strike** (1942). Short

Trois Chansons de Résistance/Three Songs about Resistance/ Songs before Sunrise. Ealing Studios. *Pr:* Cavalcanti. *Dir:* Basil Dearden. *Ed:* Sidney Cole. *With:* Germaine Sablon. Short

San Demetrio London. Ealing Studios. *Assoc Pr:* Robert Hamer. *Dir:* Charles Frend. *Sc:* Hamer, Frend. *Ph:* Ernest Palmer. *Ed:* Eily Boland. *A.D.:* Duncan Sutherland. *Mus:* John Greenwood. *With:* Walter FitzGerald, Ralph Michael, Gordon Jackson, Mervyn Johns, Frederick Piper, Robert Beatty. *Rel:* 1944

Ship Safety. Ealing Studios, for the Admiralty. *Pr:* Cavalcanti. Short

───────────── 1944 ─────────────

The Halfway House. Ealing Studios. *Assoc Pr:* Cavalcanti. *Dir:* Basil Dearden. *Sc:* Angus MacPhail, Diana Morgan, Roland Pertwee, T. E. B. Clarke, based on the play *The Peaceful Inn* by Denis Ogden. *Ph:* Wilkie Cooper. *Sup Ed:* Sidney Cole. *Ed:* Charles Hasse. *A.D.:* Michael Relph. *Mus:* Lord Berners. *With:* Françoise Rosay, Mervyn Johns, Glynis Johns, Tom Walls

For Those in Peril. Ealing Studios. *Assoc Pr:* S. C. Balcon. *Dir:* Charles Crichton. *Sc:* Harry Watt, J. O. C. Orton, T. E. B. Clarke. *Story:* Richard Hillary. *Ph:* Douglas Slocombe, Ernest Palmer. *Sup Ed:* Sidney Cole. *Ed:* Erik Cripps. *A.D.:* Duncan Sutherland. *Mus:* Gordon Jacob. *With:* David Farrar, Ralph Michael

The Return of the Vikings. Ealing Studios. *Assoc Pr:* Sidney Cole. *Dir:* Charles Frend. *Sc:* Frend, Cole. *Ph:* Ernest Palmer. *Ed:* Carl Heck. *A.D.:* Duncan Sutherland. *Mus Dir:* Ernest Irving. *Narr:* Leo Genn. *With:* Stig Nissen, Frederick Piper, Leo Genn

They Came to a City. Ealing Studios. *Assoc Pr:* Sidney Cole. *Dir:* Basil Dearden. *Sc:* Dearden, Cole, J. B. Priestley, based on Priestley's play. *Ph:* Stan Pavey. *Ed:* Michael Truman. *A.D.:* Michael Relph. *Mus:* Alexander Scriabin. *With:* John Clements, Googie Withers, Raymond Huntley. *Rel:* 1945

Champagne Charlie. Ealing Studios. *Assoc Pr:* John Croydon. *Dir:* Cavalcanti. *Sc:* Austin Melford, John Dighton, Angus MacPhail. *Ph:* Wilkie Cooper. *Ed:* Charles Hasse. *A.D.:* Michael Relph. *Original songs from 1860s:* Alfred Lee, George Leybourne. *New songs and lyrics:* Una Barr, T. E. B. Clarke, Lord Berners, Noel Gay, Frank Eyton, Billy Mayerl, MacPhail. *Mus Dir:* Ernest Irving. *With:* Tommy Trinder, Stanley Holloway, Jean Kent, Betty Warren

Fiddlers Three. Ealing Studios. *Assoc Pr:* Robert Hamer. *Dir:* Harry Watt. *Sc:* Angus MacPhail, Diana Morgan. *Ph:* Wilkie Cooper. *Ed:* Eily Boland. *A.D.:* Duncan Sutherland. *Mus:* Mischa Spoliansky, Harry Jacobson, Geoffrey Wright. *Lyr:* Morgan, Hamer, Roland Blackburn. *With:* Tommy Trinder, Frances Day, Sonnie Hale, Francis L. Sullivan

Journal of Resistance. Comité de la Libération du Cinéma Français. *Comm/Narr:* Noël Coward. Short; Eng-lang version of French film *Le Journal de la Résistance* (1944)

Dreaming. John Baxter Productions. *Assoc Pr:* Baynham Honri. *Pr/Dir:* John Baxter. *Sc:* Reginald Purdell, Bud Flanagan. *Ph:* Stan Pavey. *Ed:* E. Hunter. *A.D.:* Duncan Sutherland. *Mus:* Kennedy Russell. *Songs:* Bud Flanagan, Desmond O'Connor. *With:* Bud Flanagan, Chesney Allen. Filmed at Ealing

───────────── 1945 ─────────────

Johnny Frenchman. Ealing Studios. *Assoc Pr:* S. C. Balcon. *Dir:* Charles Frend. *Sc:* T. E. B. Clarke. *Ph:* Roy Kellino. *Ed:* Michael Truman. *A.D.:* Duncan Sutherland. *Mus:* Clifton Parker. *With:* Françoise Rosay, Tom Walls, Patricia Roc, Ralph Michael, Paul Dupuis

Painted Boats/U.S.: **The Girl on the Canal.** Ealing Studios. *Assoc Pr:* Henry Cornelius. *Dir:* Charles Crichton. *Sc:* Stephen Black, with Micky McCarthy. *Comm:* Louis MacNeice. *Ph:* Douglas Slocombe. *Ed:* Leslie Allen. *A.D.:* Jim Morahan. *Mus:* John Greenwood. *Narr:* James McKechnie. *With:* Jenny Laird, Bill Blewitt, May Hallatt, Harry Fowler

Dead of Night. Ealing Studios. *Assoc Pr:* Sidney Cole, John Croydon. *Sc:* Angus MacPhail, John V. Baines. *Add Dial:* T. E. B. Clarke. *Ph:* Stan Pavey, Douglas Slocombe. *Ed:* Charles Hasse. *A.D.:* Michael Relph. *Mus:* Georges Auric. Episodes: Linking story: *Dir:* Basil Dearden. *Story:* E. F. Benson. *With:* Mervyn Johns, Roland Culver, Frederick Valk. "The Hearse Driver": *Dir:* Dearden. *Story:* Benson. *With:* Miles Malleson. "The Christmas Party": *Dir:* Cavalcanti. *Story:* MacPhail. *With:* Sally Ann Howes, Michael Allan. "The Haunted Mirror": *Dir:* Robert Hamer. *Story:* Baines. *With:* Googie Withers, Ralph Michael. "The Golfing Story": *Dir:* Charles Crichton. *Story:* H. G. Wells. *With:* Basil Radford, Naunton Wayne. "The Ventriloquist's Dummy": *Dir:* Cavalcanti. *Story:* Baines. *With:* Michael Redgrave, Hartley Power, Garry Marsh

Pink String and Sealing Wax. Ealing Studios. *Assoc Pr:* S. C. Balcon. *Dir:* Robert Hamer. *Sc:* Diana Morgan, based on the play by Roland Pertwee. *Co-sc:* Hamer. *Ph:* Stan Pavey. *Ed:* Michael Truman. *A.D.:* Duncan Sutherland. *Mus:* Norman Demuth. *With:* Mervyn Johns, Googie Withers, Gordon Jackson, Sally Ann Howes

Here Comes the Sun. John Baxter Productions. *Assoc Pr:* Baynham Honri. *Pr/Dir:* John Baxter. *Sc:* Geoffrey Orme. *Story:* Bud Flanagan, Reginald Purdell. *Ph:* Stan Pavey. *Ed:* Vi Burdon. *A.D.:* Duncan Sutherland. *Mus:* Kennedy Russell. *With:* Bud Flanagan, Chesney Allen. *Rel:* 1946. Filmed at Ealing

───────────── 1946 ─────────────

The Captive Heart. Ealing Studios. *Assoc Pr:* Michael Relph. *Dir:* Basil Dearden. *Sc:* Angus MacPhail, Guy Morgan. *Ph:* Lionel Banes, Douglas Slocombe. *Ed:* Charles Hasse. *A.D.:* Michael Relph. *Mus:* Alan Rawsthorne. *With:* Michael Redgrave, Mervyn Johns, Basil Radford, Jack Warner, Gordon Jackson, Derek Bond, Rachel Kempson, Jane Barrett

Bedelia. John Corfield Productions. *Pr:* John Corfield. *Assoc Pr:* Isadore Goldsmith. *Dir:* Lance Comfort. *Sc:* Vera Caspary, Herbert Victor, Goldsmith, based on Caspary's novel. *Ph:* Frederick A. Young. *Ed:* Michael Truman. *A.D.:* Duncan Sutherland. *Mus:* Hans May. *With:* Margaret Lockwood, Ian Hunter, Barry K. Barnes. Filmed at Ealing

Man—One Family. Ealing Studios, for Ministry of Information. *Pr:* Sidney Cole. *Dir/Sc:* Ivor Montagu. *Comm:* Dr. Julian Huxley. *Ed:* Sidney Cole. *Mus:* Van Phillips. Short

The Overlanders. Ealing Studios. *Assoc Pr:* Ralph Smart. *Dir/Sc:* Harry Watt. *Ph:* Osmond Borradaile. *Sup Ed:* Leslie Norman. *Ed:* E. M. Inman Hunter. *Mus:* John Ireland. *With:* Chips Rafferty, Daphne Campbell. Filmed in Australia

───────────── 1947 ─────────────

Hue and Cry. Ealing Studios. *Assoc Pr:* Henry Cornelius. *Dir:* Charles Crichton. *Sc:* T. E. B. Clarke. *Ph:* Douglas Slocombe. *Ed:* Charles Hasse. *A.D.:* Norman G. Arnold. *Mus:* Georges Auric. *With:* Harry Fowler, Jack Warner, Alastair Sim

Nicholas Nickleby/The Life and Adventures of Nicholas Nickleby. Ealing Studios. *Assoc Pr:* John Croydon. *Dir:* Cavalcanti. *Sc:* John Dighton, based on the novel by Charles Dickens. *Ph:* Gordon Dines. *Ed:* Leslie Norman. *A.D.:* Michael Relph. *Mus:* Lord Berners. *With:* Derek Bond, Cedric Hardwicke, Mary Merrall, Sally Ann Howes, Bernard Miles, Jill Balcon

The Loves of Joanna Godden. Ealing Studios. *Assoc Pr:* Sidney Cole. *Dir:* Charles Frend. *Sc:* H. E. Bates, Angus MacPhail, based on the novel *Joanna Godden* by Sheila Kaye-Smith. *Ph:* Douglas Slocombe. *Ed:* Michael Truman. *A.D.:* Duncan Sutherland. *Mus:* Ralph Vaughan Williams. *With:* Googie Withers, Jean Kent, John McCallum, Derek Bond

Frieda. Ealing Studios. *Assoc Pr:* Michael Relph. *Dir:* Basil Dearden. *Sc:* Angus MacPhail, Ronald Millar, based on Millar's play. *Ph:* Gordon Dines. *Ed:* Leslie Norman. *Prod Des:* Michael Relph. *A.D.:* Jim Morahan. *Mus:* John Greenwood. *With:* David Farrar, Glynis Johns, Mai Zetterling, Flora Robson

It Always Rains on Sunday. Ealing Studios. *Assoc Pr:* Henry Cornelius. *Dir:* Robert Hamer. *Sc:* Angus MacPhail, Hamer, Cornelius, based on the novel by Arthur La Bern. *Ph:* Douglas Slocombe. *Ed:* Michael Truman. *A.D.:* Duncan Sutherland. *Mus:* Georges Auric. *With:* Googie Withers, Edward Chapman, Susan Shaw, Patricia Plunkett, John McCallum, Jack Warner, Sydney Tafler

──────────────── 1948 ────────────────

Against the Wind. Ealing Studios. *Assoc Pr:* Sidney Cole. *Dir:* Charles Crichton. *Sc:* T. E. B. Clarke. *Story:* J. Elder Wills. *Adapt:* Michael Pertwee. *Ph:* Lionel Banes. *Ed:* Alan Osbiston. *A.D.:* Wills. *Mus:* Leslie Bridgewater. *With:* Robert Beatty, Jack Warner, Simone Signoret, Gordon Jackson, Paul Dupuis

Saraband for Dead Lovers/U.S.: Saraband. Ealing Studios. *Assoc Pr:* Michael Relph. *Dir:* Basil Dearden. *Sc:* John Dighton, Alexander Mackendrick, based on the novel by Helen Simpson. *Ph (Technicolor):* Douglas Slocombe. *Ed:* Michael Truman. *Prod Des:* Relph. *A.D.:* Jim Morahan, William Kellner. *Mus:* Alan Rawsthorne. *With:* Stewart Granger, Joan Greenwood, Flora Robson, Françoise Rosay, Peter Bull, Jill Balcon

Another Shore. Ealing Studios. *Assoc Pr:* Ivor Montagu. *Dir:* Charles Crichton. *Sc:* Walter Meade. *Ph:* Douglas Slocombe. *Ed:* Bernard Gribble. *A.D.:* Malcolm Baker-Smith. *Mus:* Georges Auric. *With:* Robert Beatty, Moira Lister, Stanley Holloway

Scott of the Antarctic. Ealing Studios. *Assoc Pr:* Sidney Cole. *Dir:* Charles Frend. *Sc:* Walter Meade, Ivor Montagu. *Ph (Technicolor):* Jack Cardiff, Osmond Borradaile, Geoffrey Unsworth. *Ed:* Peter Tanner. *A.D.:* Arne Akermark. *Mus:* Ralph Vaughan Williams. *With:* John Mills, Derek Bond, Harold Warrender, James Robertson Justice, Reginald Beckwith, Kenneth More. *Rel:* 1949

──────────────── 1949 ────────────────

Eureka Stockade. Ealing Studios. *Assoc Pr:* Leslie Norman. *Dir:* Harry Watt. *Sc:* Watt, Walter Greenwood. *Ph:* George Heath. *Ed:* Leslie Norman. *A.D.:* Charles Woolveridge. *Mus:* John Greenwood. *With:* Chips Rafferty, Jane Barrett, Gordon Jackson, Jack Lambert. Filmed in Australia

Passport to Pimlico. Ealing Studios. *Assoc Pr:* E. V. H. Emmett. *Dir:* Henry Cornelius. *Sc:* T. E. B. Clarke. *Ph:* Lionel Banes. *Ed:* Michael Truman. *A.D.:* Roy Oxley. *Mus:* Georges Auric. *With:* Stanley Holloway, Paul Dupuis, Margaret Rutherford, Raymond Huntley, Barbara Murray, Betty Warren, Basil Radford, Naunton Wayne

Jill Balcon and Cedric Hardwicke, *Nicholas Nickleby,* 1947

Whisky Galore!/U.S.: Tight Little Island. Ealing Studios. *Assoc Pr:* Monja Danischewsky. *Dir:* Alexander Mackendrick. *Sc:* Compton Mackenzie, Angus MacPhail, based on Mackenzie's novel. *Ph:* Gerald Gibbs. *Ed:* Joseph Sterling. *A.D.:* Jim Morahan. *Mus:* Ernest Irving. *With:* Basil Radford, Bruce Seton, Joan Greenwood, Gordon Jackson, Wylie Watson, Gabrielle Blunt, Morland Graham, John Gregson

Kind Hearts and Coronets. Ealing Studios. *Assoc Pr:* Michael Relph. *Dir:* Robert Hamer. *Sc:* Hamer, John Dighton, based on the novel *Israel Rank* by Roy Horniman. *Ph:* Douglas Slocombe. *Ed:* Peter Tanner. *A.D.:* William Kellner. *Mus:* Mozart. *With:* Dennis Price, Joan Greenwood, Valerie Hobson, Alec Guinness

Train of Events. Ealing Studios. *Assoc Pr:* Michael Relph. Episodes: "The Engine Driver": *Dir:* Sidney Cole. "The Prisoner-of-War": *Dir:* Basil Dearden. "The Composer": *Dir:* Charles Crichton. "The Actor": *Dir:* Dearden. *Sc:* Dearden, T. E. B. Clarke, Ronald Millar, Angus MacPhail. *Ph:* Lionel Banes, Gordon Dines. *Ed:* Bernard Gribble. *A.D.:* Malcolm Baker-Smith, Jim Morahan. *Mus:* Leslie Bridgewater. *With:* Valerie Hobson, Jack Warner, John Clements, Susan Shaw, Peter Finch, Gladys Henson

A Run for Your Money. Ealing Studios. *Assoc Pr:* Leslie Norman. *Dir:* Charles Frend. *Sc:* Richard Hughes, Norman, Frend. *Story:* Clifford Evans. *Ph:* Douglas Slocombe. *Ed:* Michael Truman. *A.D.:* William Kellner. *Mus:* Ernest Irving. *With:* Donald Houston, Alec Guinness, Meredith Edwards, Hugh Griffith, Moira Lister, Joyce Grenfell

──────────────── 1950 ────────────────

The Blue Lamp. Ealing Studios. *Assoc Pr:* Michael Relph. *Dir:* Basil Dearden. *Sc:* T. E. B. Clarke. *Story:* Jan Read, Ted Willis. *Add Dial:* Alexander Mackendrick. *Ph:* Gordon Dines. *Ed:* Peter Tanner. *A.D.:* Jim Morahan. *Mus:* Ernest Irving. *With:* Jack Warner, Jimmy Hanley, Dirk Bogarde, Bernard Lee, Peggy Evans, Robert Flemyng, Gladys Henson

Dance Hall. Ealing Studios. *Assoc Pr:* E. V. H. Emmett. *Dir:* Charles Crichton. *Sc:* Emmett, Diana Morgan, Alexander Mackendrick. *Ph:* Douglas Slocombe. *Ed:* Seth Holt. *A.D.:* Norman Arnold. *With:* Donald Houston, Bonar Colleano, Petula Clark, Natasha Parry, Diana Dors, Jane Hylton

Bitter Springs. Ealing Studios. *Assoc Pr:* Leslie Norman. *Dir:* Ralph Smart. *Sc:* W. P. Lipscomb, Monja Danischewsky. *Story:* Smart. *Ph:* George Heath. *Ed:* Bernard Gribble. *A.D.:* Charles Woolveridge. *Mus:* Ralph Vaughan Williams. *With:* Tommy Trinder, Chips Rafferty, Gordon Jackson. Filmed in Australia

Cage of Gold. Ealing Studios. *Assoc Pr:* Michael Relph. *Dir:* Basil Dearden. *Sc:* Jack Whittingham. *Ph:* Douglas Slocombe. *Ed:* Peter Tanner. *A.D.:* Jim Morahan. *Mus:* Georges Auric. *With:* Jean Simmons, David Farrar, James Donald, Herbert Lom

The Magnet. Ealing Studios. *Assoc Pr:* Sidney Cole. *Dir:* Charles Frend. *Sc:* T. E. B. Clarke. *Ph:* Lionel Banes. *Ed:* Bernard Gribble. *A.D.:* Jim Morahan. *Mus:* William Alwyn. *With:* Stephen Murray, Kay Walsh, William Fox, Meredith Edwards, Julien Mitchell, Wylie Watson

———————————— 1951 ————————————

Pool of London. Ealing Studios. *Assoc Pr:* Michael Relph. *Dir:* Basil Dearden. *Sc:* Jack Whittingham, John Eldridge. *Ph:* Gordon Dines. *Ed:* Peter Tanner. *A.D.:* Jim Morahan. *Mus:* John Addison. *With:* Bonar Colleano, Susan Shaw, Earl Cameron, Renée Asherson, Moira Lister

The Lavender Hill Mob. Ealing Studios. *Assoc Pr:* Michael Truman. *Dir:* Charles Crichton. *Sc:* T. E. B. Clarke. *Ph:* Douglas Slocombe. *Ed:* Seth Holt. *A.D.:* William Kellner. *Mus:* Georges Auric. *With:* Alec Guinness, Stanley Holloway, Sidney James, Alfie Bass

The Man in the White Suit. Ealing Studios. *Assoc Pr:* Sidney Cole. *Dir:* Alexander Mackendrick. *Sc:* Roger MacDougall, John Dighton, Mackendrick, based on MacDougall's play. *Ph:* Douglas Slocombe. *Ed:* Bernard Gribble. *A.D.:* Jim Morahan. *Mus:* Benjamin Frankel. *With:* Alec Guinness, Joan Greenwood, Cecil Parker, Michael Gough, Ernest Thesiger

Where No Vultures Fly/U.S.: *Ivory Hunter.* Ealing Studios/ African Films Productions. *Assoc Pr:* Leslie Norman. *Dir:* Harry Watt. *Sc:* W. P. Lipscomb, Ralph Smart, Norman. *Story:* Watt. *Ph* (Technicolor): Geoffrey Unsworth, Paul Beeson. *Sup Ed:* Jack Harris. *Ed:* Gordon Stone. *Mus:* Alan Rawsthorne. *With:* Anthony Steel, Dinah Sheridan. *Rel:* 1952. Filmed in East Africa

———————————— 1952 ————————————

His Excellency. Ealing Studios. *Pr:* Michael Truman. *Dir:* Robert Hamer. *Sc:* Hamer, based on the play by Dorothy and Campbell Christie. *Add Dial:* W. P. Lipscomb. *Ph:* Douglas Slocombe. *Ed:* Seth Holt. *A.D.:* Jim Morahan. *Mus:* Handel, *arr:* Ernest Irving. *With:* Eric Portman, Cecil Parker, Helen Cherry

Secret People. Ealing Studios. *Pr:* Sidney Cole. *Dir:* Thorold Dickinson. *Sc:* Dickinson, Wolfgang Wilhelm. *Story:* Dickinson, Joyce Cary. *Ph:* Gordon Dines. *Ed:* Peter Tanner. *A.D.:* William Kellner. *Mus:* Roberto Gerhard. *With:* Valentina Cortese, Serge Reggiani, Audrey Hepburn, Megs Jenkins

I Believe in You. Ealing Studios. *Pr:* Michael Relph. *Dir:* Basil Dearden. *Sc:* Relph, Dearden, Jack Whittingham. *Ph:* Gordon Dines. *Ed:* Peter Tanner. *A.D.:* Maurice Carter. *Mus:* Ernest Irving. *With:* Cecil Parker, Celia Johnson, Godfrey Tearle, Harry Fowler, Joan Collins, George Relph

Mandy/U.S.: *Crash of Silence.* Ealing Studios. *Pr:* Leslie Norman. *Dir:* Alexander Mackendrick. *Sc:* Jack Whittingham,

Nigel Balchin. *Ph:* Douglas Slocombe. *Ed:* Seth Holt. *A.D.:* Jim Morahan. *Mus:* William Alwyn. *With:* Jack Hawkins, Terence Morgan, Phyllis Calvert, Mandy Miller, Godfrey Tearle

The Gentle Gunman. Ealing Studios. *Pr:* Michael Relph. *Dir:* Basil Dearden. *Sc:* Roger MacDougall, based on his play. *Ph:* Gordon Dines. *Ed:* Peter Tanner. *A.D.:* Jim Morahan. *Mus:* John Greenwood. *With:* John Mills, Robert Beatty, Dirk Bogarde

The Titfield Thunderbolt. Ealing Studios. *Pr:* Michael Truman. *Dir:* Charles Crichton. *Sc:* T. E. B. Clarke. *Ph* (Technicolor): Douglas Slocombe. *Ed:* Seth Holt. *A.D.:* C. P. Norman. *Mus:* Georges Auric. *With:* Stanley Holloway, George Relph, Naunton Wayne, John Gregson, Godfrey Tearle. *Rel:* 1953

The Cruel Sea. Ealing Studios. *Pr:* Leslie Norman. *Dir:* Charles Frend. *Sc:* Eric Ambler, based on the novel by Nicholas Monsarrat. *Ph:* Gordon Dines, Jo Jago. *Ed:* Peter Tanner. *A.D.:* Jim Morahan. *Mus:* Alan Rawsthorne. *With:* Jack Hawkins, Donald Sinden, Denholm Elliott, Stanley Baker, Virginia McKenna. *Rel:* 1953

———————————— 1953 ————————————

The Square Ring. Ealing Studios. *Pr:* Michael Relph. *Dir:* Basil Dearden. *Sc:* Robert Westerby. *Ph:* Otto Heller. *Ed:* Peter Bezencenet. *A.D.:* Jim Morahan. *Mus Dir:* Dock Mathieson. *With:* Jack Warner, Robert Beatty, Maxwell Reed, Bill Owen, George Rose, Joan Collins

Meet Mr. Lucifer. Ealing Studios. *Pr:* Monja Danischewsky. *Dir:* Anthony Pelissier. *Sc:* Danischewsky, based on the play *Beggar My Neighbour* by Arnold Ridley. *Ph:* Desmond Dickinson. *Ed:* Bernard Gribble. *A.D.:* Wilfrid Shingleton. *Mus:* Eric Rogers. *With:* Stanley Holloway, Peggy Cummins, Jack Watling, Barbara Murray

———————————— 1954 ————————————

The Love Lottery. Ealing Studios. *Pr:* Monja Danischewsky. *Dir:* Charles Crichton. *Sc:* Harry Kurnitz. *Story:* Charles Neilson-Terry, Zelma Bramley Moore. *Add Scenes/Dial:* Danischewsky. *Ph* (Technicolor): Douglas Slocombe. *Ed:* Seth Holt. *A.D.:* Tom Morahan. *Mus:* Benjamin Frankel. *With:* David Niven, Peggy Cummins, Herbert Lom, Anne Vernon

The Maggie/U.S.: *High and Dry.* Ealing Studios. *Pr:* Michael Truman. *Dir:* Alexander Mackendrick. *Sc:* William Rose. *Ph:* Gordon Dines. *Ed:* Peter Tanner. *A.D.:* Jim Morahan. *Mus:* John Addison. *With:* Paul Douglas, Alex Mackenzie

West of Zanzibar. Ealing Studios, in conjunction with Schlesinger Association. *Pr:* Leslie Norman. *Dir:* Harry Watt. *Sc:* Max Catto, Jack Whittingham. *Story:* Watt. *Ph* (Technicolor): Paul Beeson. *Ed:* Peter Bezencenet. *A.D.:* Jim Morahan. *Mus:* Alan Rawsthorne. *With:* Anthony Steel, Sheila Sim, William Simons, Edric Connor. Filmed in East Africa

The Rainbow Jacket. Ealing Studios. *Pr:* Michael Relph. *Dir:* Basil Dearden. *Sc:* T. E. B. Clarke. *Ph* (Technicolor): Otto Heller. *Ed:* Jack Harris. *A.D.:* Tom Morahan. *Mus:* William Alwyn. *With:* Bill Owen, Kay Walsh, Fella Edmonds, Edward Underdown

Lease of Life. Ealing Studios. *Assoc Pr:* Jack Rix. *Dir:* Charles Frend. *Sc:* Eric Ambler. *Ph* (Technicolor): Douglas Slocombe. *Ed:* Peter Tanner. *A.D.:* Jim Morahan. *Mus:* Alan Rawsthorne. *With:* Robert Donat, Kay Walsh, Adrienne Corri, Denholm Elliott

The Divided Heart. Ealing Studios. *Pr:* Michael Truman. *Dir:* Charles Crichton. *Sc:* Jack Whittingham, Richard Hughes. *Ph:* Otto Heller. *Ed:* Peter Bezencenet. *A.D.:* Edward Carrick. *Mus:* Georges Auric. *With:* Cornell Borchers, Yvonne

Mitchell, Alexander Knox, Michel Ray, Armin Dahlen

Armand and Michaela Denis under the Southern Cross. Ealing Studios. *Comm:* E. V. H. Emmett. *Ph* (Eastmancolor): Des Bartlett. *Sup Ed:* Jack Harris. *Ed:* Adrian de Potier. *Mus:* James Stevens. *With:* Armand and Michaela Denis. *Rel: 1955*

───────────── 1955 ─────────────

Out of the Clouds. Ealing Studios. *Pr:* Michael Relph. *Dir:* Basil Dearden. *Sc:* Relph, John Eldridge. *Ph* (Eastmancolor): Paul Beeson. *Ed:* Jack Harris. *A.D.:* Jim Morahan. *Mus:* Richard Addinsell. *With:* Anthony Steel, Robert Beatty, James Robertson Justice

The Night My Number Came Up. Ealing Studios. *Assoc Pr:* Tom Morahan. *Dir:* Leslie Norman. *Sc:* R. C. Sherriff. *Ph:* Lionel Banes. *Ed:* Peter Bezencenet. *A.D.:* Bernard Robinson. *Mus:* William Alwyn. *With:* Michael Redgrave, Sheila Sim, Alexander Knox, Denholm Elliott, Ursula Jeans

Armand and Michaela Denis on the Barrier Reef. Ealing Studios. *Comm:* E. V. H. Emmett. *Ph* (Eastmancolor): Noel Monkman, Des Bartlett. *Sup Ed:* Jack Harris. *Ed:* Adrian de Potier, David Howes. *Mus:* James Stevens. With: Armand and Michaela Denis

The Ship That Died of Shame/U.S.: ***PT Raiders.*** Ealing Studios. *Pr:* Michael Relph. *Dir:* Basil Dearden. *Sc:* John Whiting, Relph, Dearden, based on the novel by Nicholas Monsarrat. *Ph:* Gordon Dines. *Ed:* Peter Bezencenet. *A.D.:* Bernard Robinson. *Mus:* William Alwyn. *With:* Richard Attenborough, George Baker, Bill Owen, Roland Culver

Touch and Go/U.S.: ***The Light Touch.*** Ealing Studios. *Assoc Pr:* Seth Holt. *Dir:* Michael Truman. *Sc:* William Rose. *Story:* William and Tania Rose. *Ph* (Technicolor): Douglas Slocombe. *Ed:* Peter Tanner. *A.D.:* Edward Carrick. *Mus:* John Addison. *With:* Jack Hawkins, Margaret Johnston, June Thorburn, John Fraser

Armand and Michaela Denis among the Headhunters. Ealing Studios. *Comm:* E. V. H. Emmett. *Ph* (Eastmancolor): Des Bartlett. *Sup Ed:* Jack Harris. *Ed:* David Howes. *Mus:* James Stevens. *With:* Armand and Michaela Denis

The Ladykillers. Ealing Studios. *Assoc Pr:* Seth Holt. *Dir:* Alexander Mackendrick. *Sc:* William Rose. *Ph* (Technicolor): Otto Heller. *Ed:* Jack Harris. *A.D.:* Jim Morahan. *Mus:* Tristram Cary. *With:* Katie Johnson, Alec Guinness, Cecil Parker, Herbert Lom, Peter Sellers, Danny Green

───────────── 1956 ─────────────

Who Done It? Ealing Studios. *Pr:* Michael Relph. *Dir:* Basil Dearden. *Sc:* T. E. B. Clarke. *Ph:* Otto Heller. *Ed:* Peter Tanner. *A.D.:* Jim Morahan. *Mus:* Philip Green. *With:* Benny Hill, Belinda Lee, David Kossoff, Garry Marsh, Ernest Thesiger

The Feminine Touch/U.S.: ***The Gentle Touch.*** Ealing Studios. *Assoc Pr:* Jack Rix. *Dir:* Pat Jackson. *Sc:* Ian McCormick, based on the novel *A Lamp Is Heavy* by Sheila MacKay Russell. *Ph* (Eastmancolor): Paul Beeson. *Ed:* Peter Bezencenet. *A.D.:* Edward Carrick. *Mus:* Clifton Parker. *With:* George Baker, Belinda Lee, Delphi Lawrence, Adrienne Corri, Diana Wynyard

The Long Arm/U.S.: ***The Third Key.*** Ealing Studios. *Assoc Pr:* Tom Morahan. *Dir:* Charles Frend. *Sc:* Janet Green, Robert Barr. *Story:* Barr. *Ph:* Gordon Dines. *Ed:* Gordon Stone. *A.D.:* Edward Carrick. *Mus:* Gerbrand Schurmann. *With:* Jack Hawkins, Dorothy Alison

───────────── 1957 ─────────────

The Man in the Sky/U.S.: ***Decision against Time.*** Ealing

Films. *Assoc Pr:* Seth Holt. *Dir:* Charles Crichton. *Sc:* William Rose, John Eldridge. *Story:* Rose. *Ph* (Metroscope): Douglas Slocombe. *Ed:* Peter Tanner. *A.D.:* Jim Morahan. *Mus:* Gerbrand Schurmann. *With:* Jack Hawkins, Elizabeth Sellars, Catherine Lacey, John Stratton

The Shiralee. Ealing Films. *Pr:* Jack Rix. *Dir:* Leslie Norman. *Sc:* Norman, Neil Paterson. *Ph* (Metroscope): Paul Beeson. *Ed:* Gordon Stone. *A.D.:* Jim Morahan. *Mus:* John Addison. *With:* Peter Finch, Elizabeth Sellars, Dana Wilson, Rosemary Harris. Filmed in Sydney, Australia

Barnacle Bill/U.S.: ***All at Sea.*** Ealing Films. *Assoc Pr:* Dennis van Thal. *Dir:* Charles Frend. *Sc:* T. E. B. Clarke. *Ph:* Douglas Slocombe. *Ed:* Jack Harris. *A.D.:* Alan Withy. *Mus:* John Addison. *With:* Alec Guinness, Irene Browne, Maurice Denham

Davy. Ealing Films. *Pr:* Basil Dearden. *Dir:* Michael Relph. *Sc:* William Rose. *Ph* (Technicolor, Technirama): Douglas Slocombe. *Ed:* Peter Tanner. *A.D.:* Alan Withy. *With:* Harry Secombe, Alexander Knox, Ron Randell, George Relph, Susan Shaw. *Rel: 1958*

───────────── 1958 ─────────────

Dunkirk. Ealing Films. *Assoc Pr:* Michael Forlong. *Dir:* Leslie Norman. *Sc:* W. P. Lipscomb, David Divine. *Ph:* Paul Beeson. *Ed:* Gordon Stone. *A.D.:* Jim Morahan. *Mus:* Malcolm Arnold. *With:* John Mills, Richard Attenborough, Bernard Lee

Nowhere to Go. Ealing Films. *Assoc Pr:* Eric Williams. *Dir:* Seth Holt. *Sc:* Holt, Kenneth Tynan, based on the novel by Donald Mackenzie. *Ph:* Paul Beeson. *Ed:* Harry Aldous. *Prod Des:* Peter Proud. *A.D.:* Alan Withy. *With:* George Nader, Maggie Smith, Bessie Love, Bernard Lee

───────────── 1959 ─────────────

The Scapegoat. M-G-M British, a du Maurier-Guinness Production. *Assoc Pr:* Dennis van Thal. *Dir:* Robert Hamer. *Sc:* Hamer. *Adapt:* Gore Vidal, based on the novel by Daphne du Maurier. *Ph:* Paul Beeson. *Ed:* Jack Harris. *Prod Des:* Elliot Scott. *A.D.:* Alan Withy. *Mus:* Bronislau Kaper. *With:* Alec Guinness, Bette Davis, Nicole Maurey, Irene Worth, Pamela Brown

The Siege of Pinchgut/U.S.: ***Four Desperate Men.*** Ealing Films. *Assoc Pr:* Eric Williams. *Dir:* Harry Watt. *Sc:* Watt, John Cleary. *Ph:* Gordon Dines. *Ed:* Gordon Stone. *A.D.:* Alan Withy. *Mus:* Kenneth V. Jones. *With:* Aldo Ray, Neil McCallum, Heather Sears. Filmed in Sydney, Australia

───────────── 1961 ─────────────

The Long and the Short and the Tall/U.S.: ***Jungle Fighters.*** Michael Balcon Productions/Associated British Productions. *Dir:* Leslie Norman. *Sc:* Wolf Mankowitz, based on the play by Willis Hall. *Ph:* Erwin Hillier. *Ed:* Gordon Stone. *A.D.:* Jim Morahan. *Mus:* Stanley Black. *With:* Richard Todd, Laurence Harvey, Richard Harris, David McCallum

───────────── 1963 ─────────────

Sammy Going South/U.S.: ***A Boy Ten Feet Tall.*** Michael Balcon Productions, for Bryanston/Seven Arts. *Pr:* Hal Mason. *Dir:* Alexander Mackendrick. *Sc:* Denis Cannan, based on the novel by W. H. Canaway. *Ph* (Eastmancolor, CinemaScope): Erwin Hillier. *Ed:* Jack Harris. *A.D.:* Edward Tester. *Mus:* Tristram Cary. *With:* Fergus McClelland, Edward G. Robinson, Constance Cummings. Portions filmed in Africa

Bibliography

Gillian Hartnoll, Virginia Hennessy, and Joan Ingram

THIS BIBLIOGRAPHY on Michael Balcon and the British film industry was originally compiled by Virginia Hennessy and Joan Ingram of the British Film Institute for *Der Produzent: Michael Balcon und der englische Film* (1981), and is reprinted by permission of the Stiftung Deutsche Kinemathek, Berlin. It has been edited for this publication by Catherine A. Surowiec of The Museum of Modern Art, with additions and emendations by Gillian Hartnoll and Joan Ingram of the British Film Institute.

Readers seeking reviews of British films of the period 1921-77 are directed to the many newspapers, periodicals, and trade papers cited, as well as to the *New York Times, Variety* (New York), *The Times* and *The Sunday Times* of London (especially the reviews of Dilys Powell, 1939-76), *Manchester Guardian,* and the BFI's own publications the *Monthly Film Bulletin* and *Sight and Sound.* A sampling of available anthologies of critical writings is listed below:

Agee, James. *Agee on Film: Reviews and Comments by James Agee.* Boston: Beacon Press, 1964. Reviews, 1941-50, from *Life, The Nation, Partisan Review, Sight and Sound,* and *Time.*
Cooke, Alistair, ed. *Garbo and the Night Watchmen.* London: Secker & Warburg; New York: McGraw-Hill, 1971. Reprint of 1937 anthology of writings by British and American film critics.
Lorentz, Pare. *Lorentz on Film: Movies 1927 to 1941.* New York: Hopkinson & Blake, 1975. Reviews from *Judge, McCall's, Scribner's,* and *Vanity Fair.*
Taylor, John Russell, ed. *Graham Greene on Film: Collected Film Criticism 1935-1940.* New York: Simon & Schuster, 1972. Reviews from *The Spectator.*
Wilson, Robert, ed. *The Film Criticism of Otis Ferguson.* Philadelphia: Temple University Press, 1971. Reviews, 1934-41, from *The New Republic.*
Winnington, Richard. *Film: Criticism and Caricatures, 1943-53.* London: Paul Elek, 1975. Selected and with an introduction by Paul Rotha. Reviews from the *News Chronicle* (London).

SPECIAL COLLECTIONS

The Aileen and Michael Balcon Collection, British Film Institute, London. Scrapbooks 1935–72; miscellaneous files of letters, cables, data, and papers; documents relating to production technique and individual film studios and companies; scripts. Written permission from the Balcon estate is required before consulting much of this material. Held at the Library Services Department, BFI, 127 Charing Cross Road, London. WC2H OEA.

BY MICHAEL BALCON (arranged chronologically)

Books

Balcon, Michael. *Realism or Tinsel?* Brighton: Film Workers Association, 1943. Reprinted in Monja Danischewsky, ed., *Michael Balcon's 25 Years in Films.* London: World Film Publications, 1947.
———. *The Producer.* London: British Film Institute, 1945. Lecture given at the BFI Summer School.
———. *Twenty Years of British Film: 1925–1945.* London: Falcon, 1947.
———. "The Eye Behind the Camera." In Balcon et al., *"Saraband for Dead Lovers": The Film and Its Production at Ealing Studios.* London: Convoy Publications, 1948, pp. 9–22.
———. "Film Comedy." In Peter Noble, ed., *The British Film Yearbook 1949–50.* London: Skelton Robinson, 1950, pp. 25–28.
———. *Film Production and Management.* London: British Institute of Management, 1950.
———. Foreword. In Egon Larsen, *Spotlight on Films.* London: Max Parrish, 1950, pp. 5–6.
———. "10 Years of British Films." In *Films in Britain 1951.* London: Sight and Sound, BFI, 1951, pp. 23–38. Published for the Festival of Britain.
———. "The Secret of Ealing Comedy." In George Campbell Dixon, ed., *International Film Annual 1.* London: John Calder, 1957, pp. 53–61.
———. Introduction. In Alexander Jacobs, ed., *Experiment in Britain.* London: BFI, 1958.
———. *Michael Balcon Presents . . . A Lifetime of Films.* London: Hutchinson, 1969.
———. Preface. In Freddie Young and Paul Petzold, *The Work of the Motion Picture Cameraman.* London: Focal Press, 1972.
———. Foreword. In Geoff Brown, *Walter Forde.* London: BFI, 1977.
———. Preface. In John Ellis, ed., *1951–1976: British Film Institute Productions: A Catalogue of Films Made under the Auspices of the Experimental Film Fund 1951–1966 and the Production Board 1966–1976.* London: BFI, 1977, p. 8.

Periodicals and Journals

Balcon, Michael. "The Diary of a Talkie." *Film Weekly* (London), 5, 119 (Jan. 24, 1931), p. 9.

————. "Sincerity Will Make the Film English." *The Era* (London), Nov. 11, 1931, p. 10.

————. "Films We Will Make in 1933." *Picturegoer* (London), 2, 84 (Dec. 31, 1932), pp. 8–9.

————. "The Function of the Producer." *Cinema Quarterly* (London, Edinburgh), 2, 1 (Autumn 1933), pp. 5–7.

————. "Whither Film?" *Film Art* (London), 5 (Winter 1934), pp. 11–13.

————. "Putting the New British Talkie on the Map in the States." *Daily Film Renter* (London), 8, 2441 (Jan. 1, 1935).

————. "British Pictures for the World." *Picturegoer* (London), 4, 192 (Jan. 26, 1935), pp. 26–27.

————. "America Revisited: Some Views and Impressions." *Daily Film Renter* (London), Jan. 1, 1936.

————. "My Hollywood Star Captures." *Film Weekly* (London), 15, 379 (Jan. 18, 1936), pp. 7–8.

————. "Putting the *Real* Britain on the Screen." *Evening News* (London), Oct. 1, 1936, p. 11.

————. "Weather or Not: Michael Balcon Discusses Tempo and Temperature in the British Picture." *Kinematograph Weekly* (London), 239, 1522 (Jan. 14, 1937), p. 31.

————. "I'm Proud of Jessie." *Film Weekly* (London), 18, 447 (May 8, 1937), pp. 12–13.

————. "My American 'Imports.'" *Film Weekly* (London), 18, 448 (May 15, 1937), pp. 14, 26.

————. "What We Did with Conrad Veidt." *Film Weekly* (London), 18, 449 (May 22, 1937), p. 11.

————. "Talking of Directors." *Film Weekly* (London), 18, 450 (May 29, 1937), pp. 14, 25.

————. "My Baby-Star School." *Film Weekly* (London), 18, 451 (June 5, 1937), p. 14.

————. "How Films Are Made." *The Listener* (London), vol. 19, no. 472 (Jan. 26, 1938), pp. 169–71, 205.

————. "Not Even Our Best Friends Will Tell Us about the B.O. Pull of British Films." *Kinematograph Weekly* (London), 275, 1708 (Jan. 11, 1940), p. D1.

————, and Norton, Richard. "Conversation Piece by Two Producers." *Kinematograph Weekly* (London), 275, 1708 (Jan. 11, 1940), British Studio Section, p. 3.

————. "Call Up the Hollywood Britons." *Picturegoer* (London), 9, 468 (May 11, 1940), p. 11.

————. "Will 'Win the War' Films Win the Audiences?" *Cine-Technician* (London), June-July 1940, p. 42.

————. "Rationalise!" *Sight and Sound* (London), 9, 36 (Winter 1940–41), pp. 62–63.

————. "Cameramen Are Gunners." *Kinematograph Weekly* (London), 287, 1760 (Jan. 9, 1941), p. 30.

————, and Baker, Reginald. "Baker-Balcon Bout: Round Two." *Kinematograph Weekly* (London), 299, 1812 (Jan. 8, 1942), p. 87.

————. "Propaganda and the Feature Producer." *Cine-Technician* (London), Feb.-Mar. 1942, pp. 4–5.

————. "Let British Films be Ambassadors to the World: A Cogent Plea from the Head of Ealing Studios." *Kinematograph Weekly* (London), 335, 1969 (Jan. 11, 1945), p. 31.

————. "Box Office Is the Final Judge of Film." *Kinematograph Weekly* (London), 342, 2002 (Aug. 30, 1945), p. 13.

————. "Passed to You Please." *Daily Film Renter* (London), 19, 5337 (Jan. 1, 1946), p, 8.

————. "The British Film during the War." *Penguin Film Review* (London), 1 (Aug. 1946), pp. 66–73.

————. "'What Has Been Achieved?': An Answer to George Elvin's Piece 'Wanted: Increased Output.'" *The Listener* (London), 39, 1001 (Apr. 1, 1948), pp. 545, 547.

————. "Prospects of British Film Production." *New Theatre* (London), Oct. 1948, pp. 9–11.

————. "The Technical Problems of *Scott of the Antarctic.*" *Sight and Sound* (London), 17, 68 (Winter 1948–49), pp. 153–55.

————. "First Lesson in Close Harmony: Michael Balcon Gives an Imaginary Talk to a Newcomer to the Industry." *Daily Film Renter* (London), 22, 5802 (Jan. 1, 1949), pp. 9, 11.

————. "The Film Crisis and the Public." *The Sunday Times* (London), Mar. 6, 1949.

————. "Disunity within the Film Industry." *Film Industry* (London), 6, 49 (June 2, 1949), p. 13.

————. "Martyrs to Fun." *Picturegoer* (London), 18, 744 (Aug. 6, 1949), p. 6.

————. "Not Enough Creative Film Minds in This Country." *Kinematograph Weekly* (London), 394, 2224 (Dec. 15, 1949), p. 45.

————. "How to Save British Films." *Cavalcade* (London), Dec. 31, 1949.

————. "Position Steadied and Deterioration Halted." *Kinematograph Weekly* (London), 400, 2252 (June 29, 1950), Studio Review, AA.

————. "The Road to Survival." *Kinematograph Weekly* (London), 405, 2268 (Dec. 14, 1950), p. 35.

————. "The Crushing Burden on British Films." *Daily Telegraph* (London), Apr. 18, 1951.

————. "A Style of Their Own." *Kinematograph Weekly* (London), 415, 2310 (Oct. 4, 1951), Supplement, pp. 9, 11.

————. "The Feature Carries on the Documentary Tradition." *Quarterly of Film, Radio, and Television* (Berkeley) 6, 4 (Summer 1952), pp. 351–53.

————. "A View of Eady." Letter. *Financial Times* (London), Oct. 2, 1952.

————. Letter. *Daily Film Renter* (London), 26, 6395 (Oct. 6, 1952), pp. 3–5.

————. "It's the Humanities That Count." *Daily Film Renter* (London), 6432 (Dec. 30, 1952), p. 23.

————. "The Future of the Cinema." *Financial Times* (London), Apr. 4, 1953.

————. "British Film Production." *Financial Times* (London), June 8, 1955.

————. "Let's Stop This Moaning about British Films." *Daily*

The Good Companions, 1933, Victor Saville (A. W. Baskcomb, Viola Compton, Richard Dolman, Dennis Hoey, Margery Binner, Jessie Matthews)

Mail (London), Mar. 14, 1956.

_____. "Poleaxe—or Dissecting Knife." *World Press News* (London), May 11, 1956.

_____. "Let Government Clear the Air." *Daily Film Renter* (London), 7261 (Nov. 22, 1956), pp. 1, 6.

_____. "The Ealing Tradition Is Still Alive and Kicking." *Onward* (Feb. 1957), pp. 14–15.

_____. "Adapting a Story for the Screen: Sir Michael Balcon Talks to the Authors' Club." *The Times* (London), Apr. 25, 1957.

_____. "Battle of Words and Pictures." *Kinematograph Weekly* (London), 482, 2602 (June 27, 1957), Studio Review, H.

_____. "An Author in the Studio." *Films and Filming* (London), 3, 10 (July 1957), pp. 7, 34.

_____. "The Challenge Ahead." *Financial Times* (London), Sept. 23, 1957, Supplement.

_____. "The Money in Films." *Films and Filming* (London), 9, 10 (July 1963), pp. 9–10.

_____. "'It's Been Tough, but We've Survived': On Occasion of the 4th Anniversary of Bryanston." *Kinematograph Weekly* (London), 554, 2912 (July 25, 1963), Supplement, p. 25.

_____. "British Film Production." *British Kinematography* (London), 46, 6 (June 1965), pp. 164–65.

_____. "Training for Film and Television—at the Royal College of Art." *Daily Cinema* (London), Mar. 4, 1966, p. 9.

_____. "Anthony Asquith: 1902–1968." Tribute. *Sight and Sound* (London), 37, 2 (Spring 1968), p. 77.

_____. "Sir Michael Balcon Writes as One Professional Survivor to Another." *Silent Picture* (London, Cincinnati), 2 (Spring 1969), pp. 8–9.

_____. "Lord Rank." *Today's Cinema* (London), 9865 (Dec. 15, 1970), pp. 4–5.

_____. "Producers Have a Responsibility: Hope Lies in the National Film School." *Kinematograph Weekly* (London), 649, 3325 (July 3, 1971), pp. 19, 22.

_____. "Interdependence of the Film-Maker and Technologist." *British Kinematography Sound and Television* (London), 53, 8 (Aug. 1971), p. 305.

_____. "Fifty Years as a Professional Survivor." *Film and Television Technician* (London), 37, 315 (Sept. 1971), pp. 22–24.

_____. "From Korda to Bryanston." *Film and Television Technician* (London), 37, 316 (Oct. 1971), pp. 20–21.

_____. "Henry Harris, Lighting Cameraman." Obituary. *Film and Television Technician* (London), 37, 317 (Nov. 1971), p. 26.

_____. "Notes on the Film Production Board." *Journal of the Society of Film and Television Arts* (London), 2, 6 (1973), p. 18.

_____. "Balcon's Testament." *Sight and Sound* (London), 47, 2 (Spring 1978), p. 68.

ABOUT MICHAEL BALCON AND THE BRITISH FILM INDUSTRY

Books (arranged alphabetically)

Anderson, Lindsay. "The Studio That Begs to Differ." In Gavin Lambert and J. Clifford, eds., *Film and Theatre Today: The European Scene*. London: The Saturn Press, 1949.

_____. *Making a Film: The Story of "Secret People."* London: Allen & Unwin, 1952. Reprint: "Garland Classics of Film Literature." New York and London: Garland Publishing, 1977.

Arliss, George. *George Arliss, by Himself.* London: John Murray, 1940.

Armes, Roy. *A Critical History of British Cinema.* London: Secker & Warburg, 1978.

Barr, Charles. *Ealing Studios.* London: Cameron & Tayleur, David & Charles, 1977; Woodstock, N.Y.: The Overlook Press, 1980.

Betts, Ernest. *The Film Business: A History of British Cinema, 1896–1972.* London: Allen & Unwin, 1973.

Brown, Geoff. *Launder and Gilliat.* London: BFI, 1977. Essays, filmography, notes, and comments.

_____, ed. *Der Produzent: Michael Balcon und der englische Film.* Berlin: Volker Spiess, 1981. Published in conjunction with Berlin Film Festival retrospective. Essays by Geoff Brown, Rachael Low, Charles Barr, Eva Orbanz, Michelle Snapes, and Helmut Wietz; interviews by Brown, Low, Barr, John Ellis, and Heinz Rothsack. Filmography, bibliography.

_____, ed. *Walter Forde.* London: BFI, 1977. Essays by Michael Balcon and Geoff Brown; annotated filmography by Brown, Cyril B. Rollins, Robert J. Wareing, and Anthony Slide.

Brunel, Adrian. *Nice Work: The Story of Thirty Years in British Film Production.* London: Forbes Robertson Ltd., 1949.

Butler, Ivan. *"To Encourage the Art of the Film": The Story of the British Film Institute.* London: Robert Hale, 1971.

Campbell Dixon, George. "A Film Critic Reviews a Producer." In Monja Danischewsky, ed., *Michael Balcon's 25 Years in Films.* London: World Film Publications, 1947.

Cavalcanti, Alberto. "A Film Director Contributes." In Monja Danischewsky, ed., *ibid.*

Clarke, T. E. B. "Just an Idea." In Roger Manvell, ed., *The Cinema 1951.* London: Pelican, 1951.

_____. *This Is Where I Came In.* London: Michael Joseph, 1974.

Clynton, Lionel. "Michael Balcon of Ealing." In Peter Noble, ed., *British Film Yearbook, 1947–8.* London: British Yearbooks, 1947.

Danischewsky, Monja, ed., *Michael Balcon's 25 Years in Films.* London: World Film Publications, 1947.

_____. *White Russian, Red Face.* London: Gollancz, 1966.

Dean, Basil. *Mind's Eye: An Autobiography, 1927–1972.* London: Hutchinson, 1973.

Dickinson, Thorold. "The Work of Sir Michael Balcon at Ealing Studios." In Roger Manvell, ed. *The Year's Work in the Film 1950.* London: Longmans, Green, for the British Council, 1951.

Durgnat, Raymond. *A Mirror for England: British Movies from Austerity to Affluence.* London: Faber & Faber, 1970.

Forman, Denis. *Films 1945–1950.* London: Longmans, Green, for the British Council, 1952.

Hulbert, Jack. *The Little Woman's Always Right.* London: W. H. Allen, 1975.

James, David. *"Scott of the Antarctic": The Film and Its Production.* London: Convoy Publications, 1948.

Koval, Francis. "The Studio: Sir Michael Balcon and Ealing." In *Films in Britain 1951.* London: Sight and Sound, BFI, 1951. Published for the Festival of Britain.

Low, Rachael. *The History of the British Film, 1918–1929.* London: Allen & Unwin, 1971. Bibliography, list of British productions 1918–29.

Matthews, Jessie, as told to Muriel Burgess. *Over My Shoulder: An Autobiography.* London: W. H. Allen, 1974.

Montagu, Ivor. *The Youngest Son.* London: Lawrence & Wishart, 1970.

National Film Archive. *Victor Saville.* London: BFI, 1972. Booklet compiled to accompany retrospective of Saville films.

Oakley, Charles. *Where We Came In: Seventy Years of the British Film Industry.* London: Allen & Unwin, 1964.

Pearson, George. *Flashback.* London: Allen & Unwin, 1957.

Perry, George. *Forever Ealing: A Celebration of the Great British*

Film Studio. London: Pavilion/Michael Joseph, 1981.

————. *The Great British Picture Show: From the 90's to the 70's.* London. Hart-Davis/MacGibbon; New York: Hill & Wang, 1974.

Redgrave, Michael. "The Producer and the Actor." In Monja Danischewsky, ed., *Michael Balcon's 25 Years in Films.*

Rosay, Françoise. "A British Producer—By a French Actress." In Monja Danischewsky, ed., *ibid.*

Slide, Anthony, ed. *Michael Balcon: Producer.* London: National Film Theatre, 1969.

Tennyson, Charles. *Penrose Tennyson.* London: A. S. Atkinson, Ltd., 1943.

Walker, Alexander. *Hollywood/U.K.: The British Film Industry in the Sixties.* London: Michael Joseph, 1974.

Watt, Harry. *Don't Look at the Camera.* New York: St. Martin's Press, 1974.

Wilson, David. *Projecting Britain: Ealing Film Posters.* London: BFI Publishing, 1982.

Wood, Alan. *Mr. Rank: A Study of J. Arthur Rank and British Films.* London: Hodder & Stoughton, 1952.

Yacowar, Maurice. *Hitchcock's British Films.* Hamden, Ct.: Archon Books, 1977.

Periodicals and Journals (arranged alphabetically)

Agee, James. Review of *48 Hours. The Nation* (July 15, 1944); reprinted in *Agee on Film.* Boston: Beacon Press, 1964, p. 104.

"Balcon Charter for 1949 Calls for More Cuts in Costs and Union Streamlining." *Kinematograph Weekly* (London), 388, 2196 (June 2, 1949), pp. 17–18.

"The Balcon Group Get British Lion Films." *Daily Cinema* (London), 8890 (Mar. 18, 1964), pp. 1, 14.

"Balcon Has Sound Financial Backing to Buy British Lion." *Daily Cinema* (London), 9301 (Nov. 30, 1966), pp. 1, 6.

"Balcon Says He Will Not Stand for Presidency of the British Film Producers Association." *Daily Film Renter* (London), 7161 (July 4, 1956), p. 1.

"Balcon Tries to Penetrate a Bureaucratic Veil of Secrecy." *Today's Cinema* (London), 9882 (Feb. 19, 1971), p. 12.

Baldwin, Oliver. "The Romance of Gaumont British." *Picturegoer* (London), 5, 222 (Aug. 24, 1935), pp. 8–9.

Barr, Charles. "'Projecting Britain and the British Character': Ealing Studios." *Screen* (London). Part I: 15, 1 (Spring 1974), pp. 87–121. Part II: 15, 2 (Summer 1974), pp. 129–63.

Baxter, Brian. "Ealing Mainly on the Lighter Side." In BFI, *National Film Theatre Programme* (London), Apr.–May 1973, pp. 48–53.

————. "Ealing Mainly on the Serious Side." In BFI, *National Film Theatre Programme* (London), Feb.–Mar. 1973, pp. 12–17.

————. "The Glory That Was Ealing." *Films Illustrated* (London), 11, 123 (Dec. 1981): pp. 104–5.

Brown, Geoff. "Ealing's Glory: The Great Age of Ealing Studios." *The Movie* (London), 28 (1980), pp. 541–44.

————. "Ealing, Your Ealing." *Sight and Sound* (London), 46, 3 (Summer 1977), pp. 164–67.

Burnup, Peter. "Balcon Fights for British Control of British Films." *Motion Picture Herald* (New York, Chicago), 154, 9 (Feb. 26, 1944), p. 27.

"Call for Funds." *Evening Standard* (London), Feb. 24, 1971.

Chapell, C. "Michael Balcon's 25 Years in Films." *Kinematograph Weekly* (London), 370, 2118 (Dec. 4, 1947), p. 3.

Clarke, T. E. B. "The Fun Studios: Memories of the Ealing Community." *The Movie* (London), 28 (1980), pp. 554–55.

Cutts, John. "Mackendrick Finds the Sweet Smell of Success." *Films and Filming* (London) 3, 9 (June 1957), pp. 8, 30.

Danischewsky, Monja. "The Ghosts of Ealing." *Daily Express* (London), Oct. 21. 1955.

————. "University Days at Ealing." *Cine-Technician* (London), 21, 131 (Nov. 1955), pp. 168–69.

————. Editorial. *Cine-Technician* (London), 21, 131 (Nov. 1955), p. 163.

de la Roche, Catherine. "The Ealing Studios Tradition." *Picture Post* (London), Dec. 29, 1951, pp. 19–23, 37.

"Documentary Hit by Film Finance Plan." *Today's Cinema* (London), 71, 5691 (Aug. 24, 1948), pp. 3, 6.

"Ealing and After." *The Movie* (London), 28 (1980), pp. 541–57. Special issue.

"Ealing: No Release Plans Yet." *Today's Cinema* (London), 86, 7451 (Feb. 2, 1956), pp. 3, 12.

"Ealing Studios 1930–1951: For Twenty-one Years Makers of Good British Films." *Kinematograph Weekly* (London), 415, 2310 (Oct. 4, 1951), Supplement, p. 36. Articles by Reginald P. Baker, Michael Balcon, Graham Clarke, T. E. B. Clarke, Jack Warner, R. Howard Cricks, et al.

Earl, Lawrence. "The Mighty Balcon." *John Bull* (London), Apr. 19, 26; May 3, 10, 1952.

Ellis, John. "Made in Ealing." *Screen* (London), 16, 1 (Spring 1975), pp. 78–127.

Enley, Frank. "The Blue Lamp." *Sight and Sound* (London), 19, 2 (Apr. 1950), pp. 76–78.

"Famous Producer at 34 Years of Age: Michael Balcon's Romantic career." *Film Weekly* (London), 2, 60 (Dec. 9, 1929), p. 6.

"Flashback on Thirty Years of Film-Making." *The Cinema* (London), 111, 62 (June 1, 1949), Supplement "The Cinema Studio," pp. 7–9.

Foster, William. "Celluloid Tycoon." *The Scotsman* (Edinburgh), Mar. 15, 1969.

Fothergill, Richard. "The Ealing Tradition." *Screen Education* (London), 10 (Sept.–Oct. 1961), pp. 20–21, 50.

Fuller, Graham. "The Discreet Charm of Alec Guinness." *The Movie* (London), 28 (1980), pp. 550–51.

Gibbs, Patrick. "A Case for the Independent Producer: Sir Michael Balcon." *The Cinema* (London), 6 (Mar. 1948), pp. 40–44.

Gilliat, Sidney. "Ealing's Image-Maker." *The Sunday Times* (London), Mar. 16, 1969.

Graves, Charles. "More Celebrities in Cameo: Number 6, Michael Balcon." *The Bystander* (London), Feb. 10, 1937, p. 211.

Hall, Dennis John. "Balcon's Britain." *Films* (London). Part I: 1, 3 (Feb. 1981), pp. 40–43. Part II: 1, 4 (Mar. 1981), pp. 30–35.

Harman, Jympson. "Ealing's Passport to Success." *Picturegoer* (London), 19, 782 (Apr. 29, 1950), pp. 16–17.

————. "It's Still Forever Ealing." *Evening News* (London), Oct. 25, 1955.

Hitchcock, Alfred. "Hitchcock." *Sight and Sound* (London), 47, 1 (Winter 1977–78), p. 11. Part of the general tribute "Michael Balcon, 1896–1977."

Holland, Julian. "Interview with Michael Balcon." *Evening News* (London), Jan. 9, 1961.

Honri, Baynham. "The Golden Age of Ealing Studios." *The British Journal of Photography* (London, Liverpool). Part I: "Artistic and Technical Advances at Ealing over the Years" (Jan. 30, 1976), pp. 92–95. Part II: "The Reconstruction of Ealing Studios for Talking Pictures in 1931...The Epoch of Basil Dean" (Mar. 12, 1976), pp. 220–23. Part III: "The Era of Michael Balcon and the Ealing Comedies" (Apr. 9, 1976), pp. 310–12. Part IV: "The Era of BBC Films for Television" (June 25, 1976), pp. 535–38.

————. "Mick: A Tribute to Sir Michael Balcon." *The British Journal of Photography* (London, Liverpool), Aug. 20, 1971, pp. 744–46.

————. "Returning to Ealing Studios." *Screen International*

(London), 42 (June 26, 1976), p. 12.

Houston, Penelope. "Survivor." *Sight and Sound* (London), 32, 1 (Winter 1962–63), p. 15. Interview with Balcon.

Hutchinson, Tom. "Ealing Spirit Is Still as Potent." *Kinematograph Weekly* (London), 465, 2531 (Dec. 29, 1955), p. 24.

"Independent Producers Will Benefit from Big New Group." *Daily Cinema* (London), 8536 (Nov. 15, 1961), pp. 1, 4.

"I Wish I Could Join." *Cine-Technician* (London), 4, 17 (Sept.–Oct. 1938), p. 90. Interview with Balcon.

Kaul, Walter, "Der Mann, der den Film 'Macht.'" *Film-echo/Film Woche* (Wiesbaden), 9 (Feb. 13, 1981), p. 16.

King, Fay. "The Story of 'An Obstinate Success.'" *The Outspan* (Bloemfontein, South Africa), June 11, 1948, pp. 26, 27, 101, 103, 105.

Knight, Arthur. "The Balcon Situation." *Esquire* (Chicago, New York), Sept. 1953, p. 90.

Kuhn, Irene. "London Challenges Hollywood." *New York World Telegraph,* Sept. 26, 1934.

Lambert, Gavin. "Notes on the British Cinema." *Quarterly of Film, Radio, and Television* (Berkeley), 11, 1 (Fall 1956), pp. 1–13.

"Letter from Michael Balcon." *The Spectator* (London), Nov. 28, 1970.

Lewin, David. "The Sadness of the Gentle Knight of the Ealing Round Table." *Today's Cinema* (London), 9646 (Mar. 10, 1969), p. 7.

"Lion-Day: The Balcon Group Presents a Powerful Offer." *Daily Cinema* (London), 8887 (Mar. 11, 1964), pp. 1, 6.

Lovell, Alan, et al. "Interview with Alberto Cavalcanti." *Screen* (London), 13, 2 (Summer 1972), pp. 33–53.

"Making Films That Project Britain: Sue Summers Interviews Sir Michael Balcon." *Vision* (London), 2, 1 (Mar. 1977), pp. 11–12.

Mannock, P. L. "Leo Gets Mickey." *Picturegoer Weekly* (London), 6, 293 (Jan. 2, 1937), pp. 10–11.

"Michael Balcon Gives Youth Its Chance." *Film Pictorial* (London), 14, 364 (Feb. 11, 1939), pp. 6–7.

"Michael Balcon's Views on 3D." *Kinematograph Weekly* (London), 433, 2389 (Apr. 9, 1953), p. 5.

Millar, Gavin. "Typically Ealing." *The Listener* (London) 107, 2751 (Mar. 11, 1982), p. 32.

Montagu, Ivor. "Islington and the Bush." *Sight and Sound* (London), 47, 1 (Winter 1977–78); pp. 9–11. Part of the general tribute "Michael Balcon, 1896–1977."

Mooring, W. H. "I Think You're Wrong Mr. Balcon." *Picturegoer* (London), 11, 532 (Aug. 2, 1941), p. 5.

Muller, Robert. "Goodbye to Ealing." *Picture Post* (London), Jan. 14, 1956, pp. 34–35.

Myers, Denis. "The Function of a Producer: An Interview with Michael Balcon." *World Film News* (London), 1, 8 (Nov. 1936), p. 4.

Newnham, John K. "'Mr. Balcon's Young Gentlemen': The Work of Five Ealing Directors." *Film* (London), Autumn 1946, pp. 39–43.

"No Closed Shop against Americans." *Daily Film Renter* (London), 21, 5613 (Oct. 20, 1947), pp. 3, 14.

"Obituary: Sir Michael Balcon." *The Times* (London), Oct. 18, 1977.

Perry, George. "George Perry Introduces the BBC TV Season of Films from Ealing Studios." *Radio Times* (London), 233, 3029 (Nov. 28, 1981), p. 15.

———. "Ealing Studios." In BFI, *National Film Theatre Programme* (London). Part I: "The Thirties" (Nov.–Dec. 1981), pp. 24–29. Part II: "Ealing at War" (Mar. 1982), pp. 18–22. Part III: "The Great Years" (Oct.–Dec. 1982), pp. 14–20.

Pickard, Roy. "The Ealing Story." *Films in Review* (New York), 26, 2 (Feb. 1975), pp. 101–7.

Pulleine, Tim. "The English Eccentrics: Toffs, Floozies, Bumbling Old Men and Little Old Ladies." *The Movie* (London), 28 (1980), pp. 545–47.

Pullinger, W. T. "A Place of Fame: Hollywood in Islington." *Islington Gazette* (London), Sept. 21, 1956, pp. 9, 17. Gainsborough Studios.

Reed, Stanley. "Backing Britain: Michael Balcon Produced Many of Britain's Greatest Film Triumphs." *The Movie* (London), 28 (1980), pp. 556–57.

———. "Michael Balcon, 1896–1977." *BFI News* (London), 31 (Jan. 1978), p. 3. Obituary and tribute.

Relph, Michael. "Ealing and After." *Sight and Sound* (London), 47, 1 (Winter 1977–78), p. 11. Part of the general tribute "Michael Balcon, 1896–1977."

Robinson, David. "In Authentic Tones." *The Financial Times* (London), Mar. 21, 1969.

Sainsbury, Peter. "The Financial Base of Independent Film Production in the U.K." *Screen* (London), 22, 1 (1981).

Salem, Charles. "The History of Ealing." *Cinema* (London). Part I: 7 (Nov. 1982), pp. 36–40. Part II: 8 (Dec. 1982), pp. 28–31. Part III: 9 (Jan. 1983), pp. 31–33.

Shivas, Mark. "British Lion." *Movie* (London), 14 (Autumn 1965): 1–4.

"Sir M. Balcon Sees Hope for British Film Industry." *The Times* (London), July 1, 1957.

"Statements in New York and Hollywood: 'Don't Panic over 3D U.S. Tells Balcon.'" *Kinematograph Weekly* (London), 433, 2392 (Apr. 30, 1953), pp. 3, 8.

Stone, David. "Are British Films on the Rocks?" *Everybody's Weekly* (London), Apr. 28, 1956, p. 26.

Sussex, Elizabeth. "Cavalcanti in England." *Sight and Sound* (London), 44, 4 (Autumn 1975), pp. 205–11. Includes conversation with Sir Michael Balcon.

Taylor, John Russell. "Kind Hearts and Coronets." *The Movie* (London), 28 (1980), pp. 548–49.

Taylor, Max, in correspondence with Sir Michael Balcon. "Sir Michael: Today, Tomorrow, and Yesterday." *Lumière* (Melbourne), Mar.–Apr. 1972, pp. 16–18.

Tynan, Kenneth. "Ealing's Way of Life." *Films and Filming* (London), 2, 3 (Dec. 1955), p. 10.

———. "Ealing: The Studio in Suburbia." *Films and Filming* (London), 2, 2 (Nov. 1955), p. 4.

Vincent, John. "British Producers Search for Freedom." *Films and Filming* (London), 5, 9 (June 1959), p. 28.

Walker, Alexander. "Ealing Films Will Still Be British." *Birmingham Post,* Jan. 18, 1957.

Walsh, Ann. "Thirty Years of Film Production." *The British Journal of Photography* (London, Liverpool), 96, 4651 (July 8, 1949), pp. 312–13.

Index

Friday the Thirteenth, 1933,
Victor Saville (Emlyn
Williams, Max Miller,
Hartley Power, Percy
Parsons, Sonnie Hale,
Jessie Matthews, Eliot
Makeham, Mary Jerrold,
Robertson Hare)

PHOTO CREDITS

The Museum of Modern Art Film Stills
Archive:

cover, 8, 14, 16, 18, 19, 20 (top, bottom),
23, 25 (bottom), 32, 34, 35, 38 (top),
42, 44 (top, bottom), 45, 47 (bottom),
48 (top, bottom), 49 (top, bottom), 52
(top), 56, 58, 60 (top, bottom), 62 (top),
63 (bottom), 66 (right), 69, 70, 71 (top),
74

National Film Archive, London:

frontispiece, 6, 10, 12, 21, 22 (top), 24,
25 (top), 26, 27, 28, 29, 30 (top,
bottom), 31, 33, 36–37, 38 (bottom),
39, 40, 46, 47 (top), 50, 51, 52 (bottom),
53, 54, 55, 57, 59, 61, 62 (bottom), 63
(top), 64 (top, bottom), 65, 66 (left), 67,
68, 71 (bottom), 72, 114, 118, 126, 127

Howard Mandelbaum:

22 (bottom)

The Good Companions,
1933, Victor Saville
(Jessie Matthews)